PENGUIN BOOKS
The Interceptor

Cameron Addicott worked as an undercover investigator with HM Customs and SOCA (Serious Organized Crime Agency) for eighteen years. He has unrivalled experience in working at the sharp end against the biggest drug traffickers, people smugglers, money launderers and other top villains all over the world, and has used every tool available to put them inside. Cam now runs *Spooks Unlimited*, a Corporate Team Building/Adventure business.

# The Interceptor

CAMERON ADDICOTT
*with* KRIS HOLLINGTON

PENGUIN BOOKS

PENGUIN BOOKS

Published by the Penguin Group
Penguin Books Ltd, 80 Strand, London WC2R ORL, England
Penguin Group (USA) Inc., 375 Hudson Street, New York, New York 10014, USA
Penguin Group (Canada), 90 Eglinton Avenue East, Suite 700, Toronto, Ontario, Canada M4P 2Y3
(a division of Pearson Penguin Canada Inc.)
Penguin Ireland, 25 St Stephen's Green, Dublin 2, Ireland (a division of Penguin Books Ltd)
Penguin Group (Australia), 250 Camberwell Road,
Camberwell, Victoria 3124, Australia (a division of Pearson Australia Group Pty Ltd)
Penguin Books India Pvt Ltd, 11 Community Centre, Panchsheel Park, New Delhi – 110 017, India
Penguin Group (NZ), 67 Apollo Drive, Rosedale, North Shore 0632, New Zealand
(a division of Pearson New Zealand Ltd)
Penguin Books (South Africa) (Pty) Ltd, 24 Sturdee Avenue, Rosebank, Johannesburg 2196, South Africa

Penguin Books Ltd, Registered Offices: 80 Strand, London WC2R ORL, England

www.penguin.com

First published 2010
1

*The Interceptor* is based on true events, but all persons appearing in the book have had their names and identifying characteristics changed to protect their privacy. The details of all surveillance operations and information obtained during operations have also been changed.

Set in 11.5/14.75pt Garamond
Typeset by Palimpsest Book Production Ltd,
Grangemouth, Stirlingshire
Printed in England by Clays Ltd, St Ives plc

ISBN: 978-0-141-04697-6

www.greenpenguin.co.uk

Penguin Books is committed to a sustainable future
for our business, our readers and our planet.
The book in your hands is made from paper
certified by the Forest Stewardship Council.

To my cousin Ali for always being there when I need her
To Dan and Niall for being the best
To Pat, Mel, Jude, Oz, Mark and LSJ for being
outstanding colleagues and the best of friends

# Contents

# Author's Note

It is important to ensure that the details of many individuals encountered through my work are not presented in a manner that would reveal those individuals' identities. Consequently, names have been changed and background details altered where necessary. Cases on public record are reported in their original detail.

# 1. Into the Underworld

Have you ever had the thought, 'I wonder who I'm sitting next to on the train or walking past on the way into work? That guy with the frown, the stubble, the scarred chin and the duffle bag might be a crack dealer, a hit man or an undercover cop. Perhaps he's a terrorist or a serial killer.'

I do. All the time. They're all out there right now. Real living, breathing drug dealers, hit men, spies, terrorists, robbers, rapists and pornographers, all doing their bit to keep the global underworld economy spinning, recession free; dealing out misery and ecstasy, selling and seeking information and exchanging connections in equal measure. This is the underworld.

Most people never get to see it, but it's everywhere.

And I know it better than anyone else.

At 5 a.m. I walk the fifteen minutes to work from my one-bed ex-council flat in Petticoat Square. I pass, as I do every day, the bureau de change in Whitechapel. Jimmy Ashraf runs the place and changes scrunched-up coke money into freshly pressed euros for a north London outfit who've put more bodies in the Thames than the Black Death.

Although we've never met, I know Jimmy intimately. Real name: Mus Ashraf. Age: forty. Done well for himself by marrying into a good family and she's a very pretty girl. But that's not enough for Jimmy. Come the weekend, he likes to go along to a top hotel in the West End with his mates and a bag-load of Viagra, hire half a dozen failed glamour models and shag his brains out for twenty-four hours or so.

Jimmy doesn't even know who I am, yet I hold the power of life or death over the poor bastard. What he wouldn't give me to keep me from letting that little titbit of info pass under his father-in-law's murderous snout is anybody's guess.

And that wasn't even the half of it. Celebs love to dip their hands into the high-end of the underworld trough. And crims wet themselves the moment they get a sniff of a celeb. Jimmy's one of those. In fact, his eighteen-year-old daughter is regularly being beaten within an inch of her life by her British A-list actor boyfriend. Jimmy pulled him up on it a couple of times after his girl phoned him in distress but the A-lister acted all holy until Jimmy swallowed his shit, that his daughter had made it up.

I knew that she hadn't.

I'd love to greet that A-list bastard on the red carpet at Leicester Square with a winkle picker to the nuts and a recording of the evidence for the press.

But I won't, of course.

I'm a professional, after all.

The City is waking. From 4 a.m. there's another rush hour – the other rush hour, the one that normal people don't get to see.

Apart from me, a bona fide East-Ender, and one or two nightclub zombies staggering jerkily home, the streets are dead. But take a close look at the night buses as they sail past and you'll see there's standing room only. They're packed full of the cogs that keep the City of London turning; the men and women who prepare the way for the city boys and girls – the security guards, caretakers, street-sweepers, sandwich fillers, newspaper sellers and coffee-makers.

For example, I know Juan and Pedro are on the number 54 bus right now. As far as anyone's concerned they're two humble Colombian cleaners working for an international bank in the Square Mile. And they are. But they're also the connection for a load of coke that's brought in every week. They make £800 for meeting a truck driver and carrying the coke from A to B. Not much for the risk they run of ten years inside.

Here I am. Home, sweet home. Custom House in Lower Thames Street, EC3. The fortress gleams in the crisp, predawn light. Customs has had an office on this site since the fifteenth century. Presently it's home to the Investigation and Intelligence Department of Her Majesty's Customs and Excise.

That's right, I'm in Intel, but not for the Infernal Revenue, God, no.

I work for Alpha Projects. They pay me to listen.

I hear every single major deal going down in this city – every payment, every meet and every exchange. I listen to the lives of the most depraved people in London. I know what makes them tick and I know how they get away with murder.

I can tell you for a fact that all those villains who write stories about themselves – they're all bullshit. They got caught. They're failures. The real villains never get caught.

Don't believe a word those failures produce, they're liars with plenty to hide.

Yes, I know far too much about London's underworld, more than the criminals themselves. I hear what they say behind each other's backs, when they think no one else is listening; I hear what they say to their loved ones, each other, what turns them on and off and – most importantly for my job – how they get rich.

I never get to share most of it. I'm supposed to file the data, bottle my righteous indignation and keep quiet.

'You'll get used to it,' they said when I walked through those doors on my first day. But people underestimate the power of listening.

Listening can kill.

Believe me, I know. I listened a man to death just yesterday.

# 2. The Road to Alpha

Two years previously: Gatwick Airport.

My phone rang. It was Alpha.

'Drop everything,' the voice said. 'A priority-one target is in the south terminal using a TK (telephone kiosk). Find and detain him.'

Jed, my best mate, and I had been on another job in the airport when a Turk, a nasty piece of scum involved in heroin importation, popped up into Alpha's view. He needed to be nicked quickly, before he vanished in the rush-hour mayhem.

'Yes!' Jed said. 'A bit of excitement at last.' We forgot about our surveillance and moved off. Over the next ten minutes or so we identified several Turkish-looking blokes on mobiles but none using a TK.

Each time we locked on I called the Alpha case officer. 'Wrong one, keep looking.'

'Fuck's sake,' I said, 'we're on a wild goose chase here.'

Eventually, after half an hour of hunting, Jed decided to put a ten-nine (phone call) into Alpha from a TK telling them that we'd exhausted all possibilities.

Jed was in mid flow when Alpha interrupted: 'Shut the fuck up.' A few seconds' pause. 'He's stood right next to you.'

Jed looked to his right and there, at the neighbouring TK, was a Turk in a Crombie coat.

Jed slowly put his hand in his pocket and gave 'rapid

clicks' on his radio. The sign for seven-seven, seven-seven: 'target is on the move'.

He walked back to my position while I maintained the eyeball. We split up and tailed him to the Gatwick Express.

'This is gonna be good,' Jed whispered into the mic.

I grinned. Stressed passengers laden with suitcases hurried past us, oblivious to the fact that a major collar was about to get felt by Her Maj's finest.

'I'll make the pinch,' Jed said. The target bought the *Sun* and sat on a bench to read it, waiting for his train.

Jed sauntered up, sat down and started chatting. I heard everything via my earpiece.

'That the *Sun*?' Jed asked.

The target looked up, already suspicious. 'Yeah.'

'Mind if I have a quick look?'

He passed it over. Jed opened it up and started tutting. 'That bitch.'

'What?'

'It's my stars; Mystic Meg says I'm gonna have an awful day. Fucking typical.' Jed paused for a moment. 'What's your star sign?'

'Libra.'

'Libra, Libra,' Jed said, searching the paper. 'Here we are. Fucking hell, they're worse than mine. It says here you're gonna get arrested by Her Majesty's Customs. I'm Jed Heath and you're fucking nicked.'

We could hardly get the cuffs on him for laughing. Afterwards, I pulled Jed to one side. 'Alpha called. Good news, the Dutchman's flying in sometime tomorrow.'

'At fucking last. Let's wrap up our little Turkish delight, round up the team and get an early night.'

'My thoughts exactly.'

'Maybe just a quick pint in the hotel bar, though.'

At 11 a.m. the next morning, our heads pounding, Jed and I were standing near the Hertz Car Hire desk in Gatwick.

'Say, Jed, do you know how I got my nickname?'

'Duh, Cammo's short for Cameron?'

'Nope. I can't believe I never told you. It was my first ever job. I was based in Plymouth when my boss told me that this kid had been stopped at Customs. He'd walked through the "Nothing to Declare" channel when an officer noticed his shirt was wriggling. Then this fucking lizard started to crawl out between the kid's shirt buttons. He'd done a deal with a local pet-shop owner who'd paid for him to travel to Morocco and buy chameleons for about a pound each to be sold in the UK for a couple of hundred a pop. Their plan was to split the profits.

'He had about thirty of the buggers on him. Eight survived and we donated them to a zoo. He was the first person I ever dealt with. I was pretty nervous, and didn't want to mess up or miss anything, so I think went a bit over the top when I had the poor kid strip-searched.'

Jed chuckled. 'Could've had a lizard up his arse.'

'Anyway, we did him and the pet-shop owner for CITES offences [Convention on the Illegal Trade in Endangered Species]. It almost went tits-up in court when the barrister told me the case was a cakewalk. "You can go now," he said, so I went home. I got a call later asking me where the hell I'd gone. Turned out he'd said, "You can go for lunch," not, "Fuck off home." I was given a bollocking in front of the court. Everybody got to hear this story about the "chameleon guy" and soon everyone was calling me Cammo.'

'Well I never knew that,' Jed said. 'Another coffee?'

'Why the hell not?'

My phone rang. It was Alpha.

'Target's off the plane and on the phone to his girlfriend now,' said a man with a strong Scouse accent. 'He's saying he'll be with her in forty minutes and that he's just about to pick up the keys from the car rental company.'

'Roger that,' I replied. Alpha hung up.

I picked out a tall, good-looking blond guy putting a mobile in his pocket. I relayed the info to the rest of the guys via my concealed mic. 'That's a possible Zulu 10 towards the Hertz desk. Jed with eyeball.'

It was the autumn of 2000 and I was running a surveillance team based in the south-west. Alpha, Customs' elite and extremely secretive Intel arm, were coordinating the operation from their London HQ. This was my first Alpha-led operation and I was loving every moment. Even though they only had one of the target's phones hooked up, Alpha had helped us get in deep on a unique heroin job.

Our target was a Dutchman who provided an exclusive service to anyone with the right pedigree and enough wedge. He'd purchase serious weights of gear from the source country and deliver it personally right to Mr Big's door. It took balls of steel, as the risk was all the Dutchman's.

The Dutchman was bringing in tonnes of the brown stuff – literally. Alpha had picked him up after he delivered fifty kilos of heroin to a tasty firm in Birmingham who were part of a separate investigation. As the amounts were so ridiculously large and so frequent, Alpha immediately hooked up the Dutchman as a stand-alone operator.

As the elite surveillance and undercover ops A-team, we were supposed to target the Dutchman and follow him to the heart of many a drug empire before plotting his downfall.

Customs' policy at the time was one of 'upstream disruption'. The idea was to concentrate all resources in getting up the supply chain as quickly as possible to identify the major dealers operating abroad. Many managers disagreed with this because it invariably meant doing all the hard work only to see overseas agencies take out the gear and get the glory. Personally I couldn't give a toss for policy; as long as we were helping to take down bad guys then I was happy.

Problem was, the Dutchman was bloody good at his job.

We didn't even have his real name – and that was our first task, to properly ID him. He was using several mobiles but Alpha had only hooked up one so far, the one he used to call his girlfriend.

There was no way the Home Secretary was about to personally authorize the tapping of the Dutchman's girlfriend's phone, especially as she was (presumably) an innocent bystander and we had so little Intel. It was Catch 22: we needed phones bugged because we needed more Intel – but we didn't have enough Intel to warrant the bugging of the phone.

As soon Alpha called to give me the task, I put a team together. We had a total of eighteen officers trained for this sort of work. Usually we'd only be able to take on one surveillance job at a time without asking for outside help from other teams. I had a quick discussion with Gary, the other case officer, who was already running another drugs op in Devon. As my op was Alpha led, I had priority, but for this task, and to keep Gary's investigation going, I decided that four officers would be enough.

The rest of the team, Jed, Fin and Robyn, made the obligatory calls home, all apologizing to their partners yet again through gritted teeth: 'No, I don't know when I'll be back. Look, I'm sorry but you know it's the job.'

I was always amazed by the officers who would tell their wives and husbands they would be home 'tonight' and then every day around 4–6 p.m. would put in a call to say, 'Sorry, not tonight, Josephine.' Crazy. It just crushes everyone's expectations.

They did it to avoid the hassle they'd have had from their families if they'd said, 'Not back for a week, see ya,' but to my mind the shit they took every day for that four o'clock call just wasn't worth it. Madness. On Monday morning I would tell Louise I would be back on Friday. If I was back earlier she and the kids were pleased. If not, she was never surprised. Still, I was hardly in a position to talk – our relationship was not exactly one of harmonious joy.

Tracking guys like the Dutchman required extremely close surveillance – the kind that keeps you away from your wife and kids. For the past six years I'd been away from home at least two or three nights every week, following some dealer or other all over the UK. Those of us with kids and a life had missed countless school plays, sports days, friends' weddings, birthdays, funerals, christenings, bar mitzvahs, etc. While our wives or husbands, girlfriends or boyfriends watched, photographed and filmed our kids singing, dancing, acting and running with egg and spoon, we sat in cars for hours on end, recording how drug dealers made their fortunes.

It had become even worse recently. Louise and I had given up arguing and had lapsed into the hopeless silence that precedes a divorce; it was only a question of who would mention the d-word first. Ben, our twelve-year-old eldest, had been diagnosed with ADHD. He was a top lad 99 per cent of the time but occasionally his behaviour got the better of him. He'd been expelled from two schools and a third was on the cards.

While most officers made the time to go home every now and again, Jed and I were of almost identical dispositions and stayed on the job pretty much 24/7. We were obsessed. A shrink might say that this was an attempt to distance myself from a wife I no longer loved and a son I found difficult to deal with. Bollocks. Long-term ops against serious villains cannot be run by people who put their families first. Sacrifices have to be made. Family life is one of them. I loved my family and hated what the job had cost us – but I had learned to live with it.

Of course, we make our own choices. I'd always wanted an action-packed career. My original plan was to become a Marine. I'd signed up for the Territorial Army along with two mates as soon as we were old enough. We loved it; we got to shoot stuff on the weekends and it doesn't get any better than that when you're a teenage tearaway. Our troop sergeant, a crafty Royal Marine, talked us into applying for his outfit and we all swore we would – just as soon as we'd finished school.

Mum, an ex-nurse, and Dad, an engineer who built

nuclear submarines, strongly disagreed. They wanted me to go to college and university but I was having none of that. We argued about it plenty of times. I was as stubborn as my dad and signed up along with my mates, though I was the only one of us to make it through the entrance tests.

A short time later, after a week of exercises on Dartmoor, walking started to become very painful. When I finally took a look at my feet I shouted in surprise. They looked like they were rotting. 'That's you out, then,' a fellow Marine said. He wasn't wrong. I'd got a bad case of trench foot, caused by extended periods of dampness, and my feet really had started to rot. The doctors said I was particularly susceptible to the condition (worst case scenario is that your feet go gangrenous and have to be amputated) so I was booted out with a medical discharge and an invitation to join the Ministry of Defence as a civilian.

Because I'd served in the armed forces I was eligible to move on to the first level of management without having a degree, although I had to sit an entrance exam. I failed by 1 per cent. Thankfully, they were desperate for staff so they let me in anyway and I ended up working for VAT investigations in Exeter.

After my first day I knew with 100 per cent certainty that I didn't want to do VAT investigations for the rest of my life. When I saw an ad for a uniformed border investigation officer based in the south-west, I leapt at the chance. From there it was just a short hop, skip and jump into Customs' drugs investigation teams.

This, to me, was as about exciting as it could get. I drove fast cars, stayed up late, used cool equipment and got to lock up villains. In those early days it was the excitement that was most important to me.

Ten years on, I was thirty-five years old, at the top of my game and dangerously obsessed with taking villains down. Over time, winning the game, i.e., securing convictions against baddies, had become more and more important to me. There are few things more significant in life than taking away someone's freedom. If I was going to send someone to jail, I wanted to make sure it was damn well worth it, so my aim was always to hunt down and outwit the 'best' villains I could find and put them away for the maximum amount of time.

Nicking the Dutchman was very important to me. If we got on him for long enough and did our jobs properly, then he would lead us to several major players in the international drugs trade, some of the nastiest scum on the planet.

Of course, this obsession makes it all the harder to bear when an operation goes down the toilet and various Mr Bigs walk away scot-free. When you've sacrificed so much, it's hard to let these things go, especially on a psychological level. Working for our department has driven many to one or more of the three Ds: drink, divorce and depression. While I drank too much and divorce was on the cards, I held off depression by trying to make sure I won every case – and that required a fanatical approach to the job.

This was my own personal Catch 22. To stop going mad I had to succeed every time, which meant I would lose my family, which would also have driven me mad but for the fact that I was winning every case. Without my obsession I'd keep my family, but I'd lose cases, quickly followed by my job, and this was what scared me most of all. I'd spent all of my working life in Customs; I couldn't imagine doing anything other than chasing bad guys for a living. Without my job I'd be one miserable bastard – and then Louise would soon kick me out so I'd lose my family anyway. It was like a grotesque slide show looping through my brain. I tried not to let it play too often. That's where the drink came in handy . . .

Jed, Fin, Robyn and I had met every flight from Schipol, Amsterdam, to Gatwick for the past week. There was a good chance – even if Alpha picked up the call – that we would lose him as there were only four of us and about ten thousand punters in the terminal at any one time, but if we saw him and followed him to his hire car then we were on our way.

The days dragged by. This is the other thing that makes many lose their minds: the waiting game.

Jed and I were the undisputed masters of waiting around. Jed was in his late thirties, a fanatical six-foot Chelski supporter from south London with a long-term girlfriend and two kids. Our careers had roughly followed the same path, although in different parts of the country up until we'd met in Bristol two years earlier.

Both fully trained informant handlers, we considered ourselves masters of the dark art of surveillance, although I think Jed had the edge. His one flaw, if it could be considered as such, was that he was easily wound up by other people on the team. I was Mr Laid-Back in comparison.

We were there with Fin and Robyn. Fin was straight as they come. A broad 6´2˝ Irish Bristolian. Not known for being a great thinker, Fin was happy to let others worry about the decision-making. He simply went with the flow and this, along with his innate dependability and willingness to volunteer for the crappiest job of any mission, made him incredibly popular. He was also popular because he could hold his drink (most of us were serious boozers) and would go home to his wife Colleen and their two kids reeking of booze but in a straight line, still able to hold a coherent conversation. Incredibly sociable, he was always inviting other team members over for dinner.

Originally a uniformed Customs officer from the northeast, Robyn had moved down to Bristol with her old man's job. In her mid thirties, Robyn was a BOBFOC (body off *Baywatch*, face off *Crimewatch*). She was super-fit and maintained a butter-wouldn't-melt expression no matter how far up shit creek she was. She was top-notch but lacked experience. I had a feeling she preferred the quiet life doing the office paperwork to the fast cars and late nights world of surveillance.

Time wasting was a fine art. For the Dutchman, we split ourselves into two pairs and rotated our roles every day. Two of us were assigned to simply wait with uniformed Customs to help them search the target's bags before they were put onto the carousel in the arrivals hall. There is usually only a twenty-minute window before all the bags from the plane find their way to arrivals, so you have to be quick. The alternative is to hold back everyone's bags 'owing to technical difficulties', but that can make a target wary and is a trick we use only if his or her luggage contains too much 'Intel' to process quickly.

The uniformed officers could get into anyone's bags in a flash, quickly popping locks and cracking combinations.

Once open, we'd look for any helpful paperwork or clues to where our target had been, who he'd met or was going to meet. We'd always take a laptop in case we came across any hard drives, USB sticks, CDs, etc.

There wasn't too much to this job. Most of the time was spent in the uniformed team's office, drinking their coffee, studying the papers, watching the telly, chatting up anyone we dared.

Those waiting to lock on to the Dutchman once he appeared in arrivals mooched around the gate, trying to look as though they were there to pick up Granny. That's why women officers are so valuable. Criminals never think women work undercover, so relax around them. Having a male/female team in arrivals was very useful indeed. Others would be in cars outside the entrance, or sitting in McDonald's or wherever. Everyone just waiting for the call that would shoot our adrenaline levels through the roof.

All this waiting provided plenty of time for gossip, most of which would centre on the job; about who was doing what to whom, taking the piss out of colleagues, complaining about what senior management were up to and so on. It was amazing all the crap Jed and I talked about – and we never seemed to run out of material.

So, there we were, Jed and I, in front of the Hertz desk, nattering away quite happily when Alpha called. Fin and Robyn were looking out for the Dutchman's bags and were ready to move to the Avis desk if needs be. There were other car rental desks but we couldn't cover them all; we were just counting on the Dutchman choosing one of the biggest two companies.

I watched as Jed sidled up to the desk next to our possible target and asked one of the staff for some rental prices. Jed took a leaflet from the girl and strolled back to where I was, covering the natural route to where the rental cars were parked. He whispered to me as he walked past.

'Dutch accent; reckon we got 'im.' Jed kept going into the parking area where he could pick up the eyeball if this guy was indeed our target.

Walking in a small semi-circle, I kept my eyes on the target. 'From Cam: Possible Zulu 10 [the code name for our suspect], six-foot two, black on black [black top on black trousers], short blond hair, approx thirty, Dennis Bergkamp lookalike, with small black trolley bag, we *will* go with this, all call signs acknowledge.'

'Jed.'

'Fin.'

'Robyn.'

The job was on.

# 3. Interlude: Brevity Codes and Gizmos

Before we go any further, I'm going to have to brief you on some our methods and let you in on a few secrets so that what follows makes sense. So much of what we did was about communication, and like the criminals we tracked, we had to be careful what we said. More than that, we had to be fast and clear; there was no room for repetition or error, it was essential to avoid clogging up the airways. Based on a military counter-eavesdropping code, our very own gobbledegook would take a bit of cracking by the enemy.

When following a target we used ordnance survey 1:50000 maps with all major junctions given a blue spot (motorway junctions), red spot (A roads), yellow spot (B roads) or green spot (major junctions within towns and cities in addition to the others). Each spot had a number between 1 and 99.

We would use codes almost exclusively to convey what we were seeing. The five-five car, which was code for the car with visual contact, or 'eyeball', would provide a running commentary while rest of the team used alternative routes to avoid following the target in convoy and worked out how best to get ahead of the target if necessary. This way the five-five car could let the target 'run' and avoid getting too 'crispy'. Needless to say, this required some outstand-ingly fast driving beyond the ability of most mortals.

'Five-five' was just one of many number combinations

used as shorthand. 'Nine-one', meaning 'heading in the direction of', was another. A suspect's car was an 'X-ray' and each X-ray was assigned a number/letter identifier. Some words were abbreviated – e.g. 'speed' to 'S', and the police alphabet used for those letters. Finally, each officer or team had an identifying call sign.

So a typical communication might be: 'Madrid five-five, X-ray 10 Charlie, nine-one red 67, Sierra three-zero.' This translates to: 'This is call sign "Madrid": I have visual contact with suspect vehicle 10C, which is driving towards red spot 67 on the map at a speed of 30 mph.'

The six-eight car would be the car behind the eyeball car. If you called 'six-eight' it meant you were able to take five-five immediately. If the target took a quick three-one (left turn) – 'Madrid: Five-five, X-ray 10 Charlie, gone three-one at yellow 44, seven-four [handover] now' – the six-eight car would slot into place. We also used these codes in foot surveillance, e.g., 'All call signs, that's a mahogany-mahogany, sauna at the bedlight,' which means: 'Stand down, everybody; debrief at the hotel.'

Not surprisingly, many terms found their way into our everyday conversations: 'Where's the jug [public toilet]?' 'I'm in a knife [pub] on the Edgware Road opposite the bugle [post office].'

All of our gobbledegook was transmitted using the Cougar encrypted radio system. We wore radios that looked like a slab of metal about nine inches by three, and half an inch thick, in a holster under our arms. The microphones were hidden in our collars and there was a small control fob with two buttons: one to speak and another which broadcast a solid tone. If we were somewhere where we couldn't speak, the tone button would be used: rapid clicks for target moving, three clicks for yes and two clicks for no. The radio also had volume control and a channel switch.

The earpiece was similar to a small flesh-coloured digital hearing aid, almost impossible to see from more than a few feet away and even then only if you're really looking for it.

Cougar devices had varying range, a car set covered about five miles, a hand set about one mile, while a covert rig covered up to half a mile. The SAS have a similar system that uses mobile networks so a team on covert rigs can stay on comms (talk to each other) wherever they are in the world.

We had four cars designed to track targets: Wallace, Gromit, Tom and Jerry; big, powerful beasts that had been somewhat 'customized', to put it mildly. They had a huge gyro and compass under the back seat, a boot full of electronic tracking and radio kit and were souped-up so they could be driven insanely fast. Our branch had four cars: a Volvo T5 (Tom), a Saab 9000i (Wallace), a Toyota Camry V6 (Gromit) and a V8 Land-Rover Discovery (Jerry). We also had a selection of conventional vehicles crewed by the rest of the team. These were a mixture of Saabs, Fords, Nissans, vans and bikes.

Each car was fitted with a radio transmitter that could be tracked by a GPS satellite on our computerized map. The radio also picked up signals from VTDs (vehicle tracking devices) and the tracker operator (only a few officers from each team were trained to 'track' – they included Jed and me) had to work out the bearing and distance and plot it on the screen. This was by no means an exact science.

Two tracker cars were always better than one because if we drove well enough then we were able to cross vectors to help to locate the target precisely. Collectively, these gizmos were described as vehicle-mounted electronic mapping equipment, or Vmems.

We also had a brilliant interior listening device. It was basically a tiny mobile phone that could be hidden in the fabric of a suspect's vehicle. We simply rang the number, pressed 'record' on the receiver and it recorded everything. We could also listen in live; it worked off the car battery, so never needed changing.

Everyone who carried out surveillance duties had to pass the standard police driving course (four weeks), the advanced police driving course (two weeks) plus a three-week surveillance driving course and a two-week surveillance navigator's course. Mickey (one of the best officers on the team) was also a surveillance biker, so he did the advanced police motorcycle course as well, scoring so high they wanted him to go back and become an instructor. He usually rode a Blackbird or Hayabusa. On top of that, Jed and I had done a two-week tracker course. We also kept our hands in by being 'practical trainers' on all the surveillance courses, including the basic foot surveillance course.

There's a glossary at the back of the book should you need it. OK, briefing over. Back to work, people.

# 4. How to Follow a Paranoid Heroin Dealer

'From Cam: Can Fin and Robyn return to their call sign and prepare for a lift-off from the Hertz yard.'

'Robyn.'

The call signs were the two tracker cars, on this occasion 'Wallace' and 'Gromit'. Generally, it's not good practice to follow a mobile target with only two cars; you need at least four because once the target gets near home and the traffic thins out, it's much harder to stay invisible if you're sharing the tail with only two cars – especially if the target's keeping a beady eye out – but needs must. Besides, I knew if we didn't get with the Dutchman soon, the branch accountants would have an aneurysm, what with all thousands of pounds of surveillance money haemorrhaging out of the team 24/7.

Even if we lost him, as long as we managed to get a general idea of where he was headed, then we could at least spend the night searching for the car.

I put up that I had the switch (view of the target) and that Jed was covering the leek (car park) where the Hertz cars were.

In our world, targets are always labelled 'Z' – 'Zulu' in the phoenetic alphabet – and assigned a number at random. The Dutchman was Zulu 10. Zulu 10 completed his paperwork and walked away from the desk with his Hertz pouch. He walked right past me, so close I could smell his hair gel. I always marvelled at the weird world I operated in. Thousands of people were all going about their business, checking-in, lugging luggage, all unaware of the real-life spying game going on around them. Airports are always chock full of surveillance officers from all sorts of agencies and targets from all walks of life; they're a natural focus point for criminals and law enforcement officials alike.

Jed's voice sounded in my earpiece. He'd picked up the eyeball. 'From Jed: That's Zulu 10 approaching the leek, wait.

'He's activated the central locking on a silver Astra, wait.

'The bag's in the boot and he's moving towards the driver's door, wait.

''Zulu 10 complete the driver's side [he's in the driver's seat]. Engine on. Seven-seven, seven-seven.

'Silver rose mobile [a rose is a target car that has not yet been given a number – this one will later be X-ray 10], wait for twist [registration number]; that's Victor-two-three-two Yankee-Alpha-Alpha [V232 YAA], a silver Vauxhall Astra.'

Fin and Robyn meanwhile were already busy ignoring the car park's 5 mph signs and screaming onto the slip road, picking up the target at the main roundabout between the north and south terminals.

Jed and I raced to Wallace and played catch-up, weaving in and out of traffic.

'Christ, you're driving like a teenage girl again,' I said.

Jed grinned. 'Fuck off, Cammo,' he said, and took us up to sixty in a thirty zone. He quickly eased off when he spotted Fin and Robyn, about five cars back from the Dutchman. We followed the target towards Crawley. As we entered the outskirts of the town the Dutchman made various left and right turns towards what we hoped would be his girlfriend's address. Jed dropped back as the cars between us and the target became fewer. At last Fin put up.

'From Gromit: We're getting crispy, we're gonna have to drop it.'

'From Cam: Yes, yes, all call signs sauna at the bedlight.' I got on the phone and told Alpha what was happening.

'Fair enough, lad,' the Scouse voice said. 'Live to fight another day, eh?'

'I'll give it an hour or so and then we'll sweep the area for his car tonight,' I replied. 'When we find it' – ever the optimist – 'I'll get a full team down here for tomorrow.'

I phoned Paul, the senior investigating officer (SIO) boss man in Bristol, and gave him the update. He was keen to move the job on. 'OK, Cammo,' he said quickly, 'it's 2 p.m. now, so let's get a team to you tonight and you can brief in the hotel for an 0700 start. This all depends on you finding the car though,' he added.

'We'll find him. Just as long as he doesn't lift off beforehand.'

Paul hung up.

I looked at Jed. 'Time to play hunt the thimble,' I said. And it really was. The Dutchman had been travelling towards a huge collection of relatively new housing estates, all carbon copies of each other, in a rabbit warren of roads, avenues and dead ones (cul-de-sacs). Loads of them had garages, so if he'd stashed his car inside, we were already screwed.

We purchased a dozen or so street maps of the area, enough for the whole team, and pored over them, trying to figure out the most likely areas he would have gone to from the point where we dropped him. I allocated a rough area to drive round for each car and we then spent the next few hours driving up and down every single road on the outskirts of Crawley. Nothing.

What separated Jed and me from the rest of our team was that that we loved the job, and all the hard graft that came with it, far too much – far more than was healthy. Most case officers would have simply sat back and waited a few more weeks for Alpha to give us another lock-on.

Not us.

We were addicted to the elation; that tremendous feeling that follows when you find the target after hours of graft, instead of hours sat uselessly in the hotel, polishing the sofa with our arses.

Fin called in. 'Fuck me if this guy hasn't parked in a garage for the night,' he said with a yawn.

Robyn and Finbar dropped several five-tonne hints that they were pissed off spending hours pootling up and down every side street in Crawley. It was only 5 p.m. but they'd been on the plot since 5 a.m., so they had a point.

Jed looked at me. 'Fuck 'em,' he said, 'let's ditch 'em and find Mr Bergkamp. Anyone who used to play for the Arsenal deserves all he gets.'

Damn right.

I stood Fin and Robyn down to the bedlight. We lied and told them we would see them at the briefing and that we were going to have coffee in town and speak to Alpha and Paul about what to do next. We then checked all the major NCP car parks in Crawley and even sampled the delights of Horley in our hunt for the elusive Dutchman. Nothing. I checked my watch. It was 6.30 p.m.

'Fuck it,' I said. It was time to break protocol. 'How fast can you get back to Gatwick?'

Jed grinned, spun Gromit round and charged to the motorway. Soon I was watching the speedometer climb effortlessly past 110, 120, 130 mph. Crashing now would be the equivalent of driving off the top of a twenty-storey building. No airbag would save you from that kind of impact.

I had decided take a chance and approach the manager of Hertz. Usually, if you see a target meet an unknown third party, the protocol is not to approach them. You have no idea if they're criminally inclined or know the target personally, or if they just hate all policemen. If we did consider approaching a business, we would usually speak to someone at board level first before talking to employees. But by now my instincts were pretty good and after watching the manager in action for several days he seemed like a decent guy. He was always neatly turned out, kept pictures of his kids on his desk, dressed soberly, and when he talked to the girls on the front desk he spoke to their faces, as opposed to their breasts. Luckily, he was still at work when we rolled up at 7 p.m.

I flashed my ID. 'Can we have a word?'

'Sure, what's the problem?'

'A Dennis Bergkamp lookalike rented an Astra this morning. I need his name and address.'

'Oh yeah,' he said with a smile, 'I remember him, the girls kept going on about him after, saying he was really fit, and a charmer besides. What's he done?'

'Something serious,' I said. We give as little away as possible but I don't think he had much trouble putting two and two together. He was Dutch, we were Customs.

The Dutchman's name was Francis Van Schieffen. He'd given both fake Dutch and UK hotel addresses, surprise,

surprise. But it was good to know he always went to Hertz for his cars, so that would make it easier for us to pick him up whichever UK airport he headed for. Their records told us he was in the UK for about ten days a month, and had been ping-ponging back and forth for the last six months. Apart from that we knew sod all.

I gave the Hertz manager my number. 'Call us if he comes back.'

'No worries, it'll be a pleasure.'

Next, I confessed to Paul that I'd approached Hertz. He was not a happy camper. 'For fuck's sake, Cammo, you're going too far.'

But once I gave him my reasons, that an approach at senior level would have taken too much time, his mood lightened. I told him that Alpha were happy about the approach, which was a bare-faced lie but I knew he'd never check.

I then called my Liverpudlian guy in Alpha, and he was cool about it. I had already noticed that Alpha liked to see teams that had the balls to take control and make their own luck. I'd also realized that if I gave them the right attitude and was able to build the right relationship with the case officer, he'd always back me up – and no one ever questioned Alpha.

Jed and I briefed the team at about 8 p.m. and then we all retired to the pub for a proper discussion. While many frowned upon us spending so much time in the boozer, it was our very own democratic parliament, an informal briefing and debriefing area. Cunning plans were hatched, problems mulled over and tweaked – arguments and personal disagreements were thrashed out by the entire team, irrespective of rank. This was one of the things that made the team, and Customs in general, a level above everyone else.

Alpha had nothing. It was clear that the Dutchman was using other phones in the UK that they didn't yet know about. It was tempting to ask them to hook up his girl-friend's number but it was still too early. Eventually, though, they would have to do this if they wanted to continue the op. It cost about £7,000 a day to put a full surveillance team out, including capital costs, salary, accommodation, vehicles, fuel expenses, etc. Eventually, if the price rose too high, then the powers that be would pull the plug.

My bet was that his girl was working and still abroad, that's why Van Schieffen hadn't called. The team was getting severely hacked off at spending all this time sitting around without a target when other active jobs were waiting for them elsewhere. As usual Jed and I were asking them to do more and more. We now started at 6.30 a.m. and the team worked through for twelve hours straight until they were told to stand down and could clear off back to the comfy hotel for a good meal, a chat and a beer.

I didn't blame anyone who wanted a few hours off after sitting in a car all day, but we needed to get fanatical to catch the slippery bastard so as usual Jed and I would make excuses about going to the cinema for the evening, or meeting boys from one of the London teams, then spend the evening sweeping the area, looking for the target.

'Just five minutes more,' we'd say through a yawn, or, 'He could be down here, we haven't checked this road for two hours.' Eventually, come midnight, we'd drive sleepily back to the hotel for some kip, but not for long.

*

The next day, come 1900 the team stood down. 'From Cam: Jed and I have a meet with another team. See you in the morning.'

As usual, Jed and I carried on patrolling the streets. At 10 p.m. we stopped in Horley to grab a coffee and a bite.

Five minutes later, Jed walked back towards me, carrying coffees and pies on a tray. Suddenly it all went in the bin.

My heart leapt.

'Fuck, there he is,' Jed said as he jogged to the car and threw the door open, 'out of the side street gone three-one!'

He leapt into the car, Starsky and Hutch style across the bonnet. Jed floored the pedal. 'I see him' I said, buckling up. 'He's nine-one the ring road, straight on, straight on!'

Jed pulled the car into the high street. Now we'd found him, our problems were many and massive. We were the only car. There was no support. And we were a long way behind in a still busy thoroughfare. We needed to get close without drawing too much attention.

Jed pulled Gromit to the right and drove down the centre lines, forcing oncoming cars into the side.

'I can't fucking see him any more,' I said.

'Fuck this,' Jed said quietly and Gromit surged. He veered back out and drove over the centre lines again, practically brushing cars on either side.

'Astra light cluster, I see him!' I yelled excitedly. Jed was raising toots and hand gestures from angry drivers, so he eased up and slipped in and out of the cars between the target and us in a slightly more civilized manner.

Jed clung on to the Astra, dodging round cars on blind bends and blocking vehicles from getting in front of us. Eventually we were within three cars of the target; Jed had done what a team of six vehicles was designed to do. We kept with him.

We followed him through some back doubles, on a route that he must have known could throw off a shadow, into a new estate on the outskirts, somewhere we'd checked a number of times before.

We were the only two cars on the road. 'We're getting crispy,' I said.

'Just a little longer,' Jed replied. 'We're almost there.'

We knew it was very likely he'd be looking in his rear-view constantly. We 'clipped' him as he went round bends (staying far enough back so that we only saw the back end of his car as it went round the next corner, hence keeping out of his mirrors).

Another two minutes and the road straightened. His brake lights went on.

Jed speeded up a notch and we saw the car turn left into a cul-de-sac. Jed stopped short. 'I'm gone,' I said and jumped out. I walked towards the junction with the dead end. On foot, you always have to have a reason to be there. I couldn't just wander into the cul-de-sac; if the target was standing on his drive watching me, where would I go? I couldn't turn round, that's for sure.

I lit a ciggie, always a good reason to pause in the street. I gave it a moment as I took a drag and then crossed the end of the cul-de-sac, straining my peripheral vision. I could see the car parked on a drive, lights on, engine running, and the driver, tall and blond, opening up the garage doors. No wonder we hadn't been able find the fucking thing.

Van Schieffen paid me no attention and put the car in

the garage. I walked on. Jed was already waiting further up the road. I climbed in.

'Job done,' I said, 'St Margaret's Close. Let's go and check the number – it's on the offside, one before the camper van; car's in the garage.'

We gave it a few more minutes and drove into the close, right up to the end, clocking the target house as number 18. It was 10.45.

'Time for a beer?' asked Jed.

'Fuck, yes!'

I rang Alpha. Now we had stood down, the case officer could go home. He was well pleased. He would carry out phone checks on the house and also see whether it had cropped up on any previous Customs ops. In the morning, we would do all the background checks: we'd look at the electoral roll to see who was registered to vote at that address and then check the Police National Computer (PNC) to see if anyone registered at the address had a criminal record; we'd also use the PNC's vehicle on-line descriptive searching facility (VODS) to obtain a list of all vehicles registered at the address for the last few years and to whom they were registered; finally, we'd check with the Local Intelligence Office (LIO) to see if there was any intelligence about the address. This was a good one because the LIO would also be able to tell you whether the area was pro or con law enforcement – an important thing to know if you were going to approach a resident to set up an observation point in their front room.

For now, though, we went back to the hotel to find a few of the boys in the bar; they were replete after a curry, belts loosened and winding down with a few snifters.

Mickey the bike rider spotted us first. 'Evening, tossers,' he said. 'Where have you been? And why do you look so fucking pleased with yourselves?' Mickey was good-looking, in his mid forties, married to a woman also in the job, two kids. I'd known him for years and he was the one I poured my miserable guts out to whenever one of my wives/girl-friends left me because of 'that fucking job'.

'Cracked the case wide open,' Jed said quietly, beaming. 'The Addicott/Heath A-team locked on to the target, did some outstanding one-car surveillance and housed him on the outskirts of Horley. I thank you. We were gonna call you, but it all happened a bit sharpish and we didn't want to interrupt your din-dins.'

'Bollocks, no way,' said Finbar, sitting up and incredulous. 'Have you told Paul yet?'

'Nah, thought I'd leave that till the morning,' I said confidently.

'He'll not be pleased,' said Mickey.

'Yeah, right,' Jed snorted. 'There'll be no problemo when he realizes we saved him about fifty thousand quid's worth of your lazy-arse overtime; he won't care in the slightest that we have risked our lives and the mission for Queen and country.'

Eyeing the clock, which now showed 10.59, I ventured, 'Who wants a beer then?'

Now we could really crack on.

# 5. Bugs and Tags

Now we needed to know what the Dutchman did when he was in the UK. Alpha still only had the one phone for him and he was hardly using it, so it was up to us to generate the intelligence.

Now that we had a name, the Intel team at Gatwick did a daily check to see if he was booked on any incoming flights from Schipol. Invariably, he'd book a few days in advance, in which case we were ready to meet him off the plane, or if he paid cash and walked onto a flight we would get a couple of hours' notice, ensuring we spent a pleasant morning screaming round the M25 setting off all the cameras. Lots of speeding tickets landed on Paul's desk, and he had to reply to every single one. Once he mentioned Customs and hard drugs, most (but not all!) constabularies wrote them off.

We now knew that Van Schieffen's girlfriend was a very hot, twenty-three-year-old EasyJet air stewardess. She was the only person registered at the house and owned a Renault Clio. Van Schieffen never left home before about 9 a.m. and we didn't see him do anything dirty the first couple of times. He went to the gym quite a bit and took his girlfriend out for expensive meals and one pain-in-the-arse-for-us weekend away. She was away from home for extended periods and he timed his visits to coincide with the end of her shifts. He always rented a car from Hertz.

'We need more,' Jed said. 'Let's do 'is bins.'

Jed was so tenacious it was infuriating.

This wasn't a job for the weak of stomach. Now Jed and I weren't faint-hearted, but we knew only too well what going through people's bins was like, so we pulled Chrissy out of the office the day we got permission for the bin-run. Chrissy was actually the team leader but was an office boy at heart. He was brilliant at desk-based Intel but was always pestering us for a little excitement. 'Come on, Cammo, I'm going fucking mental in here, let me get out on the ground.'

I threw a pair of latex gloves onto his desk. 'Call home, tell your missus you won't be home tonight and put the Marigolds on.'

We waited until Van Schieffen put his bin out and, with call signs covering all the entry and exit points from the 'magic box' (the immediate area where we were working, mostly called 'the plot' by younger officers), we swiped the bin without anyone noticing.

Jed and I stood back while Chrissy went through it. 'Fuck me, did you ever see so many fucking used condoms in all your life, Cammo?' Jed said.

'Only in an Amsterdam whorehouse.'

Amazingly, Chrissy seemed to be having the time of his life. The bin's entire contents were divided into separate piles until eventually we had a small mound of paperwork. Nothing exciting or useful to us but it's amazing what people still throw away; no wonder identity fraud is so easy.

The next step was to bug the interior of his car so we could listen in. To do this, I decided to hatch a conspiracy with the Hertz manager. This time I got all the necessary clearance as it was a pretty big ask.

With the Hertz manager's help, we were able to prep Van Schieffen's car with listening and tracking devices, so that the next time he flew into the country we'd have him fully hooked up. Van Schieffen always rented from Hertz; his routine would be his downfall.

Legally, we had to confirm through surveillance that the target was in the car. It would have broken all the laws covering this activity if we listened in to someone who wasn't a target; this is officially known as collateral intrusion.

When Van Schieffen arrived in the UK the next time he collected a fully spammed, all-singing, all-dancing mobile tape recorder and tracking device to drive round in.

He immediately gave us gold when we overheard him set up a meet. Finally!

He took off at 10 a.m. and drove anti-clockwise around the M25. Jed and I were in the tracker car. After a while, as we neared junction 3, the signal increased in intensity. He was starting to slow.

'From Gromit: He's two of two [in the outside lane of a two-lane carriageway], that's X-ray 10 Charlie slowing, slowing, all call signs hang back. Nine-nine nine on the approach to junction 3, Madrid, can you bramble [go past the target] for a physical?'

'Madrid: Yes.'

Jed looked at me as the whine of the tracker increased. 'From Gromit: Still nine-nine-nine,' I said. 'Nine-nine-nine' meant that he'd stopped dead.

'What the fuck is he doing, stopping on the M25?'

I shrugged. 'Must've broken down.'

'From Madrid: That's a physical, X-ray 10 Charlie nine-nine-nine on the hard shoulder, hazards on.'

'From Gromit: Wallace and Gromit will maintain two-two, all other call signs plot on junctions 4 and 3.'

Still no movement. 'Smart bastard,' Jed said.

I nodded. 'There's no place better.'

Because the Dutchman was on the hard shoulder, there was no way for us to observe him other than by driving past in the traffic. I sent one of the cars from junction 4 to 3 to try and see what he was up to.

They drove past the target. 'From Berlin: There's a rose nine-nine-nine behind X-ray 10 Charlie, wait for twist . . . Twist is Lima-three-eight-two Romeo-Mike-Foxtrot, a red Rover 620.'

'Gromit,' I acknowledge.

What a place to do it. Genius. The villains would think it was almost impossible for us to plot up on. It would have been if we hadn't had technical assistance.

'Well, it must be a bloody dirty meet if they're doing it here,' said Jed.

He was right, we don't believe in coincidence. If it looks dirty, it is dirty.

It was time we made a tough call – the kind we were paid to make.

# 6. Up the Chain

'From Gromit: All conventional call signs to stay with the rose. Gromit and Wallace will maintain two-two on X-ray 10 Charlie.'

Splitting the team was a major risk a lot of people wouldn't take, but then those people wouldn't ever nick anyone. The conventional call signs were to 'house' the rose: follow it to a place that appeared to be home or work. This would take us to the next leg of the operation.

'Seven-seven, seven-seven. That's X-ray 10 Charlie mobile. Wallace tracked X-ray 10 Charlie to J3 [junction 3], where it performed a recip [pronounced 'ree-sip', a reciprocal route or return journey] back on the M25 clockwise.

This was incredibly frustrating for Jed and me. We knew that Zulu 10 would probably go home now, but because we were in the tracker car we had to follow. We wanted to be with the new target, with the excitement of trying to ID him with our limited resources. As we were heading in the opposite direction to the rest of the team we were out of comms pretty quickly.

But there was an upside.

Once we got Zulu 10 home we were free to catch up with the rest of the team – as fast as we liked. Although tracker cars were not supposed to do conventional surveillance, very few people took any notice of the rule if it meant leaving a team short.

Once Van Schieffen arrived home Jed floored the pedal and we sped off round the M25 at warp speed. We knew that if the Rover was heading in towards London on the A13 then it was likely that whoever was driving it lived or worked in that area. It could all be over if we didn't get a move on and the team lost him for lack of vehicles.

'Jed, mate, stop driving like my grandmother.'

We were in a 70 mph traffic jam yet Jed was still managing to pull 110 mph.

My stupid comment wasn't lost on Jed. 'Fuck you, sunshine,' he replied, jerking the car onto the hard shoulder.

My phone went. It was Mickey. 'Target's stopped at a small industrial estate off River Road, near Barking,' he said, adding, 'Is that the sound of a V6 being sent to an early grave?'

I grinned. 'Yeah, we'll be there in no time.' Up the speedometer climbed, 115, 120 mph. With no blues and twos (lights and two-note siren), I took delight in the shock and outrage we caused amongst other road users as our Camry barrelled past on the hard shoulder.

As soon as I hung up, the phone went again. It was Chrissy. He'd checked the PNC. 'The Rover's registered to a woman from Barking,' he said, 'Mrs Christine Matthews, 126 Houghton Way.'

'The driver's wife, then.'

'No doubt.'

Villains always do this. It doesn't ever help at all to deter us – or the taxman. Idiots.

By the time we rocked up the rest of the team were plotted around the industrial estate. The Rover drove off shortly afterwards and we followed it through Barking to the registered address of the car.

'I think we can safely assume that this is Mr Matthews,' I said as soon as he'd let himself into the house. It's a basic principle in surveillance – never miss the target entering any premises if you can avoid it; then you know if he's got a key or is just a visitor.

I booked us into a hotel on the A127. It seemed to be full of bored businesswomen and tonight was Disco Nite. Jed, Mickey, Fin and I left the others to it and found a corner where we could talk shop.

We knew nothing about the content of the two-minute-long meeting on the hard shoulder. It was clearly dirty as hell; if they were too twitchy to meet in a pub or have a coffee somewhere, it must have been important.

I always tried to second-guess the villains, to try and make sense of what we were seeing. It annoyed lots of other officers because they hated us talking shop all the time, especially in boozers, bars and discos.

But people like me Jed, Fin and Mickey couldn't help it. The Queen paid us to fuck villains' lives up and that's how we lived and breathed. We all knew it was a game, though – they do what they do, we try and stop them. It's not rocket science.

'OK, it was a quick meet,' Jed said, nursing his third pint.

'So that means it's to set up a more important meet,' Mickey concluded.

'A meeting so important it couldn't be arranged over a meal or a drink,' I added, liking where this was going.

'Van Schieffen is a fixer for a Dutch team who's brought in fifty keys of heroin, which makes him either (a) important or (b) stupid, because he went hands-on,' I continued.

'He ain't stupid,' Fin said. 'Maybe he went hands-on

because the system he uses is foolproof — for him, anyway.'

By the end of the evening we had come to the opinion that Matthews must have something to do with stashing the gear or transporting it. His little industrial unit was on the East End/Essex border, ideal for a slaughter (cutting and repackaging the drugs) and/or onward transportation. He didn't come across as a dealer, though; he didn't strike us as being enough of a pro. We hoped we would be moving one rung up the ladder in the not too distant.

The phone went. It was the boss, I made a quick exit from the disco where a number of businesswomen were succumbing to the advances of the team's swordsmen. I answered in the car park. When I returned, Jed read my expression: 'What's wrong?'

'Paul and Chrissy want me to brief in person in a full-blown sit-down-over-coffee-until-we-thrash-things-out session to see what we do next.'

I left Jed in charge and drove back home, grateful I'd stayed off the juice, getting home around midnight, just in time to have a row with Louise. Before I went to bed on the sofa, I put my head round the kids' bedroom door to see the boys fast asleep. They were still dead to the world when I left at the crack of dawn for the meeting in Bristol.

The meeting went well enough. Paul agreed to everything, he was just happy to be an operational SIO running an Alpha-led case.

It was simple:

Get Matthews hooked up and find out what part he was playing.

Get Van Schieffen's next hire car 'sorted'.

Work on both targets, switching from Crawley to Essex as intelligence dictated.

Work our way up the chain in order to identify all the components of the importation: suppliers – transport – dealers.

Meeting over. Back to work.

Matthews proved to be a creature of habit. He ran a nine-to-five business from his unit off River Road, but we had no real idea what it was or whether it was important to his relationship with Van Schieffen.

In between shifts following Matthews, I tried to get back on top of my family life. It wasn't easy. Alpha called during the boys' Saturday football match and I had to walk away so as not to be overheard while the kids looked on in outrage. I then spent the rest of the weekend getting Ben out of various scrapes with local kids, squeezing in a beer in my local, a wild Irish pub called the Ring o' Bells, before heading home to babysit while the missus went clubbing. I didn't blame her. As it happened, I spent most of the night on the phone to Jed as we had various brainwaves about the op.

My phone rang pretty much constantly. My catchphrase to the kids was 'Just a minute, son.' I spent most of my time staffing the operation for the coming week. It was a constant nightmare as people were always calling in sick or with crappy excuses when they wanted a particular day off.

I wanted to get heads-up asap and so I started bickering with Louise about lunchtime, as I packed up my gear.

'Cheer up,' Jed said when I picked him up. 'You look like a man who's been told he's got a day to live. Girl trouble?'

I glared at him darkly. He knew my situation only too well and we drove in silence until I couldn't resist the lure of discussing how Matthews fitted in once again.

We drove to Kent first, to pick up the prepped Hertz car for Van Schieffen. After dropping that off, the plan was to work on Matthews (now Zulu 20) until Van Schieffen flew in, which was any day now. Chrissy was in the office and would be listening in to whatever he said in the Hertz car.

Van Schieffen landed at Gatwick and was followed as expected to the Hertz desk. Everything was in place. The manager had arranged that Zulu 10 would be given the right car, the tracker cars had the tag number plugged into their computers and Chrissy was back in the office ready to switch on the audio kit.

The smartest villains in the world never accept the first hire car they're offered. They always upgrade, downgrade or find a fault somewhere. I'd told the manager to do whatever Van Schieffen asked; we didn't want him to suspect anything.

We needn't have worried. Zulu 10, obviously not that smart, picked up the right car, now X-ray 10 Echo, the tag was booming as we rolled off towards Crawley. As soon as we confirmed Zulu 10 in X-ray 10 Echo I rang Chrissy and he switched on the audio equipment.

'I gotta feel it in my blood – wooo-ooooh! I need your touch, don't need your love – woooo-ooooh!'

'What the fuck is this?' Jed asked as I burst out laughing. Van Schieffen may have been one of the best dope dealers we ever came across, but he couldn't sing to save his life.

'And I want – and I need. And I lust – ANIMAL!'

It was hideous. This was always the problem with listening

in to criminals. The interesting stuff we wanted usually lasted a few seconds. The rest of the time was filled with their crappy lives and bad habits. Imagine what people would hear if they listened to a socially unedited you, as you went about your business at home.

'And I waaant – and I neeeed . . .'

'Turn it down!' Jed yelled.

The next day proved to be more eventful.

My phone was ringing. I opened my eyes. The bedside clock said 04:00. I picked up.

It was Jed.

'Insomniac bastard,' I said as I sighed, forced myself to sit up and picked up the phone. 'What?'

'Let's get a couple of hours in before the others get on plot.'

Ten minutes later I was showered and dressed and in the car park, no coffee necessary. I called Alpha.

'Up already?' an impressed voice said. London accent this time. My Scouse friend wouldn't be on until 7 a.m.

Jed and I took the tracker car Jerry. We sat on high ground; elevation gives us much more range when tracking and as we were the only car out, we needed as much heads-up as possible.

Everyone else was due on plot around 8.30, there being no Intel to suggest an early lift-off. We drove up the main road past purple 10 junction, activated the tag and waited.

At 7.30 the tag sprang into life. We waited. It quickly changed from one beep every minute (stationary) to one beep every two seconds.

I said the obvious. 'He's moving.'

'Should we inform the gang?'

'Nah,' I said, 'leave them to their breakfast until we know what he's up to. If it's an early trip to the gym then we can track him ourselves for a bit.'

I sounded calmer than I felt. This was completely against the rules and Zulu 10 hadn't started that early in the morning before. But hey, we were thinking of our colleagues and just giving ourselves the adrenaline kick that we wanted – after all, if we lost him we would have a lot of explaining to do.

He drove towards the town centre. Tracking is difficult in built-up areas because the signal bounces off the buildings and gives you false vectors and ranges. I concentrated on the range and approximate direction, making Jed drive very quickly and crazily all over the place. The signal stayed good and strong.

We soon locked on to the target in his favourite supermarket. When he switched off the engine, the tag gave out a continuous tone, which became more high pitched the closer we got.

We rang the team and told them he had gone mobile and that he was in Sainsbury's. I could hear the old women amongst them muttering that we were a 'pair of bloody cowboys'.

As they rolled up, Van Schieffen was back in the car using the phone. Jed had done a drive past and asked why I wasn't on the phone to Chrissy finding out what he was saying.

'Cos he won't be in yet. It's only eight o'clock and he keeps VAT hours.'

Jed rolled his eyes theatrically. 'Fucking hell, Cammo, get him out of bed and into the office this instant; doesn't he know we've got a case to crack!'

'I'll text him and tell him to get the kit switched on, I'll say we're mobile and can't talk, I don't want any grief about being out here on our own just cos you couldn't sleep past dawn.'

'Ha-bloody-ha, didn't see you complaining at the time, or after I got the teas in.'

SMS messages were used all the time when you didn't have time to talk or, as in this case, didn't want to. If you had to tell twelve people to get their arses out of bed early because the job was on top it would take precious minutes to call them all.

I did it constantly and other officers thought I was being impersonal, but it wasn't that. I wanted to keep the line clear for Alpha and if I was engaged when they had really important stuff for me, then they'd be well hacked off.

Text to Chrissy: 'Z10 MOBILE IN X10E. CAN'T SPK NEED KIT ON. CAM.'

'That should do it,' I said as Jed blasted down a route parallel to Zulu 10 towards the M23. 'Gotta show him who's boss.'

'Quite right too,' replied Jed.

'Look out!'

Jed had already seen the speed bump. It was one of those smooth, wide ones. 'Oops – too late,' he said, as we took off.

'Shit!' The tracker cars, being very expensive and highly covert bits of kit that the department would rather not lose, each had an alarm that went off if they were jacked up off the ground – in theory, being stolen.

At the moment we sailed over the speed bump, a bell rang in our London control room. That meant Paul would

45

be getting a call right about now from an excited arse-polisher telling him: 'One of your cars has been nicked!' Paul's line was to suggest their kit was a tad too sensitive, and then bollock us for treating the car like an aircraft yet again.

Zulu 10 joined the M25 anti-clockwise and was heading for the area we last saw him meet Matthews.

'This is it, finally,' Jed said.

Zulu 10 left the motorway and headed for a greasy spoon close to Badgers Mount. Chrissy rang to say that Zulu 10 and Zulu 20 had spoken and they were meeting at a cafe off the A2.

I put this out to the team and sent Finbar and Mickey ahead to get in the caff ahead of the targets. Targets always get twitchy about being followed into meetings. If you get in ahead of them, then they're much less worried and a lot more verbal.

They arrived with five minutes to spare.

The greasy spoon was full of truckers and builders eating breakfast, so it was pretty noisy with munching, slurping, hacking and bantering; difficult for Mickey and Fin to get 'overheards'. They were at the counter when the targets walked in and stood right next to them. Van Schieffen and Matthews looked very relaxed, but they weren't chatting.

Fin and Mick ordered and picked their seats well. Just behind them was a free table, the only recently wiped one in the caff; most of the others were piled with dirty crockery.

They busied themselves with the newspaper and general chit-chat.

Sure enought, the targets picked the table immediately behind them.

Mickey passed the paper to Fin and casually leaned back in his chair with his hand on the transmit button of his covert radio in his right-hand jeans pocket.

In situations where an officer is so close to a target that he cannot transmit his voice over the air, there is a system where a series of 'clicks' can be used to send basic information via the tone button on the radio remote control.

The system is limited to yes/no answers. You can feel the anger when an officer, right up close to the target, is asked something bone-headed like: 'What are the targets talking about?'

Mickey gave three clicks that came across the air as bleeps.

'From Cam: Three clicks received, do you require interrogation?'

Mickey gave three clicks.

'Are the targets together?'

Three clicks.

'Have they ordered food?'

Three clicks.

This gave us an idea as to how long they'd be inside – if they'd just ordered drinks, then they could be out in five minutes.

'Do you require any further interrogation?'

Two clicks.

Mickey was then able to transmit what they were saying by text, a perfectly innocent activity.

Thanks to the noisy cafe and the low tones used by the targets, Mickey only got part of the story. It's very rare that overheards like this help at all, either from the intelligence angle or the evidence angle, especially when balanced against the risk of exposure ('show out') by putting officers so close to the target that they may recognize them later in the day. We are not like the security services who can 'burn' someone and then never use them again on that job. We have limited resources and therefore have to be much more sparing.

Mickey did manage to get something mildly interesting, however. One of the targets (Mickey couldn't tell which) was planning to introduce the other one to someone or something. Sounds crap, but it gave us a reason to be cheerful.

It meant that the two of them would be together later in the day to do something that sounded important.

You can always tell, in a dirty meet between villains, when the business chat has finished and the domestic chat starts. They spend the first bit leaning forward talking in hushed tones, then they laugh and lean backwards, surveying their surroundings.

This was the cue for Fin and Mick to leave. We didn't want them following the targets out of the meet, so they went back to the car before the Zulus finished up. As he left, Mickey texted me saying everyone should now be heads-up as they no longer had switch of the targets.

Mick and Fin drove off from the caff to take up a quiet plot position well away from the action. We decided to stay with Zulu 10 and let Zulu 20 go.

'He's definitely just wasting time till the meet,' Jed said.

'Yeah, but check it out,' I replied, 'he's been trying c/s on us.'

Counter surveillance (c/s) is designed to find out whether you are being followed. Anti-surveillance is designed to prevent a surveillance team from following you, whether you know they're behind you or not.

Most villains carry out c/s without knowing what they are looking for. A simple c/s route would be to drive along the main road between 'A' and 'B'. At a given point you would turn off the main and drive along a short parallel route before rejoining the main road to continue to 'B'. Comparing the vehicles that turn off the main route behind you with the ones that rejoin the main route behind you will give you a clue. Of course, good surveillance teams identify these c/s routes (or 'nips' in brevity) and will let the target run.

We'd been following Van Schieffen all day. He'd gone to Bluewater shopping centre and called his girlfriend (which Alpha got: nothing of interest). He then returned to the car and used a phone we didn't have to speak to someone in Dutch. Chrissy copied the recording of the Dutch call and sent it off for priority translation. Then he'd started his c/s nonsense. We let him get on with it and gave Fin the five-five. Now we were all waiting for his next move.

The translation had come back within an hour. It was dynamite.

The call was to a Dutchman called Rik, one of the main players in Van Schieffen's organization. The Dutch told us they already had his phone hooked up. It fitted well with what they were doing because they'd heard Van Schieffen's voice before but didn't have his phone or any other details on him.

We'd been a big help to them and Jed and I were well pleased.

But we knew our management wouldn't be happy unless the Intel was helping our job. There is a lot of bullshit surrounding drugs enforcement; senior management couldn't give a stuff if our hard work assisted the Dutch in dismantling an organization abroad, they were only judged by the number of UK organizations their teams 'dismantled'. Very short sighted.

Van Schieffen told Rik that a meeting with someone called 'Maxie' was set up for later in the day. He confirmed that the meet with the 'other man' (Matthews) had gone well and that he would call from the 'office' later. The office referred to a telephone kiosk, so called by villains because public telephones were originally called public call offices, and it was where a lot of business was done before the advent of the mobile phone.

I called Alpha with all this. They were chuffed. 'This is more like it, Cam,' the Liverpudlian said. 'Keep it coming. It's nice to be on the receiving end of new Intel for a change.' He cleared the line.

'They love us, don't they?' Jed said. 'I bet we're the only team who feeds Intel back into them instead of just sitting on our arses waiting for them to dish it out.'

Suddenly, Finbar came across the air.

'From Finbar: Seven-seven, seven-seven; Zulu 10 nine-one the jug.'

'Jerry.'

Two minutes later Zulu 10 walked towards his car. He drove up the A13 into town and parked in the underground car park of a Docklands Hotel, all glass and steel, about as homely as Stasi HQ. It had a big restaurant and the lounge/ bar area overlooking the docks were always busy.

Everyone plotted up and I kicked four footies out to cover him inside.

Zulu 10 was loafing around in reception when a call came over the air.

'Yeah, from Brazil: That's X-ray 20, driven by Zulu 20 from red three-four, nine-one generally the bedlight.'

'Jerry: Yes.'

'From foot Pedro: Zulu 10 from the handle of the bedlight nine-one the main . . . wait . . . X-ray 20 nine-nine-nine outside the bedlight wait . . . Zulu 10 complete X-ray 20, X-ray 20 mobile . . . its a re-cip, re-cip nine-one the nest, nine-one you, Brazil.'

'Brazil: Yes.'

All the footmen raced back to their call signs.

Silence.

X-ray 20 had not gone past Brazil, who was waiting at the roundabout (the nest) near the hotel. Kilo – aka Mickey the biker on a Fireblade – flashed past the traffic on the outside and saw the Rover parking up on the other side of the dock from the hotel, next to a huge Chinese restaurant.

All three targets went into the restaurant.

I could hear the team rubbing their hands. It was 5 p.m. and we'd been on the go since early morning.

'OK,' I said with a sigh, 'who wants to cover the chilli [meeting]?'

What followed was a static scramble of indecipherable volunteers. Dinner in the restaurant was claimable as 'an expense in the course of surveillance'. Similar scrambles had taken place for meets at Nobu and the Met Bar.

The rest of the team could stretch their legs and grab a

bite, anything up to £9.30 would be reimbursed – for lunch *and* dinner, mind you.

Jed grinned. 'We should cover it, mate,' he said, 'as we're the best and the bosses.'

I thought for a nanosecond how it would look if I decided to cover the meet.

In the end I sent two footies, Marion and Pedro; they were of similar age and could pass for a normal-looking couple.

A few minutes in I got the first text from Pedro: Z10 & Z20 EATING. US 2. V GOOD GRUB, SWT & SR PRAWN BALLS 2 U.

My stomach rumbled. The only thing they couldn't do was drink alcohol. A pint was OK for cover but the navigator's job was as important as the driver's. There was a Customs saying that went, 'I'd better drive cos I'm too pissed to navigate.'

I received a text from Marion describing the unknown third party. I put it out to the team:

'From Jerry: All call signs, we will be going with the unknown who is now Zulu Alpha. [Alpha indicates that this guy is a new and priority target for the moment.] Relay from Marion the unknown is an IC1 male . . . 45 to 50 years . . . clean shaven, distinctive white-grey hair . . . five-foot ten . . . wearing grey polo shirt on blue jeans. All call signs acknowledge.'

'From Pedro. Bill has arrived. Expect chilli to break up shortly.'

'Jerry: Who's Bill?'

'Pedro: *The* bill, fuckwit.'

'We'll let 10 and 20 go completely,' I said to Jed, sticking the tag into 'deep snore' (power-saving mode). 'We need to home the whole team on Zulu Alpha.'

'Well, he came with Matthews, so he'll be dropping him off somewhere.'

'Hopefully home.'

'That would be nice of him. Just as long as it's not a tube or bus stop –'

'A fucking nightmare.'

'– or a black cab.'

'Don't even go there.'

Zulu 20 and Zulu Alpha went straight to the Rover. Zulu 10 lit up and walked back across the dock towards the hotel. We let him go and stayed with Matthews.

'Let's not tell Chrissy,' Jed said, 'he'll only pack up and go home; I want any Intel from the car audio.'

I nodded. The rules governing the audio in the car were that we had to confirm (through surveillance) that the warranted target was in the car. Jed and I operated using a loose interpretation of these rules.

We followed the Rover back on the A13 eastbound. 'This is interesting,' I said as we pulled off into a side road at Ilford and a minute or two later were outside an Ilford boozer.

'Now that looks well dodge,' Jed said.

There are some places you don't send footmen into without good reason. And this was one of them. Any strange face would automatically be pinged in this crummy little boozer. Discretion being the better part of valour, we let them have their pint alone.

'Fucking annoying, though. Could be another bod they've gone to see.'

An hour later Matthews drove off alone and Zulu Alpha walked up the road, further into the backstreets. It was pretty quiet: more cars about than people. The footmen stayed well back while the rest of the team circled the side streets taking it in turns to drive past from different directions, giving lock-ons to the foot team. The problem was that for a fair percentage of time the target was out of sight of either a footman or call sign. He could step off the street and into any of the houses in just five seconds without us spotting him.

Jed and I parked at the northern end of a road filled with terraced houses. Small, two- or three-bedroom affairs, the front doors opening straight onto the pavement.

'There he is,' Jed said.

'Got him.'

The target was walking towards us from the south. I opened the car door. 'Just in case he lives here,' I said. I had my rig on and could hear the commentary as he came closer. I quickened my pace until I could see him in the gloom ahead.

He was seventy metres from a junction; one of the team had just turned the corner behind him.

'From Cam: Hold back, hold back, that's Zulu Alpha nine-one me'.

We were forty metres apart and closing.

'Cam: That's Zulu Alpha slowing, he's getting something from his pocket.'

It was a key. Yes!

'He's gone four-one [turned right] next to a red Polo, he's at the handle [door] and he's gone complete, wait for number.'

I quickened my pace, keeping a sharp eye on the spot where he had disappeared.

'Cam: Confirm the number as fourteen, that's one-four.'

The team automatically plotted up on the address, even though they knew we'd be standing down shortly. I got back to the car to find Jed searching for a hotel for us all.

I got on the phone to Alpha. 'Great one, Cam, a good day's work,' the Liverpudlian voice said, 'I'll see what I can pull and call you back.'

From Alpha that was praise indeed.

Next, Paul was on the line. He was in town and wanted a quiet face-to-face. As we were done for the day, I was happy to oblige.

'Cam,' he said, 'how would you like to run the case as your own boss?'

I think my expression of unadulterated joy might have been answer enough. Paul smiled. I quickly calmed myself down and asked: 'What about Chrissy?'

'He's not playing much of a role as "case manager", as such. He's a great commercial fraud investigator but this job isn't him. Besides, he's applied for and got a bag-carrier's job with one of the top brass in Custom House. I'm happy for you to take command and as long as it doesn't go tits-up I'll step in at the end to take all the glory.'

So Chrissy had been 'promoted' to personal ass-kisser. I suppose it was more than a simple PA job because he would be able to offer ground-level opinion and advice to someone who had been away from the coalface for far too long.

Anyway, what the fuck did I care?

This was my operation now.

*

A few years ago, this would have led me to make a very excited call home to tell the missus. Now I was full of dread. Needless to say, it didn't go down very well.

Alpha called back just as Jed and I were leaving the hotel bar. 'Your Zulu Alpha is Max "Maxie" Turnbull, a proper cockney villain. From East Ham, now residing in Ilford. Minor offences only; a bit of thievery, a dash of receiving and sprinkling of assaults, but nothing for a few years.

'He's a former a market trader turned wholesaler – and not drugs. He supplies market traders with everything under the sun – toilet rolls to frying pans. Could be a cover, but that's all for now. For all we know they could be conspiring to import fucking clogs.'

Alpha hung up.

'So what is he, then?' Jed asked. 'Warehouse? Transport? Not the buyer, surely?'

'You know what?' I said. 'I think it's time to call Sigma.'

# 7. Breaking, Entering and Bugging

Somewhere in southern England is a very special building. From the outside, it looks like a large agricultural warehouse. The only clue to its possible significance are several carefully placed, high-quality CCTV cameras.

It's only when you step inside that it gets very surreal. It's pretty much empty, except for one very striking object. In the middle of the warehouse sits a large, four-bedroom suburban house.

This is the HQ of the covert means of entry (CME) team, code name Sigma, staffed by ex-Special Forces personnel. They had built the house themselves. It had every entry system, lock, bolt and latch that's ever been made. They'd rigged it for every kind of scenario thinkable so they could refine their very specialized skills. Breaking, entering and bugging a secure property without disturbing a single speck of dust in a strictly limited time frame is not easy.

Sigma shared the space with a handful of civilian techies who fitted and maintained the 'tracker' and Vmems equipment and sourced specialist bits and bobs, such as 1000mm camera lenses and some pretty sensitive listening devices.

I put in a request to the CME to help us with Matthews' industrial unit but, thanks to our lack of Intel, I knew I'd sink straight to the bottom of their very long list of penthouses, offices, hotels, boats, planes, trains, log cabins, etc. of various Mr and Mrs Bigs that needed to be fitted with audio and visual bugging equipment for some pretty heavy-duty ops. CME always seemed to send the exotic jobs straight to the top of their list. Bugging the interior of an industrial unit in Barking just didn't do it for them.

The last thing I was expecting was a phone call a few minutes later. 'OK, you're in luck, we've had a cancellation and my lads are tooled up ready to go. How soon do you need us?'

I was bowled over. 'Fuck me, Jed, Sigma's on their way!'

We had a briefing with Sigma bright and early to go through the basics. They would spend about two hours each night attacking Matthews's security system. Matthews had a swipe card and keypad entry plus a remote lock, so it wasn't going to be that straightforward.

When we had put the target to bed, we would leave an op team on his home and move everyone to cover the Sigma attack. To minimize the likelihood of their being spotted, Sigma's plan was to work from about 1 a.m. until 3.30.

Once everyone was set, we put a tight surveillance box on the premises. Call signs would alert us to every car and person on foot around the entrance to the industrial estate. From our calls, Sigma would decide when to go in. Once at work we had to be on top of our game; if we missed anything there would be all hell to pay.

I'd met Sigma's head honcho, Kev, once before, on a surveillance course. After saying our hellos he made sure everybody heard his most important message for the team: 'First things first. We have an emergency call. If we are compromised and have to fight our way out, you won't hear a thing because we will deal with it. But if you hear "Sigma-

Sigma-Sigma" it means we are fighting and losing. That means get your arses in here.'

'Yeah, right,' Jed muttered to me afterwards, 'Kev, an ex-Para, and his team of ex-Special Forces meeting their match? I don't think that's likely unless the entire Chinese army is hiding behind Matthews' shutters.'

It was three very long days and nights before they got into the unit and managed to set about deploying the audio kit. It was all hard wired to the mains system so would run for ever. It was just like the kit in Van Schieffen's car, except that this only worked over a short range, so we kept the receiver in the back of our car.

While they were still inside, my phone rang. It was Kev. Sigma's remit was to get in. Deploy the kit. Get out. But, you know, boys will be boys.

'Look,' he said, 'we're in now and I'm just standing in front of Matthews's desk like a spare dick at a lesbian orgy. Why don't I have a nose round?'

'Sure, go for it.'

At the debrief, Kev and his team were all wearing massive grins. 'What is it? What did you find?' They carried on grinning like Cheshire cats. 'What?' I asked. 'Come on, I'm on tenterhooks here.'

'Shall I tell him?' Kev asked his team. They nodded through stifled giggles.

'Do you know what Matthews is into?'

'Of course not,' I said, exasperated.

'He's into porn. With a capital H-A-R-D-C-O-R-E!'

'Holy fuck!'

'Yes, exactly. I think there was a copy of *Sister Shag* in there, wasn't there, lads?'

Matthews was a major supplier of porn to London's West End with aspirations of becoming a producer/director. The main players in the porn biz had at one time been the O'Sullivans, but they'd disappeared down the plughole. The father was doing life for stabbing the Kray brothers' driver in the eye, while his missus was about to go down for VAT fraud. The son, Ronnie, had moved on to better things and was doing rather well at some back street pub game involving balls, sticks and a green baize table. You might have heard of him.

There was nothing to suggest what role Matthews might be playing for Van Schieffen, but we could now at least listen to him when he was in the office.

We had spent thousands on trying to increase the intelligence picture on our targets, but if you analysed it we had bugger all.

We weren't getting an awful lot from Matthews or Maxie Turnbull; they were bad lads, to be sure, but nothing we wanted to get involved in. Van Schieffen was nowhere to be seen, he hadn't been back to the UK for three months. Things were starting to look pretty grim.

# 8. I Love It When a Plan Comes Together

Jed and I were called to a meeting with Alpha. That in itself was an ominous sign. It didn't get much better when we rolled up outside their HQ in Lower Thames Street. 'Time for a few pints in the Hung, Drawn and Quartered,' my Scouser friend said, 'on us.'

'Fuck,' Jed whispered, 'if they're buying, then it must be bad news.'

'Guys, I know you're fucking gutted and that's reasonable. We love the heart you've shown, I mean you've given us more Intel than we've given you, but you know it too. You're from miles away, in the sticks. Keeping you in London is costing more than any other op. If it had been any other team, the plug would have been pulled weeks ago. Bristol's rep is rock solid with Alpha.'

'We appreciate that,' I said glumly. Inside I was burning with rage at the unfairness of it all, of this stinking job. You sacrifice everything only for it all to get pulled from under you. Fuck, fuck, fuck and fuck again.

'Let's get another round in, lads,' Scouser said and went to the bar. 'Chasers this time, eh? Listen it's not all doom and gloom, I need to have a word with you about something else.'

Jed and I sat in deep black silence.

My pager went off.

I looked at the message. It was from my old mate the

Hertz manager: OUR FRIEND AT COUNTER NOW, ABOUT
TO PICK UP THE CAR.

'SHIT!' I hissed loudly, causing heads to turn.

'What the fuck is it?' Jed asked.

'I don't believe it. Zulu 10 is at the Hertz desk now!'

We headed for the door. 'Later, guys.' I smiled as we left
the two Alpha case officers mouths agape. We had no idea
whether this changed their view about pulling the job, but
our main target had just reappeared and we didn't give a
fuck. I called the team out to get them to the Gatwick area,
pronto.

'We can get a Tommy car from the yard,' Jed said.

Jed drove like the wind through south London to a secret
garage just south of the river where all the London surveillance vehicles (Tommy cars) are kept, as there's no space
on the quay at Custom House.

The teched-up car looked like it had been there for
months; I hoped Jed could get it started. I teed up Bristol
to be ready first thing to listen to the audio and then booked
a batch of hotel rooms for the team.

By the time we got to Gatwick, Zulu 10 was in his girlfriend's house.

'Probably having the shag of his life,' Mickey said. 'It's
been a long three fuck-less months.'

'Nah, bet he's got one in every airport, good-lookin'
bastard.'

After that business was concluded, Zulu 10 finally
opened his gob in our wired car.

In a nutshell, Matthews was to supply transport while
Turnbull was the intermediary with a new set of buyers.

These new boys were major players in Essex and had

the wherewithal to get rid of as much gear as Van Schieffen could supply. It was music to our ears – and Alpha's, who quickly put the plug back in and extended to the new players as soon as they came on the scene.

Turnbull was small fry when it came to importing big lumps of class-A, but was extremely well connected and probably too smart to get involved with anything that would see him in chokey.

He was a big mate of Matthews and they discussed finding a buyer for the gear that Van Schieffen was bringing in.

Turnbull was always out and about, wheeling and dealing, and Matthews was always in his office, peddling his smut and making grand plans to become a porn-movie director, 'Cos his missus has been hit with the ugly stick more times than a Wimbledon tennis ball,' as Finbar put it.

Turnbull was good fun to follow; he had no set routine after he left home at 7 a.m.. He'd worked at Smithfield and Covent Garden in the past and was always a pretty early riser, much to the chagrin of our team. Sometimes we knew roughly what he would be up to, if it was legit, but if it was at all wonky we would have to work it out for ourselves.

He loved his golf and footy. He was a mad West Ham fan, which was popular with the footy fans on the team. Wherever the target goes, the surveillance team goes. Ascot, Wimbledon, Glastonbury – you name it, we've been there following a rich variety of targets. Most of it, of course, is completely unnecessary. Most of the time you do NOT need to know what the target is doing in the Royal Box, but as long as you can get Alpha to say, 'Yeah, could be a real important meet in there,' then you can start racking up the expenses.

The Alpha officers had all been on operational teams in the past and knew how the game was played. It's the same with foreign trips. The barristers know that a perk of the job is to carry out part of the investigation in a foreign country and that sort of evidence always looks good in court, so they are more than happy to send a letter to senior management saying how vital it is to the case that officers conduct enquiries in Spain, Hong Kong, etc.

We all loved following Turnbull. All the dirty meets were at the Hammers' ground, on the golf course or in a decent restaurant.

'Fucking ace, this is,' Jed said as we headed down to Stamford Bridge one Saturday. He was Chelski mad.

'But you're from Charlton, that's your home team.' He was from Dulwich, so this comment was always designed to wind him up.

'At least I come from a part of the world that has got a football team; you're a friggn' carrot cruncher and you support the bloody scally's.'

'Only cos my wife is one; she'd beat me up if I didn't.'

'That's about right, you big girl.'

Problem was, the meetings at the football grounds were impossible to cover. Trying to follow two unknowns discreetly out of the stadium at the same time as 20,000-odd fans proved to be impossible.

Then, finally, we had another breakthrough. Alpha gave us heads-up that Turnbull was off to play golf somewhere in Essex, possibly with the same geezers he'd met at the match.

Robyn stepped forward when she heard this. 'Cammo,' she said quietly, 'you might want me to cover Turnbull on his golfing jaunt.'

'Oh yeah? Why you?'

She beckoned me over to her car and opened the boot. 'Packed, polished and ready to hack their way round eighteen holes.'

Inside was a full set of clubs. 'She's our very own Laura Davies, Cammo,' said Finbar, who turned out to be another keen golfer.

We always had to be prepared for every possible eventuality. The unwritten rule for an investigator is to always bring an overnight bag to work. You never know where you are going to end up. You should have enough kit to last a week, and your wardrobe should be flexible enough to give you a change of profile. The more experienced officers kept a tie/jacket and a pair of filthy jeans/lumberjack shirt combo in the office and would wear smart casual to work that they could dress up with a tie or down with a pair of shorts and boots. Needless to say, a passport was essential.

Jed and I were pissed off big-style by officers who came into the office without a bag. Every time we had a shout, three or four people would say, 'I have to go home and get a bag first; I won't be there till later,' or, 'I can't do that; I haven't got my passport.'

My standard reaction was: 'Fuck off, then. I'll give the job to someone who *has* come prepared.'

But I really had to hand it to Robyn for coming prepped with golf clubs: that was a first.

Mind you, I hadn't realized she and Fin were serious when they told me they weren't going to wear their covert radios because they'd interfere with their swing.

# 9. Big Boss

Robyn made her excuses, visited the ladies' and called me using her mobile. 'Zulu 18 [Turnbull] is playing with two unknowns,' she whispered, pausing every now and again to make sure no one else had come into the toilet. 'Both white, one mid fifties, grey hair, balding, five-seven tall, heavy build, light blue on dark grey, expensive clubs. The other one is in his late thirties, five-ten, muscular build, very short dark hair, black on black, also expensively dressed and kitted.'

Robyn and Finbar's tee slot was immediately after the targets'. They could keep an eye on them and note any calls made or received. It wouldn't be a huge help, but at least they got a round paid for by the Queen.

The most important thing was to get the new targets to their cars. It was too risky to put a call sign in the car park – no one sits around in golf club car parks – so we had to rely on Finbar and Robyn.

It has not been unknown, especially by mad bastards like me and Jed, to take the registration numbers of every car in a car park in order to try and identify unknown targets. This game is all about being ahead of your enemy. If you see a car twice in separate locations it's a fair bet it's not a coincidence.

'So who do we follow?' Jed asked.

'Well, the older one might be the most important. That might also make him the most distant from the centre of the conspiracy. Chances are he'll provide far less intelligence over a period of time than his younger counterpart, who might be busier and closer to the business.'

'On the other hand, the younger might be the main man, with the older one being the lorry driver who's gonna bring the gear in.'

'You know it.' The job was all about decision-making. If you base your actions on logical analysis of the intelligence then you can't be criticized. Someone once told me that the worst thing is not making the wrong decision, it's making *no* decision.

The worst investigators are the ones who fail to make decisions on the ground. They get it into their head that a wrong decision is a black mark against them. Consequently they leave the decision-making to junior officers, using the excuse that 'it will help their development' and when that inexperienced officer makes a mistake, they hang them out to dry. Our blame culture has got a lot to answer for.Eventually we got another call from Robyn: 'Targets have finished hacking their way round. We had to drop a load of shots just so we didn't get too close.'

'All call signs from Wallace, relay from foot Robyn: Zulu 18 and two belts [unknown males] are chilli in the main broccoli [restaurant]. We are expecting an imminent departure, call signs acknowledge.'

The rustle of newspapers and crisp packets being stowed came through my earpiece.

Following two men into a car park and seeing which cars they drive off in is not as simple as it seems. It has to be timed absolutely right. You have to be 'naturally' behind the targets as they leave, if you're too close and the villains hesitate for a moment, you can't stop and wait. You have to carry on to your car, which may not be in the right place to get the details. If you leave it too late it can end up looking as if you're trying to catch them up.

'From Gromit: Activity at X-ray 18.'

'From Wallace: We will let X-ray 18 run, we will go with one of the unknowns.'

'Madrid.'

'Wallace, relay foot Robyn: That's Male A and Male B from the clubhouse nine-one the leek.'

Robyn's call sign, Berlin was handily placed to see both vehicles leave the car park. She and Fin chucked their kit in the boot and jumped in, turning on their Cougar encrypted radio so they could provide commentary to the whole team instead of having to relay it through me.

'From Berlin: That's Male A complete a green Range Rover and Male B into a grey BMW 7-Series . . . wait for twists . . . the Beamer is Tango-six-seven-seven Oscar-Yankee-Bravo and the Rover is Bravo-one-six-eight Oscar-Sierra-Sierra.'

'Hang on. What the fuck was that?' Jed asked, incredulous.

I was laughing my tits off, unable to speak.

'Well that settles it,' Jed said.

'Indeed,' I said, wiping tears of laughter from my eyes, 'a wank registration that reads BIG BOSS cannot possibly be allowed to drive around without a team of Her Majesty's finest behind it.'

I put it out over the air: 'All call signs from Wallace: We will be going with the Rover.'

The Range Rover was PNC'd to one Elizabeth Shardlow at an upmarket address in Chigwell and sure enough, that's where we ended up. As soon as the car was in the huge drive I got the team plotted up.

'Is that a Roller?' Jed asked. 'Don't see many of those these days. Sure enough, as the automatic doors to the double garage opened, I spotted a Rolls-Royce Silver Shadow. This street was pretty full of some amazing properties owned by top doctors, lawyers, accountants, brokers and their wealthy criminal clients. Jed and I drove off to check the Beamer's address in Romford. It was registered in a woman's name, with nothing else known on the PNC.

Our choice was vindicated when the LIO checks came back on the Shardlow residence. Lizzy Shardlow's husband Ronnie had been a thorn in the side of law enforcement on and off for years. He was the original East-End wide boy, born and bred in the shadow of Custom House during the war and worked his way up the criminal hierarchy in the West End clubs and pubs game during the sixties and seventies. Like a lot of villains, he'd taken a traditional path into his fifties by spending his late thirties and early forties at Her Majesty's pleasure for armed blagging before deciding it was too much effort and taking to organizing, or more importantly financing, international drug deals.

To be honest, the UK's policy on drug interdiction is a joke. Police and Customs have always assured whoever happens to be in power that they're focussing their efforts on the very highest level of criminality. But that is clearly nonsense as almost every successful operation fails to investigate or convict the people at the top: the financiers.

The cases where the police say that *everyone* in the gang

has been nicked are for the 20 to 50kg jobs, huge for the police but nothing like the 500kg-plus deals that really keep the markets supplied.

It's not surprising, because the villains who finance the mega-jobs never get anywhere near the gear, or even the money, so there is never any 'evidence' to collect.

Their problem is, of course, that law enforcers can't be seen to admit that the high-echelon criminals are untouchable.

Recent money-laundering legislation was theoretically a step in the right direction in that very rich villains must now either account for their wealth or have it taken from them, but in practice the top-level crims have, like the Mafia in the US, simply found that legitimate business is at least as profitable as their previous activities, and risk free. They now have the paperwork to disguise the proceeds of their underworld activities.

I was over the moon to see we had such a big player meeting Turnbull, but I feared we would never get anything on him, not while the law banned phone-intercept material in evidence. The upside was that his name alone pushed the job along and so we could put in twenty-four hour surveillance.

With Chrissy gone, Jed and I were now leading the op. The long hours were killing us but we couldn't stop. Shardlow was like crack cocaine to us; we were totally hooked. He was a busy bastard and went all over the country meeting Arabic money launderers. He enjoyed posh nightclubs, casinos, and Champney's health farm in Enfield where he did deals covered in a chocolate mask and while getting his back, crack and sack waxed. Alpha was up on two of his phones but they weren't getting anything; they'd yet to find his dirty phone, the one he did all the deals on.

Then we got a break. Alpha had him on the phone planning an importation with Matthews, and Matthews talking to Van Schieffen. There was nothing we could use as evidence, as they were careful about what they said and how they said it – all very ambiguous – but at least it looked as if we were going to get on the inside of a major shipment.

We turned our attention to Matthews. Jed and I were sitting outside his office when Alpha called. It was my Liverpudlian friend. 'Matthews just fixed a meet with a UKM [unknown male] at a hotel in Basildon. Sounds like a deal is about to go down.'

We followed Matthews from his unit on the A13 and ended up at a Holiday Inn in Waltham Abbey. He met the unknown in a black Merc 320, whom we housed back in Harold Hill, near Romford. He was a roofer called Tony Broom. On the face of it he was a small-time wide-boy businessman. Underneath he was supplying skiploads of coke to the white-stilettoed girls of Essex.

'No record,' Jed said after checking the PNC. 'Another smart cookie.'

This was a real leg-up after weeks of nothing at all. Alpha was really pleased; they seemed to think we were finally getting somewhere. We followed Tony and his gang all round Romford, Upminster and Hornchurch. He was always busy and it was looking good. The downside was that Van Schieffen, Turnbull and Shardlow were now nowhere to be seen. Even Matthews only occasionally put his head above the parapet.

As if running ourselves into the ground wasn't bad

enough, we started to hear whispers that another team wanted our job.

Sure enough, Paul called. 'Cam, I'm getting pressure to take you off this.'

'Who from?'

'Ipswich.'

'Fucking Ipswich,' I said, raising my eyebrows at Jed, who made the time honoured 'wanker' sign. Essex was on Ipswich office's manor.

'Yeah,' Paul continued. 'Well, they're getting highly aroused by the sound of all this sexy intelligence. As far as they're concerned, you're in deep on a massive job in their territory and they want it.'

'We're not having it, Paul. This is our job and I'm not handing it over right at the endgame. I know what will happen. They'll get too excited and shoot their load too soon. They'll just grab a big consignment and let the Dutch-man and Shardlow escape. You know yourself, Paul, that's what happens when you hand a job over. The new team always go for the quick score, a pat on the back and lots of media-friendly Brownie points.'

'OK, Cam, I'll tell them no deal.' Paul hung up.

'We need to wrap this up soon,' I told Jed.

'Too damn right,' he replied.

We were both knackered. Christmas was a week away. I hadn't even thought about presents for the boys or what we were going to do (I suspected my main present would be a quickie divorce).

Our surveillance had taken us all over the London and the Home Counties but, when it came right down to it, we had nothing concrete to show for it.

On Christmas Eve I was really ready to lose it. Jed and I were sitting outside another fancy house in Chigwell where we listened to the muffled sound of Slade's 'Merry Xmas Everybody' being sung along to by a bunch of pissed-up east London criminals and their partners.

'At least someone's having a happy Christmas,' Jed said.

I grimaced. My phone rang. It was Paul. 'Oh . . . right . . . OK, then, see you in a minute.' I hung up.

'What is it?' Jed asked.

'Paul's here; he wants to meet us.'

We both knew this was bad news. Paul hardly ever came out to see us in the field. I drove to a nearby pub and we saw Paul's long face as soon as we walked in. He took one look at me and said, 'Jesus, Cam, you look like shit.'

'What, me?' I replied. 'I'm as fresh as a daisy and smell twice as good.' Inside I was falling apart.

'Boys, the job's going to Ipswich in the New Year. It's from the top. We're spending upwards of twenty grand a week to keep you up here and the Ipswich team can do it for a quarter of the cost.'

'Simple as that, eh? The economic argument always wins.'

'Cammo, you should be relieved to be relieved. Go home. Spend Christmas with your family. You've done an amazing job, now just get some rest.'

We left the pub gutted. I drove past Shardlow's house one more time. 'Look at those fucking fairy lights,' Jed said. 'The national grid must be about to pop a fuse.'

'Yeah, and they're paid for with the miserable cash scratched together by thousands of junkies.'

Jed put on an Irish accent and sang: 'You scumbag, you faggot, you cheap lousy maggot, Happy Christmas your arse!'

We went home. Louise wasn't expecting me and her face wasn't exactly a picture of pleasant surprise when I stomped in. We had ourselves a shitty little Christmas.

A few days later I handed the job over to a very self-satisfied looking Ipswich case officer. I couldn't blame him for looking smug. We'd done all the crappy work and now all he had to do was follow the gang and piece together a couple of exchanges and he would be able nab loads of drugs and some decent players. I spent a long time with them, giving them the low-down on the targets, their habits and working patterns and left them to it.

I kept in touch on a weekly basis but my heart wasn't really in it. Part of me wanted them to fail. I knew that Alpha wouldn't get as good a service as we'd given them.

The knock came a couple of weeks later, when Ipswich tried to stop a BMW and a truck on the M25. The truck came quietly; inside was half a tonne of cannabis and a few thousand tabs. The driver of the Beamer decided to floor it as soon as he realized what was going down. He took off round the M25 and chucked bags of coke at the pursuing team. A couple of officers wound up high as kites after a kilo bag hit the front of the car and clouds of white powder came straight through the air-con and up their noses. All in all, they recovered about 25kg of coke.

Broom was arrested and got fourteen years. As I suspected, the Muppets had shot their load too soon. Van Schieffen, Turnbull, Matthews and Shardlow were never even nicked, let alone charged or taken to court.

Jed was as frustrated as me. 'I can't believe they're still out there, after all that, and after all we learned.'

'Fuck knows how much gear they're still bringing in and where it's all going.'

We were gutted, totally pissed off.

And that's when Alpha called.

# 10. Leaving the World Behind

'I'll write you up, of course,' Paul told me, 'but you should know that there are some very strong candidates.'

I walked away thinking, *Thanks, Paul, why don't you just chuck it straight in the bin?* Paul knew I'd put my soul into bringing down the Dutchman and his friends and he wanted to help me get into Alpha. But he clearly didn't want to write me up above Jed. I knew I was one of the best, but even so I was pretty sure I was third officer in line from the Bristol office, behind Jed and one other bloke.

Until 2001, Alpha had never recruited outside of Custom House, their London HQ. They always picked the brightest and best, without interview, and 'invited' them to join. The problem was that Alpha's workload was rising exponentially (villains now all owned about ten phones each), so officers were being picked from an ever-decreasing pool. A three-year stint in Alpha used to be a direct pathway to senior management, but now over-worked officers were being asked to stay in the intense world of Alpha for longer periods, without even the carrot of promotion. Many were becoming burnt out, so senior management was being forced to look further afield.

Before the Hertz manager had called the night Alpha had tried to take us off the case, the Alpha officers were planning to tell Jed and I to apply, that we were in with a good chance. We'd still have to go through the application process, but they said our reputation with them would stand us in good stead.

Those who thought they could do the job had to explain why on a side of A4, with the application being counter-signed by an SIO (in my case, Paul) and an assistant chief investigation officer (ACIO – my branch commander).

Most people knew very little about Alpha and its myst-erious workings, which made it almost impossible to fill out the application, especially as the people who applied tended to be similar characters with a similarly wide expe-rience. The difference between each application would be minimal – the smallest thing might make the biggest differ-ence. After about fifty rewrites of my A4 page I thought I was going to go mad, so stopped and ran it through spell-checker, fired it off and got on with my life.

By early September Jed and I had pretty much forgotten about our applications and were in Bristol with an informant-handling team. Charlie, the recently promoted controller had an informant with fantastic access to a crew who were planning a big importation into north Devon. Charlie needed us to follow his informant to see if he was kosher and passing on the right Intel. Better to spend a few grand now than waste months of work finding out the guy was a time waster or feeding misinformation.

After a couple of meetings to lay out the ground rules (when we could fit in a deployment amongst our other work, who was paying the overtime and expenses, etc.) Jed and I arranged to meet Charlie and the handling team in an anonymous hotel outside Barnstaple. North Devon was a very difficult place to work in; everyone knew everyone else and the local Customs and police had a fairly crap reputation for keeping secrets.

To get round the surveillance problems that tight-knit communities throw up, we had a specialist team of 'CROPS' (Covert Rural OPerationS) officers. These guys were trained to establish observation points in challenging rural areas, using methods that would not be detected by the baddies or members of the public. They lived and worked in holes in the ground, fields, derelict buildings, etc., for days on end, in areas that had no other view of the target premises. In these days of modern surveillance equipment their role has been reduced to installing mini-cams in telegraph poles.

We were about twenty miles short of Barnstaple when Charlie called. 'I'll be there at 10.30 a.m.; just head straight up to room two-zero-four.'

'Got it.' I said. 'See you then.'

'Have you guys got the radio on?'

'No, we prefer to talk shop than to listen to Sheep-Shagger FM.'

'Stick it on. Someone's crashed a plane into the World Trade Center.'

'Fucking hell,' I replied and hung up. I switched on the news and it was full of reports about a light plane crashing into one of the twin towers.

'Crap pilot,' Jed said. 'The biggest building in the world should be pretty easy to miss.'

I knew a few New York cops. There's a discreet bar in the back room of one of the more popular tourists haunts near Times Square that is 'law enforcement only'. British officers on assignment, or even on holiday, rubbed shoulders with officers from the US Drug Enforcement Administration, the NYPD, US Customs and the FBI. When our people went over there, they were treated like royalty. I can't remember anyone ever allowing a Brit to buy a drink. Their wit was drier than ours; nothing ever seemed to faze them. I knew they'd be making plenty of wisecracks while taking this odd little tragedy (as we thought it was then; we assumed it was a single light aircraft) in their stride.

But the further we drove, the worse the news became, and when we arrived at the hotel we marched straight to the room, where Charlie was already watching TV. We walked in just as the first tower fell.

None of us spoke, not even saying hello. Just the occasional swear word as new footage kept coming in. Eventually, we got the kettle boiling. None of us felt like going out on the ground.

But as the day progressed and the TV started repeating the same images and story over and over, we went out and did our job and followed the informant. It took us five days and proved to be uneventful, the sort of thing we could do standing on our heads, and the Intel he provided Charlie matched what we saw him do.

At 11 o'clock on the Friday, job done, we were in the hotel watching the news when Jed's phone rang.

'Hi, Paul. What's up?' This was followed by a lengthy silence as Jed listened. 'Oh, right. Yeah, well, thanks. Right. No. It's OK. Yeah, I'll see you Monday.'

'What was that?'

'Alpha's a no-go. Didn't get in.'

'Christ, sorry, mate. I can't believe it. Why the fuck not?'

'Holborn State Penitentiary, I reckon.'

'Christ almighty, are they still making you pay for that?'

When Jed was a young officer he had borrowed the team obs van, with his line manager driving, to move house (from one beautiful young lady's flat to another) and while it was chocka with his stuff, the senior officer managed to crash it into an MG Maestro. The senior officer coughed straight away to being in Customs and the member of the public, seeing pound signs, sued. It all came out and Jed was sent to the God-awful VAT office in Holborn for four years.

He wasn't allowed back in investigation until senior line management felt he had learned from his mistake. Nothing happened to the senior officer.

The people who had sent him to Holborn were now part of Alpha's senior management.

'I can't believe those wankers are still making a point, even after seventeen years,' Jed said.

Ten minutes later Jed received another call from Human Resources, telling him that he hadn't been promoted either (this was a separate application he'd put in months before).

Jed and I took things very personally. Jobs that we had been in charge of that went awry knocked us right back, unlike others who didn't seem that bothered if they screwed up, or if management pulled the plug. Being turned down for promotion was about as bad as it could get for Jed.

I was equally gutted for him because I knew how much both applications had meant to him. To have the pair of them turned down on the same day seemed like pretty bad timing, but we both suspected the same thing: somebody wanted to rub it in Jed's face.

We went our separate ways home: me to Gloucester, Jed to Wiltshire.

As I drove, the mobile rang.

'Cam?' It was Paul. 'You're in.'

'What?'

'Congrats, mate, you're in Alpha.'

'What?'

'Get your bags packed and clear your desk, you're moving to London on Monday.'

My life was about to change big time.

I'd moved out of the family home and had been sharing a house in Gloucester with Mickey, our surveillance biker. He'd had a fair bit of domestic turbulence too; sharing reduced at least the financial pain of our separations. I said sorry and told him he'd need to find a new flatmate. 'No worries, Cammo,' he said. 'I'll speak to you on the other side.'

I thought about Jed. It took me hours to pluck up the courage to call him. He put on a brave front, but I knew my call would be followed by a long, angry conversation between Jed and a pint of Jack Daniel's.

Joining any other team would have meant spending weeks handing over casework and making sure every man and his dog was *au fait* with the situation. Alpha was completely different. No one ever questioned their decisions; it just wasn't done. Most people weren't even allowed to know their phone number.

So I went into the Bristol office on Sunday and did a Reggie Perrin. I cleared my desk, got my personal kit, left a couple of goodbye messages on Post-it notes, shut the door behind me and vanished.

I had to admit, I liked their style.

# 11. Day One

I arrived in the Alpha admin office at 0900. I was dressed in a dark pinstripe suit, shoes buffed to a blinding shine. Accessing the legendary, almost mythical Branch Ten on the third floor of Custom House on Lower Thames Street required two swipe cards, a code number and a thumbprint – through three different doors.

Another newbie had arrived just before me. Ranjiv – also in a smart new suit – looked as apprehensive as I felt. We were the first two officers from outside London ever to be selected for Alpha.

We were joined by a third guy dressed in a tatty rugby shirt, jeans and trainers. He clearly knew the score. My shirt collar closed around me.

'Simon,' he said, holding out his hand. 'Came here from Branch One.' Branch One was the London heroin team. I marvelled at his accent: he sounded like Prince Philip. 'Hope you don't mind me saying, but you're a bit over-dressed. I think you can loosen the tie and breathe out.'

After the intros we were met by our tour guide, a dark-haired, balding man of about forty with a stocky, powerful frame; I could tell from his manner and the way he carried himself he was ex-military, even though he was casually dressed.

He looked Ranjiv and me up and down and then across at Simon. It was obvious they'd met before. 'Hello, Si. Nice to see you joining us at long last.' He turned back to Ranjiv and me. 'So, what do you two arse polishers know about Alpha?'

I rattled off what I knew, which wasn't much.

'Right, so naff all then. I'll start from the beginning. My name is John. Welcome to the legend that is Branch Ten. It needs to be accessed by lots of electronic wizardry for obvious reasons and we'll sort out your passes shortly.

'A long list of chief investigators have described Alpha as the "Crown Jewels" of British law enforcement. Without it, there'd be no significant drugs seizures of any description. Alpha is absolutely the most invaluable weapon we've got in the so-called "war on drugs".

'We don't get many visitors. And we don't speak to strangers in here. There are three other top-secret departments on the same floor and you don't want to know what they are, what they do and to whom they do it. In this building, there are no uncomfortable silences in the lift: there are long, comfortable silences. There are *never* any casual visitors and no loudmouths. People talk quietly and only ever about football in the corridors. Each team keeps tight. You will never get to know anyone outside Alpha in this building. It just isn't done.

'And yes, the general dress code in Custom House is smart casual. I know it's your first day at school and I appreciate the effort, but you're going to be locked in a windowless room for twelve hours a day and no one cares what you wear.'

We were introduced to the three SIOs who ran Alpha and the ACIO (this was Jed's old boss with the long memory). We were given various forms to fill in and our eyeballs and fingers were scanned and our faces photographed and filmed from every angle.

While this went on, our tour guide gave us a history lesson.

'When Alpha was set up in the early eighties it was staffed by about a dozen senior officers [an old Customs grade equivalent to a detective inspector in the CID; the only grade below that in investigation was 'officer' – equivalent to a police detective sergeant]. The dirty dozen were split into the A shift and B shift, covering 0600 to 2200, seven days a week, 365 days a year. Each operation had two case officers, one from each of the shifts, so there was someone with intimate knowledge on duty at all times.

'All investigation teams were given names and roles. In the early days it was known as "Intel A". Alpha always had nicknames, originally to disguise what anyone was talking about, and has been variously known as "Zero-One", "Upstairs" and "The Other Office". Now we just do it for fun.

'In the early days intercepted calls were recorded on bulky tape machines, the reels of which had to be changed every few hours. A lot of space was given over to storage.

'Each operation only had a couple of phones hooked up, and Alpha only ran half a dozen ops at any one time. The number of ops and staff was dictated by the phone-line capacity. It started with about forty lines. Today we have five hundred lines manned by twenty-five officers.

'One tradition we've maintained is the "Bat phone" and log book in each team SIO's office. Only the SIO can answer it. Every morning he gets the same update as the operational team on the ground. He writes it out, by hand, into a hardback A4 book, which goes into a locked safe. This book never leaves his office.

'In fact, the old system worked so well that nothing much has really changed, except for one major aspect. In the good old days the villains had to plan much further in advance, so we got our heads up nice and early. That has all changed with the advent of the greatest tool ever provided to the discerning criminal: the cheap pay-as-you-go mobile phone. Nothing else has done more for the drug-importing criminal, or any criminal in fact, over the last thirty years.'

We entered the main room. There was a sense of hushed intensity in the air. Our guide lowered his voice. 'Welcome to the heart of Alpha. Over there we have Cocaine Corner, over here Smack Central.

'Whichever way you look at it, drugs are pouring into the country, whether it be via mules from Jamaica and eastern Europe or truck drivers from southern Spain. Just the other day a couple of teenagers were seized at Gatwick with nearly four kilos of cocaine in their stomachs. They were both from a Croatian family living in east London.

'As things have tightened up through Europe, the Colombians are starting to use Africa and so we're getting more coke coming into the UK that way. At least sixty drug mules arrive in Britain from West Africa every week. Thirteen mules were found on board one flight from Ghana after local customs did a surprise sweep of the plane and X-rayed all the passengers. A dealer who uses drug mules might expect that one in four won't get through customs. A haulier will estimate that forty per cent of his consignments will get caught. Despite this, he'll still have a healthy tax-free profit that more than mitigates the risk and effort involved.

'So we try, but we can't stop it all getting in. But what we can do at Alpha is take out the bastards who are ordering and buying all the gear based here in the UK by getting onto their phones. They're not going to stop, because the risk and effort will always be justified by the rewards, so we have to make it impossible for them to work. Just how effective we are at disruption is a matter for speculation, but what nobody can deny is that we are running some of the biggest operations in the country, if not in Europe.

'Right now, Perry over there is working a heroin job on a bunch of Turks bringing gear in fresh from the fields of Afghanistan; he's linked up with German cops who have been tracking the bad lads across ze Fatherland. He's onto the phones of the receivers in Liverpool. This way we can remove an entire European chain of smugglers in one fell swoop.

'Nige, meanwhile, is working on a smack dealership in the north of England with some Mancunian bastards and I believe he's got a Dutch ecstasy job running too. Carmella's working with the Royal Navy and the Spanish authorities, who have been following ten million quids' worth of coke from Colombia via Jamaica and southern Spain to exotic Harwich, where a bunch of eager East Anglian beavers are anxiously awaiting their fix. Then you've got Dave and Mike currently following about three tonnes of coke, which is pinging its way around the motorways of the UK, not to mention all the one-tonne hash jobs in Spanish lorries and the cash bouncing between London and the Middle and Far East and more offshore accounts than you can shake a stick at.'

*Fuck me*, I thought. I might as well as said it out loud. I think my expression said it all. This was like Aladdin's cave.

It was all I could to stop myself from rubbing my hands together in glee.

'Welcome, gentlemen,' John said smugly, 'to the dog's bollocks of British law enforcement.'

The training to become a 'number' – a fully trained Alpha Officer – took two months. It was all on the job. It wasn't that the work was particularly difficult; it was just that everything had to be done very quickly and once you were on your own, you alone were the intelligence case officer. It was your job – you would dictate how it progressed.

This all depended on how well you could sell the job to the SIO and this was a real skill as Dave, my mentor, explained.

'This job is all about the sales,' he explained. 'You can't sell, you're screwed, no matter how orgasmic the Intel is.

'Take these Muppets I'm working on now; a couple of drug dealers, Vinnie and Vinnie (I kid you not), who've expanded into carousel fraud. They've started shifting the same old computer chips back and forth between various countries and the UK, issuing false invoices and claiming back the VAT, costing our beloved chancellor millions. You see, Vinnie is Vinnie's accountant. I need to get on a lot of their contacts' phones. But this all sounds a bit boring really, don't it?'

I nodded.

'Well, Vinnie's also the accountant for Rick James, a Mr Big in south London, and when I say "accountant", I don't mean in the chartered sense. No, he's the guy who makes sure there's twenty grand in untraceable cash waiting for a hit man in the left luggage office at Euston Station.'

'Oh, *that* kind of accountant.'

'When you look at the transcripts of their calls, I know and you know this is about drug importation, but presented like that in a court of law it could easily be argued that they're drinking buddies discussing next week's match. They might be about to commit a major crime, but equally it might be a small bit of insurance fraud, something we really don't need to spend eight grand a day on ground surveillance to prevent. I need to show that this bloke is worth extending to.

'So the first thing I'll mention to the SIO will be that one of the targets pays off hit men for one of London's drug kingpins. I'll see his eyes open wide at that. "Aha, a sexy job," he'll think. Killers and drugs, lovely. Never mind the carousel fraud. But that's the main point of the phone tap – not to nab them for coke but for laundering and VAT fraud. It's the only way of getting to someone that senior; they're too far removed from the drugs.

'In the end, it comes down to how well you sell against all the other numbers, mixed with our current capacity.

'Problem is that the most outrageous sexing-up comes from the average Intel officers based in Customs buildings across the UK. They are supposed to work up potential jobs for the operational teams. They get immense kudos if their Intel package gets taken on by Alpha. Remember, we only take on the absolute cream, probably less than one per cent of all operations being run by law enforcement across the UK.

'So, the intelligence officer produces an "intelligence package", claiming that his subjects are all involved in dealing or smuggling class-A. It's all backed up with loads of phone billing showing "contact with known drugs dealers" or "links to organized crime" or "connections to Latin America".

'Because everyone is obsessed with their job being taken on by Alpha, no one actually checks the original intelligence, resulting in us spending about a quarter of a million pounds on surveillance and man-hours before it's actually revealed to be a load of old pony. We may be an elite department but we end up mining a mountain of bullshit to get to the gold seam. It's probably the single biggest problem for law enforcement and is caused by a complete failure of the training and recruitment system.

'Military intelligence officers are psychologically vetted before going through an eighteen-week training programme; Customs and the cops aren't vetted and train for two weeks.'

Dave looked at me closely before continuing, perhaps worried he was saying too much. He carried on, nonetheless. I was riveted.

'The intelligence officers who produce this crap are usually rubbish at everything else and end up in some nice cushy Intel post, regardless of their suitability. Honestly, I have probably spent half my career working on absolute bollocks.'

At the end of each day, Dave and I handed over to Ranjiv and his trainer. Apart from this, and even though we worked the same jobs, Ranjiv and I almost never saw each other. Like me, he was divorced with two kids. Despite the lack of interaction, we got on pretty well during the brief handovers.

Once Dave had completed my training, official and un-official, I settled into 'cocaine corner'. I soon had a routine of sorts. I was on earlies and usually entered the building before dawn. I swiped my card through the reader, stepped beyond the security gates, keys and coins in and out of pockets for the metal detector, and took the lift to the third floor.

I entered the outer office and passed through yet another swipe door before finally entering Alpha's inner sanctum. The lights were out. I was nearly always the first one in. Most of the other guys preferred to blow their £1,200 a month housing allowance on fancy addresses in north and west London. Not me. I liked to be able to walk to work and besides, my family originally came from the East End, so it felt like home to be within chiming distance of Bow Bells.

First things first. I headed into the fully fitted kitchen that contained the largest range it's possible to get, along with an industrial-sized dishwasher. It was also home to the world's largest tea urn. While it started to hiss, I passed through the cosy dining room, checked that no one was sleeping in any of the bedrooms and noted that the show-ers had been cleaned. Where the hell do they find cleaners that can clear that much security?

The tea point was right behind my desk. Every twenty minutes or so someone, we took it in turns, would fill a giant teapot from the urn, bring it to the tea point and yell 'FRESH TEA!'

The inner sanctum was a massive L-shaped room, home to twenty-five of us, so some people were miles away. This was one of the few times in the day you could have thirty seconds off for a stretch of the legs and a quick chat.

The urn fired up, I walked over to my desk in Cocaine Corner (Smack Central was at the other end of the suite) and prodded my computers awake.

Each operative had two computers. One was the 'live board' which showed all the lines connected to the jobs you were running; the other was for recording everything from a précis of an important call to the note you'd leave your co-case officer on the overnight shift detailing briefly what had gone on during your stint.

The computer told me we had almost five hundred lines running, nearly at full capacity. 'Fuck me,' I muttered to myself, reaching for my Sennheiser headphones, 'someone's been busy.' The Sennheisers were the dog's *cojones*, kept out all ambient noise and made sure nothing escaped.

I studied the screen. The top of the first page looked like this:

| Line | Job | Target | Number |
|------|-----|--------|--------|
| 26 | Op Fix | Kevin | 078888234552 |
| 102 | Op Fix | UKM | 012165552882 |
| 156 | Op Fix | Sanjeev | Unknown Dutch number |
| 255 | Op Undo | Billy | 07222772991 |
| 301 | Op Undo | Jimmy | 078822281004 |
| 435 | Op Undo | Elton | 079211010191 |

The 'line' number was just a reference to a slot on the system. The target names were usually only first names. Villains NEVER give their real full name over the phone. We only knew them by the names they gave themselves, or what others called them. UKM and UKF stand for unknown male and unknown female. It's mainly up to the operational team on the ground to figure out who all these idiots actually are.

If one of the targets used or answered his phone, the line would light up green. If I felt like listening live, I'd simply click on the line. Once he hung up it went yellow until I clicked to listen. It was all digitally recorded so I could click in and out of live calls and recorded calls all day, never losing any product. All calls were recorded, and by clicking on another part of the board, I could see a list of all the calls that phone had made over the day.

With about twenty lines running on one job, and villains being busy little bastards, it was impossible to listen to every call live; I'd have to play catch-up to get the old ones when I had the time. My objective was to draw all the relevant Intel out of the calls and write a 'note' about it on the second computer. From this info the operational team were updated. If it was about to come on top then I'd have to listen to as many live calls as possible and ring the ops team to tell them what was going on. If the team were trying to cover a handover you had to tell them everything 'as-soon-as-fucking-possible'.

If all the info was coming through one particular target I could set an alarm on my live board so that the line flashed red and the product went straight into my headphones, even if I were in on another call. With twenty or so targets each using their mobiles once every ten minutes or so, a ten-hour shift shot by very quickly. You can't help but become deeply involved in these people's lives. You get to learn all kinds of things you'd rather not. As I said, you get used to it.

Voice recognition was crucial. With thirty targets or more and all the 3Ps (third parties) they talked to, I could be dealing with a hundred voices. Luckily, I had a gift.

Kevin's line lit up red. 'You're early, aren't you, mate?' I said to myself. 'What are you trying to do, ruin my warrant-time?' Most villains conducted their business between 9 a.m. and 9 p.m. The wee hours were nearly always dead but the calls would be recorded anyway, ready for us early-shift guys. Usually, the early morning was spent playing catch-up with any calls made overnight and filling out enormous warrant applications, a sixteen-page beast, trying to get more lines wired.

Intruding into someone's life is quite a big deal. A lot of civil liberties people got their underwear in a twist about some of the things we got up to and so asking for a new wire wasn't easy. Each sixteen-page application went through three lines of management authorization, mainly to make sure at least ten times that the right number has been written down.

The application would then go straight to the desk of the Home Secretary, in this case David Blunkett. In any given year Blunkett would receive about 1,400 warrants from Customs, police and the Secret Intelligence Service. I had to give it to him, he was really on the ball: he didn't just read and sign, he remembered each job, and asked how they were going.

Curious, I tapped Kev's line.

Kev: Fagoctdaory or wadarehouse?
UKM: Wadarehouse, shidit lodogoda chedogeap pilgodals.

Villains use all sorts of backslang that's a nightmare for us to interpret; these lads were Scouse and used a formula where they'd insert the letters 'G' and 'O' or 'D' and 'A', or a combination thereof, sometimes in reverse order, into every word they could. Listening to two Scallys talking nineteen to the dozen was one hell of a challenge and often necessitated a few playbacks before it could be deciphered.

Kev was setting up a meet to buy some pills; the ops team would want to know about that.

Even worse than the Scousers were the travelling community (less politically sensitive officers had other words for them). Their dialects had us in a permanent state of confusion. Every word was shortened amid weird intonations. Like the Scousers, they spoke at a hundred miles an hour, and a typical call lasted for just a few seconds. It was only after several hours' listening that you gradually came to absorb the lingo – it was a bit like listening to Chaucer or Shakespeare.

My most high-priority job was Jimmy Ashraf's bureau de change, passed on by Dave. Jobs were usually given to us by the SIO but very often other operatives would pass on solid leads once their area of interest had expanded beyond one person's listening ability, or went off on a juicy-looking tangent. These referrals tended to be a lot more reliable than the ones we'd get from officers across the country.

'Vinnie's henchmen have rinsed a tonne of Rick James' coke money there,' Dave said. 'Jimmy sounds to me like a busy little bee, he's getting lots of other visitors, so get onto him.'

Most Asians connected to the underworld were given Western nicknames by their white criminal colleagues. 'His real name's Mus Ashraf,' Dave told me. 'He says the bureau belongs to his uncle, but I'm thinking he's making that up. I've not heard him speak to uncle anyone, and no one else has referred to him. He's fantastic; he can change any amount of sterling into euros or US dollars, no questions asked, usually within twenty-four hours. I think you'll enjoy it, but,' he paused, leaned forward and looked me dead in the eyes, 'don't forget, *sell* the job to the SIO.'

People like Jimmy were a breeze; I had his home, office and mobile hooked up, and although he was careful, he at least spoke plain English. Jimmy didn't know it but with a bit of luck and skill on our part, he was going to take us to some fantastic scores.

The serious players were a nightmare, chucking phones left right and centre; we spent all our time chasing warrants so we could get back on their line. We relied on those at the bottom of the food chain who couldn't afford to change their phones all that often, the guys that the Mr Bigs needed to run their errands.

Billy and Elton were a pair of twins from north London, a right pair of Muppets. I christened them the Scrote twins. They spent their whole lives on the phone, mostly to each other, while they lived out their crappy little lives. They were crack addicts and would do anything to make a buck. Every two or three days they'd bring £100k to Jimmy to change into euros; somehow these hopeless twats were bringing in a £5 million wedge each year.

And they were just one customer of Jimmy's. His tiny bureau de change was dealing out more money than all the Barclays Banks in east London. And it's like this all over the country. Of course, none of this would go through Jimmy's records. He would then use dozens of routes and methods to get the money to Dubai, via Hong Kong and Singapore. He would provide this service for any number of villains around London and the UK. For the Colombians he'd ship the dirty cash out of the UK with foreign lorry drivers headed for Spain. From there it was shipped by container to Latin America.

Trouble was, I'd been listening to their inane nonsense day after day to get the pick-up and drop-off details and, of course, to get hold of those all-important numbers further up the chain. I had no idea what the Scrote twins looked like but they sounded like they had a thin, ratty, pasty and downright dodgy look about them. They were into so much, I couldn't understand why they hadn't been picked up for something else already. For example:

Billy: 'Ow many of these fuckin' things we need?
Elton: Many you can get in the farking van.
Billy: 'Ow the fuck am I gonna take 'em off the wall without blowing the 'ole fuckin' block up?

Where on earth were they? Blow up what fucking building? I'd have had London's finest round there in a flash if I'd known their location. Unfortunately we didn't yet have the ability to track quickly all of the five hundred mobiles we had wired, just listen in.

Elton: Dunno. Just rip one o' the fuckin' things off the wall. No
skin off our nose if the block goes up.
Billy: Easy for you ter say, ya wanker.
[There was a bang: Billy had tripped over something in the dark.]
UKM: Shut up, you twat!

The call ended. The line came on again an hour later.

Billy: Fuckin' nightmare. Got 'em, though. Water's all over the
shop and there's a hissing noise.
Elton: Great, get round to mine, we got a bit o' work from the
Asian fella; we can meet the other geezer on the way.
Billy: Sweet. There in twenny.

I could only guess that they'd been robbing boilers from a
new as-yet unoccupied block of flats; they'd be worth a
pretty penny on the black market.

In time, I'd gradually get the low-down on the Scrote twins,
the Davis gang and Jimmy Ashraf – far more knowledge than
I'd wanted and far more than anyone should have to know.

There were three of us running coke jobs. Brian and Mike
were both really experienced and had been there about five
years.

Mike Harrison was a very likeable and charming Scouser
and was the most successful coke job officer. He was nick-
named 'Lord Harrison of Scouseland', because he had the
knack (mostly by working his arse off) of getting with the
villains who were bringing in tonnes of the stuff. A month
hardly seemed to go by during which his hard work didn't
result in a massive seizure of coke. Management loved him.

'You know what my tip would be for you starting this job?'

I shrugged.

'Learn Spanish. On this job you can end up listening to Spanish all fucking day and having to find and work with an interpreter can be a real pain; really winds me up, anyway.' *El Pais* and *El Mundo* were on his desk, open at the sports section. 'Learning Spanish also helped me to chat up the hot interpreter.' Mike thumbed over his shoulder where a very attractive *señorita* was bending over another guy's desk; we all took a moment before Mike regained his thread. 'But at the same time the disadvantage is that Monique and I hardly ever spend any time with each other at work any more. She's free to concentrate on you linguistically challenged bastards.'

'It got you fit, too,' Brian added.

'True. She's so hot, she drove me to go on a massive health kick.'

'He even ran the sodding London marathon.'

'Blimey.' I could see why he wanted to impress Monique. I decided to hold off learning Spanish for a little while.

Translators were a key part of Alpha. London remained one of the world centres of the drugs trade and we listened to Turkish Cypriots from Green Lanes, Latin Americans and other Spanish speakers in Hammersmith, Arabs in Finsbury Park and Brompton, West Indian Yardies in Harlesden and Chinese money-men in the East End, all speaking in their own languages, so Alpha employed a number of interpreters. We had full time Turkish and Spanish speakers; everyone else we called in when we needed them. Of course, these translators weren't just pulled from any employment agency; they'd gone through the necessary clearance and worked full time for the security services.

As was normal procedure, the name for my first operation came from a folder full of randomly generated words. The next word on the list was 'Undo'.

I typed Operation Undo into the system. *Sounds perfect*, I thought. *Let's undo Jimmy's little operation, a nice easy one to start.* Little did I know.

I started with just one line: Jimmy Ashraf's office. I couldn't believe that my first job was in Middlesex Street, literally round the corner from where I lived in Petticoat Square. I wondered whether I should change my walk home so I wouldn't pass Jimmy's office every day. In the end, curiosity got the better of me. *I'll just have a quick peek every now and again*, I thought. *Just a passing glance through the window . . .*

I popped on the Sennheisers and sat waiting, staring at the screen. Hardly the most exciting start to an operation, but inside I was buzzing. Our top-secret, soundproofed office was pretty damn quiet but there was an intense, electric atmosphere. Deals were going down all around me. Shipments were being ordered, brought in; people were getting warned, kidnapped, tortured and whacked and I was about to join the game.

I spent the morning twiddling my thumbs and tried to ingratiate myself by making everyone cups of tea and coffee.

At 11 a.m. Jimmy's line went green.

'Here we go.' I clicked on the line to listen live.

UKM: It's Chamo. I got real big one t'do.

Jimmy: I can't do that all at once man. Be free trips at least and
that's free days, bruv.

UKM: OK, Jay, whaddabout tomorrow?

Jimmy: All day, but me got prayers in de arternoon.

UKM: Beun. Tomorrow, den.


The line went dead. The UKM, Chamo, had a Latin American accent. I guessed he was Colombian. I knew that a 'big one' meant something like £100k, so I guessed a 'really big one' was £300k. Carrying anything over £100k in crumpled coke-stained readies would require a super-kingsize suitcase.

Obviously, neither Jimmy or Chamo had mentioned drugs, but I put in the application to get Chamo's phone hooked up. To me it was obvious what he was talking about but in terms of the transcript they could have been discussing anything.

Jimmy's line went green again. A girl's tearful voice.


UKF: He's hit me.

Jimmy: C'mon, Melia, not now, baby. I'm at work.


It soon became clear that this was Jimmy's daughter and that her husband was apparently beating her. I felt like hanging up but it was fascinating in a morbid kind of way. I wanted to know what Jimmy was going to do about it.


Melia: I'm gonna leave him Dad, I don't care who he is or what
you say.

Jimmy: Look, calm down, let me talk to 'im.

They hung up and Jimmy rang a new number. It went straight to voicemail.

'Hi, this is ———. I'm not here right now, but leave a message and I'll call you right back.'

'Fucking hell!'

Mike and Brian both turned and looked at me in amazement. Hardly behaviour becoming an Alpha operative.

'What's up with you?' Brian asked.

The son-in-law was a British A-list actor and director, quite a bit older than Jimmy's daughter. Over the next few days it became obvious that he was indeed beating her. Problem was, he was a real smooth talker and did a good job of defending himself with excuses about how Melia was making it all up. Scumbag. Stupid Jimmy bought every last word.

'Fuck me,' Brian said, 'who'd've thought? I thought the bastard was great in ———' He named a well-known film.

I started to fill out the initial warrant application to get both Chamo's and Melia's phones intercepted. There was a chance Jimmy would talk to her about his travel arrangements, client details, addresses and financial information, that sort of thing. She was probably innocent, but this invasion of her privacy had to be balanced with the seriousness of her father's crimes – he helped fuel a significant part of the UK's drugs trade.

Brian suddenly threw down his Sennheisers. 'Fuck it!' he hissed.

'*¿Que pasa?*' Mike asked.

'That's the third one this week. I swear I'm gonna kick that Intel officer's lardy arse from here to fucking Colombia!'

'Another dead 'un?'

'For three weeks now, according to the shit-hot Intel I've been fed by NCIS [National Criminal Intelligence Service], I've been listening to an East-Ender arrange a shipment of marching powder from Bolivia to a dealer in Southall. What I've actually been listening to, I've finally found out, is a bloke arranging a small shipment of hookey porn DVDs and the purchase of a second-hand Mondeo, a surprise for his missus.'

'The car or the porn?'

'Ha-bloody-ha.'

'Bugger,' I said, 'that's going to be a tough one to explain to the boss.'

'Nah,' Mike said. 'It's easy; this happens all the bloody time. Sometimes it's our fault, but usually we've been fed crap Intel by idiots from outside Custom House. We're forced to make educated guesses from short and shifty phone conversations after listening to these Muppets for hundreds of hours. Every now and again we get it wrong and end up listening to an innocent bloke and his family going about their day-to-day business, real soap-opera stuff.'

'All we do,' said Brian, 'is cancel the line by filling out the appropriate paperwork and send it through to the SIO with comments like: "Believe the target is now using another mobile, this one is no longer in use." So if you have a phone that's illegally hooked up, you just put in a cancellation as if it was one of your legitimate phones.'

The Office of the Surveillance Commissioners (OSC) carried out audits to make sure the right checks were in place to prevent this sort of thing from happening. Unfortunately, the breaches Alpha admitted to the OSC were rather fewer than actually occurred. It was simply the nature of the game; no one I knew ever abused the system – apart from one guy, but we'll come to him later.

That's why the application forms were such monsters. There needed to be so many checks because we were violating people's privacy to a Big-Brother-like extent. If an innocent person ever found out we were listening to and recording their private lives, I'm sure we would've been sued to bankruptcy.

I was still filling out the warrant forms when a strange smell wafted over me. I sniffed and looked at Mike. 'What the hell's that?'

'Buggered if I know.'

We sniffed again. 'Something's definitely burning,' I said. 'Smells like . . . pasta.'

Just at that moment, I saw Nigel from Smack Central suddenly leap up from behind his desk with an 'OH CHRIST!' and sprint into the kitchen.

Mike picked up the phone. 'I'll order pizza, shall I?'

I nodded gratefully.

Everyone on lates took it in turns to cook dinner. That meant cooking for twenty-five people. You only did it once every five to six weeks. It cost around £80, but the rest of the time you got free dinners. I love cooking, but my experience was dinner for four, BBQs and the Christmas turkey. Cooking for twenty-five supercritical connoisseurs all bent on outdoing each other's culinary skills was extremely daunting. Being on lates was like being on a never-ending series of *Come Dine With Me*.

At least I had cooked before. Nigel had never so much as boiled an egg. He'd started with Alpha shortly before me and had the misfortune to come up first on the rotation. I could see his screen was lit up with green lines. Obviously he'd had a lot come on top that day and managed to forget about his precious ravioli. I don't know how, but even the rocket leaves in the salad were burnt. It did *not* go down well, and poor Nigel was sent to the rear of Custom House to pick up and pay for twenty-five pizzas, assorted garlic breads and fizzy drinks.

Mike nodded towards the board. 'It's a good idea to get to know each other's ops in case you ever have to babysit,' he said. 'You know, if we take leave, get sick, head of for training, kill ourselves from boredom or burn the dinner.'

'Babysitting's tricky,' Dave added. 'You've got to get familiar with the voices really quickly and make sure you know what Intel there is already, so it's good to talk shop whenever we can.'

I liked nothing more. 'Fine by me.' After another half-hour of nothing I switched the system to record and popped out the back of Custom House for a smoke.

James 'Snapper' Sandford was already there; he was in his mid thirties, 5′ 9″, pretty stocky and the same rank as me. He ran ops out on the ground, based on our Intel. Like all ground officers, he wasn't actually allowed in our suite but we would end up seeing each other quite often. The most surprising thing about him was that he was a total scruff bag; he had long hair and was unshaven. He didn't look at all like 'law enforcement', a bonus really, I suppose.

He'd just lit up. We nodded our hellos and stared out over the Thames at HMS *Belfast*, puffing away in the bright cold winter's morning.

Snapper broke the silence. 'What do you think so far?'

'Well, it's early days, but it's already been full of surprises.'

'You come from the ground, don't you?'

'S'right.'

'How long?'

'My first op was in '93. My first ever night away in a big London hotel, in fact. I was with a bloke called Mickey. We were booked to share a twin room to save money and we marched back down to the concierge to complain in a very macho way that we had been given a double. "I think you'll find it's what we call a 'continental twin', sir," he said, all snooty. "The beds move apart after you take the double bedcover off." Ah. Did we ever feel like hicks from the sticks.'

Snapper laughed.

'Alpha prefers to sleep in a separate bed to everyone else as well,' he said. 'We're not interested in six months of surveillance and intelligence gathering with one big seizure at the end. We go wherever the job takes us and nick and seize as many people and as much gear as possible. If there's one thing we've learned it's that the criminal fraternity is not organized at all.

'Criminals are a disparate group of opportunistic little bastard capitalists and most of them work on the principle of highest return for the least amount of work and never mind who gets stitched up in the process.

'So, hook up any phone you think will give you a chance of a seizure of gear. It doesn't matter where or what. All we're interested in is the most sure-fire method of putting people away.'

I nodded. 'Got it. Can I ask you a personal question?'

Snapper took a drag and looked at me. 'What?'

'Why are you called Snapper?'

'I have no idea.'

# 12. Los Huevos del Perro

Jimmy: We set for Saturday?
UKM: Yeah bruv, got the blue one, rooms booked at the Maryle-
bone.

This sounded interesting.

Jimmy: Girls?
UKM: All sorted, Jiiiiimmmmy. C'mon man I told you already,
leave it to me.
Jimmy: Yeah, yeah, I know, I know. This week's been fulla stress
and I really need this.

Come Saturday I was listening in as Jimmy called his
mates from his mobile.

Yeah, man, I'm the hotel now; these girls are hot and the pills
are working, you know what I'm sayin'!

He was wired, completely off his trolley on booze and
Viagra. He'd hired half-a-dozen prostitutes and was going
at it hammer and tongs with a few of his mates for forty-
eight hours straight. Poor Mrs Jimmy.

This was, of course, the downside of listening in to
criminals. The stuff we wanted to hear took a minute at
most. So that left another 40,000-odd minutes every month

to listen to them doing everything else but deal drugs.

Finally, after a couple of weeks spent listening to Melia, Jimmy and his Viagra-fuelled shagging weekends, I caught my first break:

UKM: Hi, mate, it's Steve, we met last week at that place. I was wiv Chelsea Barry.

Jimmy: Oh yeah, yeah; how you doin', man?

Steve: Good, mate, good. Look I need to change some up.

Jimmy: How much and how often?

Steve: Fifty large, every two weeks; sweaty ones [Scottish notes].

Jimmy: OK, bruv, I'll do it at one pound forty-six to start, see how we go.

Steve: Sweet, I'll call you later.

Jimmy: Yeah, mate, you want it out as well, I can put it anywhere.

Steve: I'll bell you. Later.

This opportunity was too good to miss. I spoke to my SIO and told him we could get a quick hit if we got Steve's phone on ASAP. He listened to the calls himself.

'Sounds good, Cam, a genuine smuggling op, nice one. He sounds like a regular though, so no need for an emergency application. Should take about a week.'

Ranjiv and I were dying to hear the product from the phone and we weren't disappointed. As soon as we got it on the board, there was lots of dirty talk.

Steve was also in regular contact with a lorry driver who travelled to the Continent on a weekly basis. The lorry driver brought in around twenty-five kilos of coke from Holland every week or so, quite a big deal.

We got the lorry driver's phone up. Then I called Customs

at Dover with a time, date and description of the lorry and made sure they understood that, no matter what, it needed to be tugged, that they should make it look like a random check and they should let the driver make as many phone calls as he liked while they searched. They were happy to oblige; anything for a nice easy seizure to boost their confiscation rates.

I could hardly sleep the night before. On the day, I was in early and Ranjiv handed over the headset with no little reluctance.

A few hours later the driver rang the supplier, whose name we never discovered; I could smell the fear in his voice: 'I've been fucking pulled by Customs.'

I smiled. Yes! 'Keep your fucking toupee on,' the supplier said, 'they'll never find the fucking gear, all right?'

About an hour later, Dover Customs called me. 'We've taken the truck to bits but there's nothing there. My men are calling you every name under the sun.'

'Don't worry, keep your flaming toupee on,' I replied, sounding a lot more confident than I felt. 'I'm just waiting for one more call from the driver. Let him go.'

'What?!'

'Trust me,' I said.

The trucker's line went green. The supplier picked it up on the first ring. 'Thank fuck for that,' the trucker said, 'just a routine stop.'

'See, I told you,' the supplier said, 'I put proper people on it. No fucking cowboys. Those idiots would never think of looking in the fucking oil filters.'

Thank you and good night.

The next call from the driver: 'They've called me back and gone for the filters. See you in twenty-five years.'

The phone went dead as the supplier rushed off to the airport.

The driver was nicked under Section 170(2) of the Customs & Excise Management Act 1979, that he was knowingly concerned in the importation of class-A drugs contrary to Section 1 of the Misuse of Drugs Act 1971.

'Knowingly concerned' is a very important premise. In English law, under this Act, we have to prove that the suspect both 'knew' about the importation and was also 'concerned' in it, i.e. he played an active part in it. For example a villain's wife who knew the details of a job, but wasn't involved in setting it up, couldn't be convicted under this legislation. Equally, we could not convict a lorry driver who was 'concerned' inasmuch as he had the gear in his truck unless we could prove that he also knew it was there.

Using lorry drivers to bring gear into the UK remains very popular because of this loophole (under French and Spanish law, a lorry driver with gear in the back of his truck is guilty, regardless of whether he knew it was there or not). If the gear is hidden in the load and is stopped on a cold pull at Dover, it is almost impossible to get a conviction and rightly so. But if the job is part of a long-term op and the driver was in constant contact with the main man it was a bit harder for him to claim he was not 'knowingly concerned'.

In this case the driver coughed and got twelve years while the main man vanished into the ether. *C'est la vie.*

By then, however, I was already up on another job thanks to Jimmy. Up until the early nineties Customs had kept the Intel generated from Alpha *very* close to their chest. It was where all the major seizures of drugs came from and they were reluctant to get the Old Bill involved. But the expansion of Alpha meant that there were not enough operational resources to react to everything.

So, if we had a quick, one-off job and the ops team were too busy, we'd simply call someone we knew at the local police's drugs squad.

We'd always start the call with: 'Don't ask too many questions but I happen to know . . .'

'A big meet is going down in McDonald's in Eltham, the one near the A2 roundabout,' I said. 'That's where the handover will be.' I gave them the target's details. 'He's planning to meet a third party with a blue and white striped T-shirt, driving a Ford Focus. You have fifteen minutes.' I could hardly contain myself as the drugs squad sergeant, now suddenly full of adrenaline and thoughts of promotion, yelled for his team to get their shit together. I grinned.

I paced the silent office for thirty minutes. The phones stayed quiet; I heard no more from my targets. Hopefully, this meant they were too busy having their faces rubbed in the tarmac to make a call.

Eventually the landline rang. 'Thirty-five kilos of coke in the boot of the car and another eighteen back at the Focus driver's flat.' Reee-sult. I punched the air.

While the coppers celebrated with many beers, I got a quick nod and a handshake from the lads in Cocaine Corner. On to the next job.

In just two operations, I'd helped take almost a hundred kilos of coke off the streets and it actually felt like I'd achieved the impossible and made a dent in the coke trade. I don't mean to sound unprofessional but Alpha really was the dog's bollocks.

# 13. Another Short Lecture

Time for another (very quick) briefing.

One of the great things about Alpha was that we would never, ever have to appear in court. When I'd been a surveillance officer, I'd never been that keen to spend too long under cross-examination, but sometimes it was inevitable. Lots of my experienced colleagues positively relished giving evidence. Pat was the extreme example; every time he appeared in the witness box he made it his personal mission to make defence counsel look as stupid as possible.

It was even known for him to round on his own prosecution counsel from the box if he felt they weren't making enough of an effort to protect him from over-aggressive interrogation. He even sacked our counsel on one drugs job, something no one had ever done before, probably because most officers automatically gave barristers far too much respect. But Pat knew the score. 'Customs employ barristers,' he reasoned. 'Ergo, if I can employ 'em, I can sack 'em!'

But all that was over for me now. As far as the jury were concerned, Alpha did not exist. The judge would be informed about the existence of intercepts but that would be it.

There's been a lot of legal argument about admitting intercept material as evidence. It mostly relates at present to terrorist cases where the intelligence is very strong but the prosecutions are not being made because of lack of evidence. The case for admission is that if you arrest someone for blowing someone up, you should be able to use the phone calls in which he discussed the act with his co-defendants prior to the event.

The case against is that when it comes to the disclosure of material relating to the case, you will have to disclose *every single minute* of intercept material relating to the case. The defence/judges are not going to let one-minute's evidence be adduced without reviewing the thousands of hours of material that the prosecution do not rely on.

My view is that it should not be used in evidence. What someone says in the course of a phone call can be interpreted in many ways. Take, for example, a phone call where the conversation in full is:

'Yeah, it's me.'

'Everything OK?'

'Yeah, cushty, see you later.'

Now I know that these two individuals have been discussing importing twenty kilos of heroin for the past two weeks, and so as prosecution QC I would argue that the phone call meant that the gear had arrived in Dover and that they would meet later in the evening to hide the packages. Of course, the defence would be able to argue that it was perfectly innocent, about something completely different.

Each operation could have over 5,000 hours of intercept material, especially if there were multiple targets. There is no disclosure officer alive who would sign his name to say that in the material that is not being relied on, there is nothing that harms the prosecution case or assists the defence.

The disclosure officer would have to analyse every

minute of material, listening again and again to parts he did not understand or hear, before signing the disclosure schedule. The analysis would take (at eight hours a day, and allowing for holidays) at least two years! When it was finally disclosed to the defence, they would want to go through it with a fine-toothed comb as well, all on legal aid.

Trials are already getting completely bogged down by these 'show me everything' tactics. Even though disclosure rules say that the defence can only see material that the prosecution relies on (or which hinders the prosecution or assists the defence), judges are scared of creating 'appeal points' and all too often allow the defence the chance to see it all.

So that's why we don't use Alpha recordings in evidence.

Disclosure procedures were already a nightmare without having to worry about intercept evidence. The first few days were the worst. Before the trial everyone would get a 'prosecution bundle' – one for the judge, one each for the defence teams and one per person for the jury and our team of four. Each bundle was about five hundred pages thick and included copies of all the evidence and witness state-ments (the jury bundles did not include a copy of witness statements, they had to rely on the testimony of each witness in court).

From the date of committal, when the core evidence and witness statements are served, to the start of the trial, there is a constant flow of additional evidence served on defence. These are called NAEs or Notices of Additional Evidence. It is reasonable that as the investigation progresses and we gather more witness statements and pieces of evidence, copies would be passed to the defence. Every couple of weeks we would let the new evidence accumulate, then serve it on defence as NAE1, NAE2, etc., until a point close to the trial where the judge would rule that no additional evidence could be served.

During this 'disclosure' process a couple of things would also happen. Our disclosure officer would sign a statement to say that we held no material that assisted the defence or undermined the prosecution. The defence would also have to provide a 'defence statement'. This statement had to outline their arguments for their clients' innocence. It was brought in so that defence could not 'ambush' the prosecution in court by mentioning something in their favour that we did not know about and could not investigate. That is why the police caution made at the time of arrest has been changed to 'it may harm your defence if you do not mention something you later rely on in court'. For example if someone refused to give a statement and then claimed in court to have committed the crime under duress, the judge could instruct the jury to ignore the belated claim and find the defendant guilty as charged. This would certainly 'harm your defence'.

In reality, the defence statements usually just say, in effect, 'our client is not guilty of the charges'. They are supposed to give a story that the prosecution can investigate but they are never held to account for it.

The amount of material the jury sees is but a small percentage of everything we have seized. By signing the declaration that there was nothing in the material that has not been disclosed to defence that either harms our case or assists the defence we are saying that defence do not have to see all the material. In the past, the defence would be entitled to examine every piece of paper, every witness statement to confirm that we were not hiding any evidence that would cast doubt on their client's guilt.

These days we just make a legally binding statement and, in theory, the defence should take our word for it. If only. The defence love to see everything, mainly because the more hours they can put down, the more they get paid. And as it all comes out of a bottomless legal aid budget, then who cares?

Defence teams are the absolute worst for wasting taxpayer's money looking for evidence to help their clients that just doesn't exist. And the judges don't help either. They know the law. We say there is nothing to assist. The judges should put defence teams in their place.

But they don't. They roll over and agree that 'it might be better if defence were allowed to see all the material'. So we spend literally weeks babysitting some paralegal who hasn't a clue what they're looking for anyway, as they bill their way through mountains of paperwork. You can't leave them alone for minutes for fear of them stealing material, then claiming that 'item 5643 on the list of unused material' is missing and then suggesting that the reason it's missing is because it is the one piece of material that proves their client is not guilty.

OK, OK, I'll get off my soapbox now.

# 14. The Million-Pound Risotto

Chamo's application came through. He was indeed Colombian, part of a small 'cell' of three. The other two, Rico and Martín, worked as cleaners in the City. Despite their lowly position, they had a huge responsibility for shipping large amounts of coke into the UK and then getting the proceeds out to Spain, where their superiors arranged onward transport to Bogotá.

They were paid pretty badly considering all the risks they took. They had to meet the transport from the Continent, receive the gear and get it across London to the stash. They had to change the stash every week or so and then arrange to sell the gear in lumps of five to twenty kilos. All for about £800 a week. At every stage they were at the sharp end of the whole business, as I was about to try and demonstrate.

The best place to 'swoop', as the papers like to describe it, was at the handover of the main amount of gear, or at the point when the cash was handed over to the lorry driver for export.

'You know what *chamo* means, don't you?' Mike asked me.

I shook my head.

'It means "mate" in Spanish; nice and anonymous,' he said. 'I think you'll be requiring the services of our glamorous assistant.'

Funnily enough, the IC2s (Latin American/Spanish)

mainly spoke in pidgin-English. Indigenous Spanish speakers from Latin America, especially Colombia, Peru and Ecuador, have a very different accent from the rest of the Spanish-speaking world. They liked to clip words short. So instead of *buenas dias* they would say *beuna dia*. They did the same with English. World, food, football becomes worl', foo', foobaa and so on:

Chamo: Hiya, may, es me [Hiya, mate, it's me].

UKM: Wo' you up to? [Flat 'o' in wo']

Chamo: I pick you up layer, bou twel, we go an' see aar fren', you know wi' de two seesters?

UKM: Sure, may, I be raydey. Where we go' go?

Chamo: Tha' play up the row, near where we saw the gain [That place up the road, near where we saw the game – they also often replaced 'm' with 'n'].

After listening to Chamo and Jimmy for a while longer, I realized that a 'big one' actually meant £1 million. Jimmy had explained that he couldn't change all of it in one go and it would take three drops over three days.

This was looking bloody good to me, and when I took it to my SIO he thought it stood a decent chance of ranking highly at the weekly prioritization meeting. 'I think Ali will want this one,' he said. 'Have you met her yet?'

Although I hadn't, I recognized Ali Mooney as soon as she came over to introduce herself. She was a legend in Customs. Thirty years old, tall, with short spiky hair, she was half Scandinavian, half cockney. Athletically built (she used to be a kung-fu champ), Ali's appearance was intimidating to some (several of my non-PC colleagues called her 'geezerbird'), but I thought she looked pretty damn good. She was often accused (behind her back) of sleeping her way to the top. Not by me, though. Sure, she had a few long-term relationships with senior investigators, but these were the only men able to understand and put up with the demands of her job.

'Hi, Ali, great to meet you at last,' I said as we shook hands. There was a little bloke with her carrying a large A4 binder; he looked about fourteen. Some kind of office junior, I presumed.

'How about a cup of tea?' I asked, raising my eyebrows at the young lad in the hope that he'd get the hint and bugger off so that Ali and I could talk shop.

'Sounds good,' Ali said. Her companion stayed just where he was. I was just about to give him directions to the tea urn when Ali introduced him.

'This is Thomas,' she said, turning towards the little guy. 'He's our SIO.'

Whoops! I cleared my throat awkwardly. 'I'll put the kettle on.'

That done, we sat down in a meeting room for a confab. 'So,' Ali said in her soft Swedish-cockney accent, 'Jimmy's bureau looks like it might take us far and wide. I'd love my team to take this one on.'

'Great,' I said, chuffed that my first really major investigation was getting this much attention already.

Thomas, who'd been virtually silent until this point, finally chipped in. He spoke quietly. 'In terms of selling this job at the prioritization meeting, it should be a shoo-in. Perhaps, as you're a newbie, you'd like to sit in? See how it all works.'

The prioritization meeting was where Alpha's agenda was thrashed out. We had a finite number of lines, so there was a limit to how many ops could be run at one time. Operational team SIOs would pitch to get their op placed as high on the Alpha board as possible. This was a prioritized list of jobs to be taken on by Alpha. Depending on its urgency and general sexiness, a job could move up and down the list, sometimes for weeks or even months, before being allocated an operational team – or dropped altogether.

The meeting was a revelation. It started politely enough but it soon broke down into a combination of tantrums and secret handshakes as frustrated SIOs had good jobs kicked to the back of the queue by the head honchos who'd already agreed to take on 'sexier' jobs, discussed with their SIO drinking buddies in the pub the night before.

Thomas, to give him credit, did us proud.

'We have an inside track into a major money-laundering operation in a central London bureau de change run by a Pakistani who is able to turn more than £250,000 round in less than twenty-four hours.' That got everyone's attention. 'The target is working for a number of major players from across the UK. He's clearly the financial lynchpin of several drug-dealing operations and has significant links to overseas organizations.'

Thomas had not only painted a picture of Jimmy's bureau, he'd turned it into masterpiece. The combination of Pakistan and 'overseas organizations' got everyone's imaginations running wild with the 'T' word.

Like many other officers in my position, I'm reluctant to describe such a set-up as an 'organization'. In my experience, these dimwits are anything but organized. I agreed with Snapper UK-based criminals almost never formed tight, long-lasting organizations. There is no English equivalent of the Mafia, Triads, Yakuza or Solntsevskaya Bratva, never mind what you read in the tabloids. Crime in the UK is and always has been very disjointed, and British crims are famous for their lack of loyalty.

Returning to my desk I sat down next to Mike. 'Thomas is a real smooth talker,' I said, 'better than guys twice his age.'

'He has to be good if he can talk his way into Ali's bedroom.'

'Fuck off!'

Mike and Brian both nodded. 'It's the worst kept secret that they're in the first flushes of an affair, old boy.'

I was all ears in the office when Ali took her team out on the ground on the hunt for Chamo. They were waiting for a Colombian no one had ever seen to arrive at a bureau in the middle of Whitechapel, one of the most ethnically diverse boroughs in London, with one of the busiest markets in full swing and with the rush hour just about to get underway.

'This is going to be impossible,' I said to myself. I'd walked through that market a hundred times and I was often the only white face. I couldn't do anything to help; the villains hadn't talked to each other since the day before and Chamo's phone had stayed silent.

Lots of possibles were called from the two observation points (a white van and one of our black cabs parked up across the road), but they all walked straight past.

Call-sign Joseph (cockney rhyming slang for taxi – Joe

Baxi, a boxer from the fifties) was invaluable in London, utter gold dust. It was as if it had a Harry Potter invisibility cloak around it. Villains simply did not see it behind them.

Finally, Chamo's line turned green:

It's me.
Jimmy: OK?
Chamo: In five.
Jimmy: Yeah.
Click.

I was already dialling Ali.

'It's Cam. He's here, just out of the tube.'

'Got it.'

Ali had stationed two guys between Aldgate and Aldgate East and she gave them the heads-up.

It should be almost impossible to single out a lone Colombian with a bag in Whitechapel on market day but when you factor in the way he walks, the bag, his general demeanour and that he's just out of the tube and should be getting off the phone, then an obs team should at least have a fighting chance.

'From Bill: I'm five-five, the belt [male suspect] is out of the trench [underground] with bag, on his flyer [mobile phone], nine-one east.'

'From Ali: Bill will go.'

I prayed they had the right guy.

'From Bill: Belt complete the dryer [bureau de change].'

I could hear the satisfaction in Ali's voice. 'All call-signs stand by, this belt is the target.'

He was there five minutes and left without the bag. Great

evidence. Now Ali's team needed to 'house him', follow him to wherever he slept. This was going to be tricky. In those days, our radios didn't work underground, so officers on the tube weren't able to guide those in cars above them. Plus, keeping close to a target travelling on the underground without being outed was nigh impossible.

'From Ali: All footmen to go complete the trench; confirm.'

Six guys followed the belt into the tube. Now Ali had to wait until the first officer got off the tube and sprinted out of the station.

'From Mo at Tower Hill: The belt is westbound on District Line.'

All five vehicles drove as quickly as they could towards Bank, the next large interchange.

'From Maggie at Bank: Belt southbound on Northern Line.'

The fleet flew over London Bridge and so on it went until there was just Bill left following the target on his own. The entire team waited.

'From Bill: Belt exit Kennington, nine-one the [Elephant and] Castle.'

Before he got too crispy, Bill was relieved by a male/female 'couple' who managed to house the belt in Kennington.

The obs van plotted up on the address overnight, ready to pick him up in the morning and follow him to where he would pick up the next bag for Jimmy. Then they'd follow the guy he met to see where *he* went. Hopefully, at some point we'd ID a main player in the drug network that we could farm out as a separate target to another team, and on it would go.

Following targets was a long, gruelling process, especially if you were unlucky enough to be in the back of the obs van. Trying to stay interested in the back of a stuffy obs van at 3 a.m. in a Kennington side street just in case the Muppet decides to do business at some ungodly hour takes a special kind of stamina. There is no way on earth you can risk getting out, which means you could end up in the back of a van for more than twenty-four hours. As well as food and water, you need plenty of cling film and empty plastic bottles. It's not a job for the faint hearted, or the claustrophobic.

Over the next few days Ali and her team managed to house the person Chamo was collecting the dirty cash off. Now all that was left to do was to follow the clean money from the bureau to the point of exit from the UK. Simple.

It was while we were tracking Chamo that I first got to hear about Billy and Elton, the Scrote twins. They were utter plankton, right at the bottom of the food chain. They never changed their phones, had huge gobs and had fewer brain cells than most minnows. They were also given the new phone numbers of those higher up the chain who constantly changed their numbers. Perfect Alpha fodder.

Billy: I got a long 'un for ya, cuz, day after tomorra.
Jimmy: Usual rate. Come round anytime –
Billy: 'Cept during prayers; yeah, yeah I know.

This call was repeated every two or three days. A 'long 'un' was £100k, and the rate they were going meant they turned over £5 million a year. I put in applications to get their phones hooked up.

Almost straight away they got a call from a guy called Oliver.

Oliver: Awight, bro, pick up a long 'un from me. I gotta collect it off the train. See you at five-fifteen, say.

Billy: Usual place?

Oliver: Yeah, man. How's the little 'un?

Billy: Ain't seen im in a while.

Oliver: Tch. Fer fuck's sake, Billy, he's your son. I got six of the bastards and I see 'em all.

Billy: I'll see 'im soon; been busy making a crust, you know?

Oliver: Yeah well, you heard from Dublin Dave?

Billy: Nah, man, ain't you 'eard?

Oliver: 'Eard wot?

Billy: He's been pulled, held for ransom. Owes a kay to Bazza.

Oliver: Bazza? Fuck me, he ain't comin' back in one piece no matter how much they pay, that's one sadistic fucker.

Billy: When's the pick-up again?

Oliver: Today, five-fifteen, dickhead; make sure yer straight by da time I get there.

I put in an application for Oliver's number. He was the Scrote twins' older brother; his head was a tiny bit more screwed on. I badly wanted the number of the courier Oliver was going to meet; there was a good chance he would take me to his boss.

I listened in later as Billy called Jimmy to let him know about the incoming dirty cash. I also learned that his job was not just to take the money to Jimmy's bureau; he also negotiated the best deal.

That's when Jimmy gave away how he did it. As soon as he and Billy had finished negotiating, he made a phone call.

Jimmy (translated): Hi, Suresh, I've got a large transfer for you.
Suresh (translated): Black or white?
Jimmy: Black. Three, no, hang on, four trips, each twenty-four hours.
Suresh: Come by tomorrow, before prayers.

Needless to say, I wrote up an application for Suresh. 'Black' identified the money as being dirty and there was only one way to launder money in twenty-four hours: hawala.

Anyone selling drugs, from the guy who sells grams on the street, through his supplier to the people bringing in multi-tonne shipments, generates *huge* amounts of cash. From £30 a gram to £28k per kilo wholesale, the value of the drugs trade is well documented. They all have to get rid of the money. They can't deposit it in their bank accounts, because UK money laundering legislation is the most draconian in the world. Every business in the UK has an obligation under this legislation to notify the authorities of any suspicious transaction. With banks this usually means cash deposits higher than £5,000. It also applies to all other businesses, so if you are running a BMW dealership and a bloke comes in and buys a £25k Beamer for cash, you have to notify the authorities.

So, the drug gangs from Glasgow, Manchester, Liverpool, London, Birmingham who are generating maybe £100 million per week need to replace their drug-stained cash with clean bills, which in turn need to be hidden and invested.

Hawala is the answer. This traditional system of money

transference exists and operates outside of, or parallel to, 'traditional' banking or financial channels. It started in India about three hundred years ago and is still widely used by subcontinental and Middle Eastern communities to send money around the world.

Unlike traditional banking, hawala makes minimal use of any sort of negotiable instrument. 'Transfers' (the money doesn't actually have to be moved) take place based on communications between members of a network of hawaladars (hawala dealers). Ironically enough, for a system that is widely abused by money launderers and tax dodgers, its key component is trust. It also depends on family connections and regional affiliations.

Unlike banks, you don't need an account, a passport or a National Insurance number to transfer large wedges. Also, hawala traders don't have any hidden charges such as a delivery and transfer fees, nor do they require expensive bankers' drafts, nor do they take seven working days to complete. They may charge a five per cent commission but their rate of exchange tends to be much better than a bank and they don't care where the money's come from. Although the law varies and is quite fuzzy, hawala is generally recognized as being illegal in India and Pakistan. This doesn't seem to stop anybody, however.

In the UK, hawala banking services are advertised openly in newspapers, trade magazines and shop windows. For drug dealers who need to launder large amounts of cash quickly it's a perfect system: it's cost effective, efficient, there's a distinct lack of bureaucracy, there's no paper trail and it's fast and very reliable.

If the financial cops decide to investigate the financial

transactions of a Mr Big and they find they've been using the hawala system, then all they can do is throw their hands in the air in despair. Hawala transfers leave a sparse or confusing paper trail, if any. Even when invoices are used, the mixture of legal goods and illegal money, confusion about 'valid' prices and a complex international shipping network creates a convoluted, impossible to follow set of tracks. And that's if you can find the hawaladar in the first place. Some operate using a table in a tea shop for an office; a mobile phone and notebook full of coded writing are their only other overheads.

Policing the international financial system is hard enough as it is, thanks to the development of free trade zones, extraterritorial banking, electronic money transfers and smart cards, all of which have made the movement of capital much easier over the past twenty years. Every day there are 70,000 international money transfers, shunting £1 trillion to and from accounts around the world. In 1979 there were seventy-five offshore tax havens. Today, there are more than three thousand and nearly half of the world's money supply passes through them. Once Jimmy had cleaned the money there were almost unlimited options as to where his customers could hide it.

In a nutshell, hawala sticks two fingers up at the Western banking system and neatly sidesteps all the wizardry of modern law enforcement. It is the perfect money laundering system. It was this, alongside pay-as-you-go phones, that kept the drugs trade ticking along so smoothly (besides the insatiable demand, of course). It was also the reason we needed fifty Alpha squads across the country, not just one based in London.

And just in case you're wondering, it's very rare for a hawala trader who deals with a client face-to-face to disappear with a client's money. In fact it never happens. Traders earn plenty of money (they also use the hawala system to avoid paying taxes) and the more trusted they are, the greater their income.

As far as this op was concerned, hawala could work one of two ways. Jimmy could either take the cash from Chamo (or Billy and Elton) and give it to Suresh, his hawaladar. Suresh would then contact Ganesh, his hawaladar in London, who would arrange to have the clean money delivered back to Jimmy in euros. Jimmy would take a tasty 15 per cent commission and the euros would then be smuggled abroad.

An even better way would be if Jimmy were to contact Vinod, his hawala trader in Dubai. Vinod would then take clean cash straight to whoever Mr Big wanted (could even be Mr Big himself) in Dubai, and the recipient would then deposit the cash into various accounts, completely legally, no questions asked.

A significant proportion of Dubai has been built on laundered drugs money. There are two reasons for this. The first is the large population of expatriate workers from India and Pakistan who use hawala to send money home. The second is Dubai's large gold market, which is the source of much of the gold sent (legally and illegally) to India and Pakistan. Dubai, unlike many other South Asian nations, allows pretty much unregulated financial dealing.

Because of this, many South Asian businessmen have offices in Dubai, and money is often wired there to circumvent regulations elsewhere in the world. In addition, Dubai offers a neutral meeting place for Indian and Pakistani businessmen, as tension between those two countries makes travel between them difficult, if not impossible.

Once the money is in Dubai, it can be deposited in several bank accounts and then used to buy shares in hotels under construction. This is why Dubai is one big building site and why it's awash with 6-star hotels. Dubai is up to its neck in black cash transferred through the hawala system, which is thought to make up about 50 per cent of south Asia's economy.

As it turned out, Chamo wanted his cash changed into US dollars in the UK and sent to Colombia via Spain.

Chamo: Everythin' OK?
Jimmy: Yeah, anytime 'cept during prayers.
Chamo: I'll come by after, today.

'Bollocks!' I exclaimed. 'Any other day than today, Chamo, come on!' I was on lates and it was my turn to cook. Prayers were at 4 p.m., so Chamo would be coming to pick up the money after then, just when I'd have to have started dinner. Twenty-five hungry and irritable officers would be expecting a nice meal at half-past six and I still had to do my own work, and be part of the op to catch Chamo's cash before it vanished abroad. Now that's pressure. After seeing the dreadful reaction to Nigel's disaster, I was in a real flap about not disappointing everyone.

Mike said not to worry; I could put an alarm on Jimmy and Chamo's lines so a red light on my desk would flash if they called. Mike promised to come and get me the moment it did. I could then play the call back and update the team on the ground.

Come five o'clock I was sweating like a pig in a sausage factory, battling with a mountain of fresh shellfish. Why on earth had I thought seafood risotto would be a good idea for twenty-five people?

Mike stuck his head round the door. 'Christ, Cam,' he said, looking at the mountain of mussels and the half-smashed crabs in the sink. 'What the hell are you going to do to us? Anyway, get out of there, the alarm's gone off.'

Ali's team had been waiting patiently since dawn in Kennington for Chamo to emerge. He finally appeared after lunch and mooched about for a few hours in a half-arsed effort to convince himself he wasn't being followed.

We had no idea what he was supposed to do once he'd been to the bureau.

'Let's hope he'll try and take it straight out of the UK,' Ali said. 'It's the best we can do evidentially – keep the bag in sight from bureau to border. Pretty hard for Chamo to deny what's going on.'

'What if it goes to a stash?' I asked.

'We bash the door in. We can't afford to lose sight of the cash for too long. The chain of evidence would be broken if the cash were sorted and broken up between several couriers.'

'Fingers crossed the Colombians are greedy bastards and want the money in their sweaty hands ASAP.'

'My thoughts exactly.'

'Zulu 1 mobile complete the shaker [taxi], nine-one the Castle. Paris has five-five.'

Finally, Chamo had decided to get the gear. Black cabs are a nightmare to follow but call signs Denmark and Belgium stuck to him with little trouble.

He took the shaker to a cafe in Kennington, then took another up to Elephant and Castle to meet the guy he'd been given the money by in the first place. Whoever was in charge had decided that it wouldn't be wise to let just one man walk around with $1.5 million in untraceable notes.

'Denmark, Zulu1 and Zulu 2 are complete a white Sierra, X-ray Alpha, wait for twist.'

The team did really well to stick with it. Ali could have let it run all the way to the bureau but she couldn't be sure that Jimmy wouldn't send someone to meet them halfway with the cash.

On their way through town the car stopped. The supplier went to a TK to make a call.

'Bill: On foot marking call.'

As soon as Zulu 2 finished his call, Bill went into the kiosk and 'marked' the call by dialling the speaking clock.

This would appear immediately after the target's call on the itemized call list we'd get from BT. Combining the surveillance team's observations with the number appearing on the itemized billing was a good way of 'evidencing' the number called by the target.

'From Bill: TK reference number 5961, number 02075557645. Timed at 13:24.'

My phone rang.

'Cam.'

'Ali. Received?'

'Roger that, checking now.' After making a quick call to BT, I looked up the previous number. A Portuguese mobile. Interesting but not much use to us. I put it in the system. If that mobile ever cropped up again, we'd know its history.

The team got the targets to Whitechapel.

The supplier dropped Chamo five minutes' walk from the bureau. A team were already plotted up round the bureau but Ali sent a couple of guys with him, just in case they were going to do the handover at a cafe instead of the bureau.

'Foot Andy: deployed.'

'Foot Maggie: deployed.'

'From Andy: Zulu 1 Hanbury Street, possible recip.'

'Denmark: I have five-five; foot Andy, let Zulu 1 run.'

'Foot Maggie: I'm in Greatorex Street, trying five-five.'

After about five minutes walking down side streets and doubling back round, doing a crap job checking he wasn't being followed, Chamo dived into Jimmy's bureau. Jimmy closed up.

The supplier, meanwhile, parked up round the corner, right in front of call sign Joseph. The 'cabbie' read his paper with one eye.

A few minutes later: 'Foot Andy: Zulu 1 out of dryer with back-pack.'

'Belgium: With flourish [taking photos]. Zulu 1 is nine-one for Zulu 2.'

'Foot Andy: Bloody hell, it's stuffed full. Packets are poking out.'

I grinned. 'We've got the right guy and he's fully loaded,' I said to myself.

Chamo walked round the corner, straining under the weight of his back-pack. Then he froze. He'd stopped dead. He turned and surveyed the busy street. Before him were a dozen or so officers and four of our cars, all in plain view and desperately trying to keep their cool. Had Chamo smelled a rat?

The surveillance team's adrenaline levels shot off the scale. Was a hot pursuit on the cards?

Finally satisfied, Chamo jumped in the supplier's car, right under Joseph's nose.

Suddenly, Dave was beside me. 'What's that smell?' he said, 'Smell's like . . .'

'SHIT!'

I stormed out to the kitchen and got to the risotto in the nick of time. I broke out the French bread, grated the Parmesan, bashed the dinner gong, dished up and ran back to my station.

The team took the target west on the A4 then the M4, M25 and eventually the M3. The south coast. Portsmouth, perhaps?

Mike appeared next to me. 'Risotto's going down a storm, mate. Aren't you joining us?'

I wasn't hungry, but now was the best time to join the rest of the office for a bite, so I set everything to record and went to receive my culinary judgement. Fortunately it had indeed gone down a storm and the dish quickly disappeared.

As soon as I returned, Ali called. 'Hi, Cam, it's game on. Portuguese mobile phone; M3 south towards a port that serves the Iberian Peninsula.'

Eventually the target pulled into a warpath Swede (motorway services) just outside Portsmouth. There's a set system for dealing with this situation during surveillance. The two closest cars, the five-five and six-eight cars, in this case France and Denmark, followed the target to the parking area. The third car, Belgium went to the flood (fuel pumps), while Dublin, the fourth car, covered the slip road back onto the warpath.

'From France: Zulu 1 and Zulu 2 nine-one for the cafe, Zulu 1 with the rucksack.'

'From Denmark: Bill, Mark, Andy, Maggie, split into two teams and rotate on their plot. The objective is to stay with the bag, all call signs acknowledge in sequence.'

It didn't matter what these Zulus decided to do now, Ali's team would stick with the bag. This is one of the hardest parts of surveillance, a bag can move between any number of hands/cars/vehicles in a short space of time. It's extremely difficult to keep up with it and not end up showing out.

All I could do was listen. It was frustrating, not being able to see everything, not being able to help on the ground. But I knew Ali was at the top of her game and at least I could hear everything.

'From Bill: Zulu 2 nine one the jug. I have five-five.'

'From Maggie: I have five-five, am going with Zulu 1 . . . Zulu 1 is nine-one the canary [public telephone].'

Maggie was brilliant. She was just the wrong side of middle-aged and dressed conservatively, real Women's Institute stuff. As I've already mentioned, villains never thought women might be undercover officers, let alone some old biddy. Maggie could stand right behind Mr Big and he wouldn't give her a second thought. Maggie looked over Zulu 1's shoulder as she went past.

'From Maggie: Zulu 1 dialled three-five-one.'

The international dialling code for Portugal.

They both returned to their seats and sat there for another twenty minutes. After Maggie and Andy had supper, they swapped with Bill and Mark.

Ten minutes after another phone call, Zulu 1 and Zulu 2 returned to the car.

It was 9 p.m. The team had been on plot since seven that morning, and most of them had been up at least a couple of hours before that.

'From Belgium: All call signs standby, a Portuguese registered slug [lorry], white unit, red trailer nine-one the lorry park.'

'Denmark: Yes.'

'Yeah from France: The slug is nine-nine-nine in the leek.'

'From Denmark: Clear the air, clear the air, that's seven-seven, seven-seven. Zulu 1 mobile, wait . . . Zulu 1 nine-one the lorry park.'

'Belgium: Switch of the slug is about to take place . . . Zulu nine-one the slug slowly, slowly.'

'From Denmark: Belgium eyeball, this is a three-way chilli, Zulu 1 and Zulu 2 plus unknown at the rear of X-ray Alpha.'

'Belgium: Five-five, this is now a three-way chilli, a third party has joined them, I can't see from where, they're all stood at the rear of X-ray Alpha.'

'From Denmark: Remember, stay with the bag, stay with the bag.'

'Belgium: that's foot Andy deployed.'

'Belgium – Andy: radio check.'

'Belgium: OK.'

'From Andy: The chilli is between Zulu 1, Zulu 2 and a UKM. The boot's up on X-ray Alpha, wait.'

'Wait' means no-one else can transmit until all the info is passed.

'From Andy: Zulu 2 has taken the bag from the boot and is walking round to the drivers' side of the tractor unit. Wait.

'They're at the door, UKM is complete the slug, repeat, UKM is complete the slug.'

'From Denmark: We will go with the slug.'

I knew that a lot of officers wouldn't have the balls to run this any further. Most would have knocked it the minute the bag went in the cab. A money laundering charge looks so much better if you trace the money from the bureau to the point where it's supposed to leave the country. And luckily Ali had bigger balls than most of the guys in Alpha. This decision was all hers and the Alpha office always left operational decisions to the head of the operational team out on the ground.

The team carried on commentating on Zulu 1 and Zulu 2 going back to their car, but everyone was now locked-on to the truck.

As it went mobile the details were passed over the air.

My phone rang. 'Cam, it's Ali. Any joy on the truck details?'

'No dice. Truck has no record.'

The team stuck with the lorry to Portsmouth docks. I called local Customs to get it tugged. 'Only nab him once he's got his ticket and is driving towards the ferry,' I warned, and then put them in touch with Ali.

They waited until the moment when the lorry driver must have thought he was in the clear and then brought his world crashing down. In his cab was a rucksack containing $1.5 million in clean bills.

Funnily enough, when Ali interviewed him, all he had to say for himself was '*Não comentar.*'

Didn't do him any good, though. The phone numbers of the supplier and Chamo were still on his mobile.

Ali picked up Chamo and the supplier the next day. They pleaded total ignorance and refused to turn supergrass. All of them went down. Except Jimmy. We left him there as bait.

It was a clinical operation and so I was riding high in Alpha. Any jobs that came from Jimmy would shoot straight to the top of the priority board. The only problem was that he had so much going on; I wanted to choose the next one carefully.

This time, murder and mayhem were just a phone call away.

# 15. Everyone Digs Their Own Grave

I stole a look from the other side of the street. Jimmy's bureau just looked like any other independent bureau in inner London. Small and drab, it had a board with his current exchange rates in little red lights propped up on a shelf behind the plate-glass window. Its location was entirely incongruous; it was on the edge of Petticoat Lane Market and was surrounded by clothes shops selling African-style clothing and materials.

A bored-looking man was sitting behind the counter. Was that Jimmy? I guessed he was in his early forties but I couldn't make much else out from the opposite side of the street. This was against all the rules but my curiosity had got the better of me. There was no way I was supposed to be on the plot – but it was literally on my way home (if I stood on tiptoe and bent my neck a little I could just about see it from my kitchen window), and I told myself that I'd only glance as I walked past. Still, it was the first step across a line – and it wouldn't be the last.

I imagined his shop would be pretty busy with law-abiding customers. His rates were quite good and he was just a short distance from the City, so handy for anyone wanting to order currency for business trips and weekends away. He was also on the route of one of the Jack the Ripper tours that attracted hundreds of ghoulish sightseers every day, so I suspect he got quite a bit of passing trade. As I watched, a couple of Japanese tourists stepped out. And then a skinny man in jeans, trainers and ski jacket arrived. He was carrying a sports holdall. It looked very heavy.

Holy shit!

Skinny guy gave a nod and the man behind the counter buzzed the door open and let him straight into the back.

He stepped into the hallway and disappeared down some stairs into the basement.

Yep, business was booming, right enough.

UKM: I've changed up but don't feel comfortable walking back to the bureau with so much. I need to book a taxi. Come on, Jimmy, it won't be much.

Jimmy: No, absolutely no, man. You know what biz is like, knife edge and all dat.

UKM: But I can't take the bus with all this, er . . .

Jimmy: I'm not payin' for a bloody taxi to tek you 'arf a mile down the road! Why mus' you do this to me? With my 'eart condition. You know I can't take stress. Take the bus! Now go!

UKM: OK, OK, I'll get the bus.

What a skinflint. Jimmy was making £50,000 from Billy and Elton's latest consignment and he wouldn't cough up six quid for a short cab journey. God knows what he'd do if his runner got held up. Have a heart attack, probably. If ever there was someone to try and turn into an informant, it was Jimmy's runner.

So I now knew his counting house was in the basement. He must have had guys on the go 24/7, counting and playing hunt the forgery. It takes days to sort through £500,000 by hand; a counting machine might be able to do a thousand notes a minute but checking for forgeries would take a while longer.

Billy's line lit up. He was calling his twin.

Billy: You 'eard?
Elton: Yeah.
Billy: Cunts stuck a knife right through the top of his fucking head. Then, just to make sure, they done him through the throat as well.
Elton: Jesus, you can't mess with the northern monkeys, man. They top people if they even *think* they're grassing, even if they dunno for sure.

The Scrote Twins, God bless their big ugly mouths, had provided me with yet another charming little update from the underworld.

Billy: Anyway, I have Slim's goods, five long. Who's Ollie sayin' it's gotta go to?
Elton: A geezer called Ivan is taking it to Harwich. Text you 'is number.

The next call Billy made was to a Russian immigrant called Ivan. Now I had Ivan's number. And it was registered in his name to an address in east London. I typed his name and address into the Police National Computer, more in hope than expectation.

Miraculously, his vehicle details materialized before my eyes. 'Stupid fucking bastard,' I said with no little wonder and plenty of appreciation.

All that was needed was a quick call to alert Harwich and they made it look like a cold pull. A quick half mil in the Queen's kitty. Job done.

I noted the name 'Slim'. Billy and Elton's voices changed ever so slightly whenever they spoke about him; there was a definite and very unusual (for them) hint of respect.

Ivan's money was 'detained' as suspected proceeds of crime. The 'owner' had to turn up in the Magistrates Court in three days to prove the money had come from a legitimate source. Sometimes a gopher would turn up with a bullshit letter from a fake solicitor saying the money was to 'purchase a bar in Spain', but the fact that it might as well have been written in crayon usually persuaded the beak to find in our favour.

I wanted Ivan's line hooked up on the hurry-hurry. My fingers raced across the keyboard in double-quick time and I thrust it under Thomas's nose. 'Need this one fast,' I said, explaining how Ivan wasn't exactly the Brain of Ukraine and that there was a good chance he'd take us further up the supply chain. 'If anyone can sell it, you can. You think it's possible to get it under the Home Sec's nose today?'

Thomas looked at the form and then back to me and grinned, knowing I'd owe him one. 'Sure, why not?'

Sure enough, once we let him go, Ivan still didn't think he was bugged and used his phone to call the mysterious Slim.

Ivan: It's me.
Slim: So what the fuck happened, comrade?
Ivan: Sorry, man; they pulled me and took the cash.
Slim: Yeah, well I'm gonna need to see some proof.

Ivan: They gave me a receipt.
Slim: What's it say at the top?
Ivan: Err . . . Seizure Notice.
Slim: Well bring it over. I need to see it a-s-a-fucking-p, all right?
Ivan: OK, OK, I'm coming.

Understandably, Slim didn't believe the seizure was legit; criminals are not in the habit of trusting one another. Even though he could probably afford to lose a load or two, he still wanted to see our paperwork – bizarrely, our own bureaucracy is regularly used to reassure the gangsters that their courier isn't pulling a fast one. If the courier was dodgy then, even if Slim could afford to lose the load, the courier would have to be punished – it just won't do in the drugs world to let yourself be seen to be doing nothing when someone rips you off. Needless to say, the couriers were eternally grateful for our receipts as that meant they wouldn't get topped (or at least not for a while).

I was delighted. I had Slim's number. He was obviously someone much higher up the chain, someone very well connected. I typed out yet another form and his line was wired. It was clear from the amount of money that Billy and Elton were moving for him that Slim was a quality drug target in his own right.

Sure enough, at the next prioritization meeting, Slim was shoved to the top of the board. Ranjiv and I would manage the intercepts and Intel while Snapper was penned in to lead the ground ops. He could hardly sit still with excitement. 'I've got a good feeling about this one,' he said, rubbing his hands together, 'and my instincts are rarely wrong.'

Snapper reminded me of Jed; they were definitely cast

from the same mould: work hard and play hard. Myself aside, I didn't know anyone other than Jed who put as much into the job as Snapper did. He lived and breathed it. I could ring him at two in the morning with a snippet and he'd be out of bed and pulling his jeans on before I had finished. He was thirty-six, the same rank as me, had the cold blue eyes of Terence Stamp and was a real hell-raiser to boot. He looked the part, too: scruffy, long hair, unshaven, into weird hippy music and loved to drink. He was ridiculously well connected, he seemed to know everybody in law enforcement and picked up more whispers than everyone else in our office combined.

This became apparent when I asked Snapper a question. 'I reckon we could turn Jimmy's runner, you know. Jimmy treats him really badly and won't even stump up for his bus fare to a handover, let alone a cab.'

'Nah, mate. Sounds like a good idea but I'm not going down that route.'

'Why not? I've handled plenty of informants in my time and this seems like the best candidate going.'

Customs were having a nightmare with bureaux de change. Understandably frustrated at not being able to penetrate the closed circle of hawala and the bureaux (one money laundering outfit in Bradford took £3.3 million in notes in a single day and paid over £80 million into the banks for just one client), officers had taken a chance and tried to turn an employee of one London bureau into a confidential informant. In the end, they had several informants from three bureaux in the same street.

'I'm telling you, bureaux de change move more money than the City every week of the year,' Snapper said.

'Hundreds of men and women bombing up and down the M1 loaded with dirty and freshly laundered cash. I can understand why they recruited informants, I mean how else are you gonna get these bastards? It's impossible. They're getting away with murder and no one can stop them.

'These informants were so good that Customs started using them as witnesses of truth in money laundering prosecutions,' Snapper told me. 'They produced the financial records of the bureau, which apparently recorded the illegal transactions.

'Problem was, they weren't telling Customs about all the other dodgy deals they were doing. They eagerly touted for other business, thinking that the Excise had given them a licence to launder. And it was bloody obvious. They should have spotted it and simply arrested their informants but no, the idiots paid them for their services and carried on instead.

'Well, it all went tits-up when a Customs prosecutor looked at the information relating to the informant and concluded that the bureau was "rotten to the core", so they could hardly be presented as credible witnesses. Cases against loads of money launderers were overturned – some were even paid compensation for time served, courtesy of the taxpayer.'

He went on to describe one incredible meeting, the likes of which I've not heard before or since, where about 150 top barristers appeared in a south London courtroom to learn from Customs whether their convicted clients had ever passed through this particular bureau while Customs were running their corrupt informant and whether their corrupt informant was the man they'd concealed behind a screen to give evidence before a jury.

'Needless to say, the powers that be don't want to go

down that route ever again. The bosses would run a mile if you came at them with an informant working for a BdC.'

That was me told. 'No informants for us, then,' I replied.

'Fuck yeah, stick with our phones; they're watertight by comparison. Everyone digs their own grave that way.'

Unsurprisingly, Slim was a lot more cautious than the Scrote twins and Ivan. His phone was pay-as-you-go and was one of many he owned. I was getting a tiny piece of the big picture and I knew I wouldn't have this line for long before it was chucked.

I still depended on Billy and Elton's big mouths. It was clear from their chatter that Slim was dealing E's, speed, coke and heroin, but I needed more. I needed someone close to Slim, someone who didn't change their phones. Someone like Terry, his dad, a black cab driver.

Slim: Dad?

Terry: Awight, son, what's up?

Slim: Me and Unc have got some of those bits of paper . . . you know.

Terry: When and where?

Slim: I'll text it to you from my safe one. Usual pay. Conner wants it done asap.

Terry: Yeah, well, give us a bell when you're ready, I'm off the golf early mind.

Terry was about to move a load of laundered cash that the Scrote twins had picked up from Jimmy Ashraf. Now I had Slim's dad's phone number, I had another way into what was obviously a family business.

It was a perfect set-up, having a black cab on board – as we knew only too well, nobody ever got suspicious of a black cab and if Terry was ever pulled he could just say he was doing a delivery for some unknown bloke.

Once the application was done, it was home time. I briefed Ranjiv and was on my way out when Snapper called me over. 'Me and the lads are gonna have a few jars in the Hung, Drawn and Quartered. Coming?'

I was footloose and fancy-free. I owed my sons a phone call but that could wait. I'd ring them tomorrow. Being invited out on the piss with the ops team was a good sign.

'A lot of good work's done in the boozer,' Snapper said as we exited Custom House, threw on our coats and lit up.

'You'll meet lots of ops team members who you'd never see otherwise; they like to put a face to the mysterious "voice-on-the-phone". Senior management don't like it but it works really well.'

It was true. All we could do was talk shop, it was the one thing we had in common. I thought it was great to be able to have a semi-social relationship with officers on the ground.

It wasn't yet 5 p.m. so the pub was quiet. I returned to a corner table with pints for Snapper and Mike. 'So what's the score with Slim, then?' Snapper asked.

'Well, I put in an application for his dad today.'

'Nice one.'

'Yeah, it seems as if Slim is running a family business, all right. He mentioned an Uncle Conner.'

Snapper choked on his pint.

'What's up?' I asked. 'What did I say?'

'You sure he said Uncle Conner?'

'Hundred per cent.'

'Fuck me,' Snapper said. 'Well fuck me sideways with my uncle's marrow.'

'You don't think . . . ?' Mike added.

'Could be,' Snapper said, puffing out his cheeks.

'Fucking hell,' Mike said to Snapper, 'I'd pay to be in Cam's shoes.'

Snapper nodded silently as he swallowed the dregs of his pint and burped.

'Would someone mind telling me what the fucking hell you two are talking about?'

'Well, Cam,' said Snapper, with no little condescension, 'you told me a while ago you felt like a hick from the sticks. You've just done it again. If you'd spent a bit more time in London then you'd have a fair idea who Uncle Conner was.'

I kept my gob shut and tried not to look as blank as I felt.

'You're deep into Finnegan territory.'

I'd heard the name and knew it was part of London gangster folklore, but nothing else.

'Barry and Conner Finnegan are proper mentalists,' Snapper said. 'Bad as they come and twice as mad. Came over to London in the fifties and after messing about in the Irish stronghold of Kilburn, they settled on the messy area between Camden and Islington: Somerstown, North Holloway, Caledonian Road and Pentonville. The rest is an all-too familiar story of protection, blagging, supergrassing, the odd gun battle here and there with rivals before discovering there was easy money to be made from drug dealing. Then came the nineties rave scene and Barry and Conner became multi-*multi*-millionaires. Anyone who's ever popped a pill, then it was very likely supplied by these guys.

'Those two have done it all. They're in their sixties now and are still operating, albeit more as financiers. Their money's squirrelled safely away in Dubai and Lichtenstein and they're far enough away from any drugs so as to be untouchable. UK law enforcement can't be bothered with them; to be honest, they're just too difficult.

'And now –' I started.

'And now we know they use Slim to set up the deals and move the money while Slim moves the drugs,' Snapper said, slapping the table with his hand. 'Anything that Slim's planning is going to involve the brothers and we've got an ear on. It's incredible, I would never have believed their operation was so localized.'

'Fuck me, Cam,' Mike said. 'That is either the worst or best beginner's luck I have ever seen. Dave's gonna shit a brick when he realizes what he's given you.'

Why the worst? Well, the bigger the criminal, the bigger and more expensive the operation and the more likely it is to go tits-up. If it all came together and we got some decent seizures then all well and good, it just depended how far the phones would force us to go.

The days passed; Slim didn't let much slip. The best info I got was that one of his cousins, a bloke called Neal, was also heavily involved in the family business. Snapper was busy with other ops but whenever he saw me having a fag on the quay he came down to ask me what was going on. He was desperate to get his teeth into the Finnegans.

'Remember, Cam,' he said, 'here it's all about the seizures, taking out weight and nicking whoever we can.'

'I haven't forgotten, it's just nothing's happening at the moment. Terry's too far out of Slim's ops, the Scrote twins have been fairly silent, for them anyway, and Slim's at the top of his game, the best at personal security I've ever seen. He doesn't just have street smarts, he's actually intelligent.'

Slim: Dad, 'ow many times do I have to tell you? Change your bloody phone.

Terry: But son, I need a regular number for the cab work.

Slim: You don't 'ave to work, Dad, you know that.

Terry: It's what I do. I like it. I'm a cabbie.

Slim: I know, I know. Look, I just change the SIM cards. You can keep your contacts on the phone and do a group text to let them know the new number. It's 'undred per cent safe.

Terry: Defeats the object, dunnit?

Slim: They can't get texts yet.

Terry: Yeah, well, I dunno. How's the little 'un?

Slim: Great, about to start school, well excited. Got 'im into St Dunstan's. Had to register 'im to do it.

Terry: He'll go far, that one.

Slim: I'll make sure of that.

Terry: And Sandra?

Slim: She's right 'ere, blowing you a kiss and inviting you up for dinner. Why don't you come up for a bit o' lunch on Sunday?

Terry: Awight, son, see you then.

Slim: I've got another fing to ask you too. Love you.

Terry: Love you too, son, bye.

Slim knew if he changed his phone every week he'd be safe. He'd let slip to his dad that he used six handsets, and put a new chip in one of them every week. I was playing Russian roulette. The one phone I had would soon be gone.

I rang the technical services department of a leading mobile-phone company to ask for help. They always had to keep someone on hand to talk to the security services, not exactly your average customer advisor.

Their resident geek had some interesting info. 'Your man's not been careful enough,' he said. 'If he's got a new model – which I presume he has, since he changes them so often – we're now able to hold and use information from both SIM cards and phones. If someone puts in a new SIM card [i.e. changes the phone number] into the same handset as the old SIM card, we can still extract the information from the handset.'

'So you can tell me what the new number is?'

'Yup.'

'Sweet!' The only remaining problem was that Slim had six phones on the go at any one time, and I still only had one of them, so I was only getting one in six of his calls and most of those were clean. I didn't yet have his dirtiest phones, the ones he did his business on.

But now I had a school name. St Dunstan's. Slim's son was starting there so it was an infants' school. There were five St Dunstan's Primary Schools in London. I guessed from the family history that Slim was based north of the river. That narrowed it down to Finchley or Hammersmith. Hammersmith was way out west so I figured Slim lived in Finchley, which was quite a bit closer to the family manor.

We pinged Slim's mobile for a few days to see which masts it was using most and, sure enough, they were clustered around Finchley.

Snapper checked what Intel we had with a mate at the National Criminal Intelligence Service. They came back with Slim's real name: Nigel Barker. He'd been of interest, but they'd not managed to get anywhere with him. Slim had a clean record; he lived in a nice house with a girlfriend and son he clearly adored. He was close to his old man and his uncles Barry and Conner. He also owned a couple of trendy shops; nothing flash but something that covered his income.

In the end, though, it was Billy and Elton who proved to be the key to getting to Slim's phone. It doesn't matter how clever you are, if the people who know your phone numbers aren't as security conscious as you then you're fucked.

Slim would change his numbers and pass the new ones in code to his nearest and dearest, who would at some point put the number in the address book of their phone.

But instead of going through the 'add name' and 'add number' menu, Billy and Elton did it the lazy way by dialling the number and then saving it. As soon as they pressed the little green icon I got Slim's new number. *Voila!*

Whenever Billy did the dial-and-save method, I got the new number hooked up. It was just a case of waiting to see if it was one of Slim's and whether he used that phone to talk to anyone but the Scrote twins.

The next one proved to be pure gold.

Slim: Yeah it's me.
UKM: OK, mate.

Slim: You sorted wiv those little fellas [ecstasy]?

UKM: All done, matey. We're ready to rock and roll.

Slim: What about the fast [speed]?

UKM: Whatever you need, mon braaav.

Slim: Sweet as. I might want some of the shiny [coke] as well.

UKM: No prob.

Slim: How fast is it?

UKM: Super-good, eighty miles an hour. It's real flaky, fish scales you know. Come and 'ave a look at a bit.

Slim: Cush. I'll send me mate over, you know, the one you met at that place last time. You still got 'is number?

UKM: Nah, I got a new one since then, send it me in the . . . you know.

Slim: Yeah, yeah, sweet as. If everyfing's cool I'll send the paper round wiv a fast black. What we lookin' at?

UKM: Twenty-fives's [£25k per kilo] for the shiny, sixty [60p per tab] for the little fellas. Got some garden furniture [skunk marijuana] as well, that's three [£3k per kilo].

Slim: Got loads of four-by [four-by-four: herbal marijuana].

UKM: Bet you ain't got stuff this good, it's the white one [white widow: really powerful skunk].

Slim: I'll fink abaht it and bell you later.

UKM: Later.


That was it, a deal was set. Slim was planning to buy twenty kilos of coke with eighty per cent purity from an importer at £25,000 per kilo that he'd sell on the very same day in smaller amounts to local dealers for a £3,000-a-kilo profit.

Sixty thousand quid for a few phone calls from his bedroom and a trip by one of his gophers to check that the gear was kosher. Not bad.

People bought all that Slim could get. He was working his way through millions. It always amazed me that there seemed to be no limit to the number of people ready to snort, smoke and shoot every last crumb of coke that made it into the UK. Most politicians seem to forget (or avoid talking about) the fact that demand, not supply, is the main reason for the coke trade and that's what needs to be reduced. Criminals are in it for the money and would drop drug importation like a hot coal if they weren't getting the rewards.

Despite his one communication flaw further down the line, Slim was the smartest career villain I'd ever come across. He could have got a job working for us no trouble, and if he didn't happen to get his jollies from selling smack that would end up putting boys and girls on the game, I might even have liked him.

Slim had massive ambition. His whole life was spent on the phone moving gear around, buying and selling without ever getting his hands dirty. On a good week he could turn over £10 million for the Finnegans and others and he would personally make about £250,000 profit. There was no question: Slim was one of the central cogs spinning right at the heart of the UK's drugs importation system.

Something told me he was going to be incredibly difficult to nick.

# 16. What Criminals Really Talk About

Chelsea Barry: I'm feelin' so horny, babes. What are ya wearing?
UKF: Nuthin', honey.

Oh no, please not again. I covered my ears.

UKF: Why don't you take down your pants and put your hand
round your, big, fat –

Enough! There could not possibly be any illegal business
being discussed while that was going on. This particular
suspect was always at it on the phone (with several different
women) and often I'd hit play or start listening in, only to
hear:

Chelsea Barry: Oh that feels so good.
UKF: Put it inside me . . .
Chelsea Barry: Lick your tits . . .

Or there was always the good old-fashioned heavy breathing and passionate moaning before I cut out again. Chelsea
Barry did it so often I did start to wonder whether this was
a clever use of a new coding system designed to put us off.
These telephone trysts really made for agonizing listening,
so if this was a strategy then it definitely worked.

  This was of course one of the problems with this line

of work. We listened to the same people for weeks at a time for just half a dozen or so innocuous and ambiguous words: 'It's me.' – 'Tomorrow?' – 'Usual?' – 'OK.'

The rest of the time we'd listen to their entire lives play out on the telephone. Working for Alpha showed me a side of criminality I hadn't really seen before. When you're on the ground you're just following bods and cars; once the knock came, I often disappeared (always if I was undercover) and never spoke to the criminals. But now the underworld had truly opened up.

Listening in made them appear – well, human (even if they were proper scumbags). So what did they talk about? Paranoia ruled. Top of the list was avoiding the authorities – they constantly debated whether they were being followed. The top villains continually changed their phones and were always calling their mates to give them new numbers, always in code. They'd all talk about their fellow villains for hours, whether they thought they'd ever grass, what they'd do if they were nicked, whether they were respected enough, if they could be 'eased aside'.

A lot of time was devoted to kidnappings; there are loads of kidnappings of villains and their relatives, usually over debt. No one ever reports them to the police.

They gossiped about beatings, robberies, stabbings and shootings, but mostly the focus was money and what they did with it – which was to spend it on the latest cars and gadgets and gamble it away at the tracks and in casinos. The top villains loved to moan about how much their wag was spending. Family was very important, on the surface, but all the blokes played away and would lie to their dying mother for a fiver.

One time Slim called his missus on one of the phones we'd had. It was the first time I'd heard him speak to his wife and I listened, intensely interested. He'd dialled her from a dirty phone as well, so it seemed to me he must have been muddled by something, and the panic in his voice soon revealed this.

Slim: Now don't lose it, but I killed the cat.
Sandra: Wh-wh-what?
Slim: I was backing out the drive and he was stretched out under the car.

Ouch.

Sandra (sobbing): I told you before to always check for Snuggles before driving off!

*Snuggles?*

Slim: Sorry, luv, it —
Sandra: Don't you 'luv' me! Idiot!
Slim: I'll get you another just like 'er —
Sandra: Tosser!
Slim: Spare a thought, love, I've got to sort it out now. It's a mess here and I'm late. And the fucking cat should've known better, anyway.

Whoops. Slim had lost his patience. His wife hung up the phone; Slim would be sleeping in the spare bedroom for quite a few days.

*

The one thing all these calls told me was that life certainly wasn't all gangsters in paradise. A collection of choice overheards that have stuck in my mind include: 'Terry, your wife's sleeping with the gardener' ('I'll kill the bitch,' said Terry) and, 'Ted's locked up in a garage in Canning Town. If you wanna see 'im again, pay up the ransom or I'll FedEx his bollocks to his kids.'

And, in a variation on a theme: 'They dropped his pinkie through his fucking letter box.'

There were dozens of exchanges like this:

UKM1: The missus is in Sloane Street giving it large to those posh bitches in the shoe shop. Cunts fought she weren't good enough to shop in there. Soon set those stuck-up twats straight, should've seen the security Muppet's face when I pulled out ten grand cash. Practically shat 'is keks right there and then. Told 'em I robbed it from the poxy Bank of Dubai, which is half-true as it goes.

UKM2: Which shop you at?

UKM1: Err . . . Fucking hell, how the fuck d'you say it? Sir-geo Rossi.

UKM2: Wanna have a pint? I'm in Pickles [Harvey Nichols].

UKM1: Wotcha doin' there?

UKM2: Gettin' a snowboard. Goin' to Char-monicks [Chamonix] next week, gonna 'ave to 'ave it large, know what I mean?

UKM1: Awight, then. There's a boozer in the Mandorental [Mandarin Oriental], see you there in twenny?

Every now and again, one of their conversations would have me in stitches:

UKM1 (in his car): I think I'm bein' followed.
UKM2: It's me, yer twat.

Many of them were obsessed with soap operas. This was because dealing drugs involves a helluva a lot of waiting around, either in hotels or at home, and they don't seem able to find anything else to do — although some were fans of the Xbox. I ended up knowing the plot of *EastEnders* better than my missus ever had.

In a nutshell, their lives were debauched, materialistic, extremely violent (often senselessly so) and fraught with peril, not so much from us as from each other.

As I said earlier, the bits we were interested in were tiny snatches of conversation, sometimes just five or six ambiguous words. Take this Alpha extract, for example:

[Baz to Mickey]
Baz: Yeah, it's me.
Mickey: How's it going? Everything OK?
Baz: Yeah, it's all good.
Mickey: OK, I'll call you later.
[Mickey to Viktor]
Mickey: All right, mate? I've just spoken to my mate; everything's sorted his end.
Viktor: OK.
[Viktor to each of the three unknown customers]
Viktor: Hi, mate.
UKM: How you doin'?
Victor: Good, good. We're good down here, no problems; it's all ready when you are.

UKM: OK, I'll bell you when my mate is in the area, maybe you
    can meet up.

Viktor: Yeah, that'll be fine.

[Viktor to Courier]

Viktor: Hey, mate, it's me.

Courier: OK?

Viktor: Yeah, might need your help later tonight or tomorrow,
    there'll be a few quid for you.

Courier: Good, just give me a call when it's on.


Because everyone knew what everyone else was talking
about, it took just a couple of minutes to let all parties know
that the drugs had arrived safely, had been extracted from
wherever they'd been hidden and were now packed and
ready for collection by the customers.

Of course, this also meant it was a good time for twenty
boot-wearing, baton-carrying Customs officers to knock
on Viktor's door with a thirty-kilo battering ram.

# 17. The Ozzies of Whizz

Our office was usually a place of hushed but intense activity. So when a voice suddenly screamed out 'OH SHIT!', heads turned. It soon emerged that Perry had mistakenly tapped the line of the criminal he had been listening into and called him instead of a police officer.

This was the first time anyone had ever heard of this happening. Apparently, the geezer answered before Perry realized his mistake and said 'wrong number' and hung up.

The guy was a suspicious so and so and he called back, he got straight through to Perry's phone and demanded to know who was talking to him. Perry came up with some bullshit story about misdialling and the matter was left there, but only after a memorandum went round the office, much to Perry's embarrassment. What made it worse was Perry was a real know-it-all and came across as immediately dislikable whenever he was introduced to someone. He was extremely good at what he did, but he had a rather unpleasant attitude so the office particularly enjoyed this stupid mistake.

We were still sniggering about Perry when Slim's line lit up.

Neal: So the little ones are going from the flat place [Amsterdam] to Ozzie Steve?
Slim: S'right.
Neal: How about the paperwork?

Slim: Seventy to us; one twenny-five to them. Three point six big 'uns.

Neal: Who's doing the pick-up?

Slim: Fat Dave; I'll call 'im now.

Slim certainly had all the right contacts. He'd set up his cousin Neal with a Finnegan based in Australia. Together they planned to import 360,000 Ecstasy tablets from Amsterdam to Sydney, hidden in DHL and TNT packages.

The plan was to buy for 70p and sell for £1.25 per pill. Almost £200,000 profit for a few phone calls.

Snapper and his team couldn't do it. Thanks to his enthusiasm and habit for taking everything going, he'd managed to get his team snowed under with other jobs.

So the job got punted around the office, but all I got in response was, 'Yeah we'll do it when we're not busy,' or, 'We know best, you need to wait for the next bit of Intel to come in to confirm it.'

'They've got it too good,' Ranjiv said when I filled him in. 'The lazy bastards can afford to miss one Alpha-led seizure because they know another one will come along soon.'

In contrast, the police were so desperate for the job they were about to bite my hand off. So I went back to Snapper.

'Not to worry,' Snapper said, 'I can spare one man; he can run things for you on the ground with the Martians (police) from the crime squad. He'll be your point of communication.'

In the end Snapper went on the job personally. 'The Martians think it's about thirty thousand tabs and we'll keep it that way. Best to make that look of surprise on their faces as genuine as possible.'

Alpha policy was that the operational team were never told how much gear was expected. You didn't want some bonehead to mention the figure in the presence of the targets, otherwise the crims might start to wonder how we knew how much gear there would be before the seizure – then the disclosure nightmare would begin.

As it was a significant importation with good Intel I got Fat Dave's phone hooked up just twelve hours after Slim called him, and within an hour of that the ops team were in place outside his home.

Ranjiv had stayed on overnight in the suite instead of going home, and I had come in early at 4 a.m. We were both as keen as mustard to make sure we got a result.

Snapper was already out with the Martians outside Fat Dave's home in Wanstead, east London. He was sitting in the back of the command car with the police Bronze commander (Bronze directly controls police resources at the incident, Gold and Silver commanders manage the op from the cop shop). They did what operational detectives do best: chatted about 'jobs what I have done'. Of course, Snapper would win hands down; his list was endless.

It had taken a lot of phone calls but the baddies had eventually decided on a plan. A Dutch flower lorry would stop off somewhere in north London, just off its usual route. They had to be careful, the Dutch use tachographs, and they wouldn't want to show a stop or deviation that could be questioned in the future.

Fat Dave: Yeah?
Slim: Everything cushty?
Fat Dave: Yeah. Just about to head off now.

Slim: OK, give me a bell when you're at the first stop.
Fat Dave: No probs.

As usual, Slim was nowhere near the gear and ran the show from his bedroom. I could hear BBC breakfast news in the background and the stirring of a coffee mug. I called Snapper. 'Fat Dave's about to head off now.'

'Got it. Here he comes.'

Snapper and the Martians followed Fat Dave from Wanstead to a truck stop off the M25 near Waltham Abbey. I had to wait patiently for Snapper to call as, this now being a police op, I couldn't listen into their comms. Fat Dave had a full English and then sat around waiting for the truck to turn up.

One hour passed, then two. Lots of time for Snapper and his Martian friend to swap stories. Too much time. Soon the silences would grow longer, the interior of the car smellier. I knew it all too well and was grateful for my luxurious office space. I stretched, wandered around a bit. All of my phones were silent. It was still pretty early in the day, after all. I put the urn on and made a brew for everyone.

A third hour ticked by.

Snapper called. He was irritable, to say the least: 'What the fuck's he waiting for?'

'Not a clue,' I replied.

'Typical. Bet the bloody lorry driver's lost or been pulled already by some bushy-tailed muppet at Dover.'

'Let's hope not, eh?'

'Such a stupid idiot. How's he gonna explain this? It's always the same. Villains end up waiting for hours in cafes and service stations up and down the country. And that's the first thing a prosecuting barrister will kick off with.'

He put on the voice of an 'East-End geezer'. 'Well, Yer Honour, I was waitin' for me mate to play a rounda golf. He never turned up, so instead of goin' home and watchin' Jeremy Vyle, I sat in a truck stop constantly on the blower. No, I carn't remember who to . . . No, I dunno no Dutchmen and I carn't understan' why me bill shows a dozen calls to a Dutch lorry driver who was arrested with me in possession of a 'undred an' ten killergrams of class-A fuckin' drugs.'

Finally, as the fourth hour approached, the lorry rolled up.

Snapper called. 'Cam, the Old Bill want to follow Fat Dave and the pills to the next handover.' That would be the gopher for whoever Slim was selling the gear to.

'They can do that, can they?'

'I know we need to get Gold's authorization for a live run, but the Bronze in his wisdom reckons you have to speculate to accumulate.'

This was extremely risky, if you lost the load you were screwed. It wouldn't be easy trying to explain to the powers that be that you had the pills under control in the lorry park, had watched them being handed over in four large holdalls from the truck to van, only to lose them on the M25.

If you are not completely on top of things, it can easily go spectacularly wrong. We very rarely conducted live runs without pulling the truck and replacing the gear with 'dummied' packages. Now the Old Bill were doing it without any authorization or dummy load.

The flower truck drove off. The Martians arranged for

a traffic car to pull it over as soon as it got onto the M25. The tricky part was to do this quickly, before he had time to call anyone further up the chain, but in this case they managed with little trouble.

Snapper followed Fat Dave away from Waltham Abbey towards north London. He did lots of amusing anti-surveillance and counter-surveillance before stopping in a supermarket car park in Camden.

Fat Dave: I'm here.

Slim: Keep going.

Fat Dave: Going where?

Slim: Drive around some more; make sure no one is following you.

Fat Dave: But I've been driving round Camden for an hour now and I'm telling you, no one's fucking following me.

Slim: Keep going for another hour. I gotta run the money hand-over.

'He's gonna drive around for another hour, while Slim sorts the money.'

'Oh, fer Pete's sake.'

'Needless to say, we don't have the phones for that transfer and won't have time to get them wired up today.'

Snapper and the Martians stuck with Fat Dave, who was clearly as bored as they were and drove around listening to some tuneless house music with the windows down. Sure enough, one hour later, Slim called.

'OK, the transfers are set. 'Ere's the number of the guy you're meeting. Call it now and get a sample of the gear ready.'

Fat Dave drove to a retail park off the A406 near Muswell

Hill, parked up and sat in Tesco's coffee shop. He rang the buyer.

Ten minutes later Snapper called me. 'Looks like the buyer's gopher just walked into the coffee shop.'

Fat Dave and the gopher walked with the sample to the buyer's car, a big black Range Rover with tinted windows. Two minutes later Fat Dave emerged. He was on the phone to Slim.

Slim: Yeah?
Fat Dave: Everything's cushty. Quality's good.
Slim: OK, give them the gear.

I called Snapper. 'The gear is A1, handover imminent.'

While Fat Dave went to get the gear, the gopher called his boss to confirm the sample was OK and that he should release the cash.

'All foot move in, slowly.'

The baddies had chosen a busy car park because they thought they'd be invisible amongst the hundreds of shoppers. This actually made things a lot easier, as the Martians could amble casually towards them; some had even pulled out shopping trolleys.

I knew that underneath the forced calmness, the coppers' adrenaline count would be sky high. Mine certainly was.

Fat Dave got into his van and drove between two rows of parked cars. He pulled up behind the gopher's van. The gopher got out and opened the back doors.

Unknown to us there was a third party waiting in the back of the Range Rover. He climbed out of the back seat and opened the tailgate.

As soon as the first bag had been taken from the van and placed in the back of the Range Rover, the Bronze called it.

'From Bronze: It's a STRIKE! STRIKE! STRIKE!'

All foot officers and cars screamed into the area, cutting off the two vehicles, blocking off the aisles.

With all exits blocked, the targets starburst on their toes, but the foot units pounced waving fists, batons and handcuffs and a proper old-school punch-up ensued. Shoppers caught up in the melee either froze or ran for it.

The driver of the Range Rover didn't even have time to get out of the car before he was cuffed.

Everything was in the Old Bill's hands and Snapper could withdraw after receiving the thanks of the Martians. We had only told them we were expecting a 'significant amount' of Ecstasy.

They were thinking maybe 30,000 pills. They were jumping with joy at getting twelve times that amount.

'Well, I'll be off, then,' Snapper said. 'No need to mention us to anyone, OK?'

The Martians were only too happy to oblige and Snapper took himself down to the Hung, Drawn and Quartered, where he drank until he was carried outside by the bar staff at midnight and pushed in the direction of Canon Street.

Of course, while this was all well and good, we'd only nicked the monkeys.

I thought about Slim. He would've been curled up on the sofa with his son, watching Saturday morning kids' TV, waiting for the call to say that it all had gone well. Nothing. After half an hour, he was experienced enough to know it had all gone Pete Tong and simply stopped using his phones.

Slim would have been well out of pocket. He had already paid up front to the Dutch, who were his regular suppliers. So instead of making his money back and a £220k profit, he was suddenly half a mil poorer than he'd been expecting.

Round one to Alpha.

# 18. Temptation

The zone behind Custom House, specifically Cigarette-Butt Alley, aka Smoker's Corner, appeared to be the area where all inter-departmental knowledge was shared. What couldn't be said inside was said there.

As I lit up, Mike appeared beside me with a cough. I held out my pack, but he declined. 'Did you hear about what happened to Snapper last night?'

Why did I never get to hear any of the good stuff first? 'No, what?'

'After he left the Hung, Drawn and Quartered he borrowed a Tommy car and drove home.'

'Why the hell didn't he take a taxi? The Tommy cars are a twenty-minute walk away.'

'I expect the booze helped him think it was a good idea at the time,' Mike replied with a grin. 'And that's not the half of it.'

'Go on.'

'He only crashed into a member of good old Joe Public.'

'He didn't!'

'Not finished yet.'

'Oh God, he didn't beat them up, did he?'

'No, better than that. It was a black cab; you know how precious those guys are about their shakers. The slightest ding and they have to take it off the road for repairs immediately.'

'And?'

'Well, the cabbie went mental and Snapper decided the best thing to do was jump over a hedge and vanish into the night.'

'What?'

'As soon as he saw the cabbie was OK he ran off, left the Tommy car and the scene of the accident.'

'Bloody hell.'

'Turned up this morning looking sheepish as hell. Right now he's with Thomas and some of the other SIOs trying to talk his way out of this mess.'

That wouldn't be easy. It'd take the mojo of Austin Powers to get out of this one. Snapper had broken the law and practically written off a £50,000 tracker car. I thought about what had happened to Jed, his four-year stretch in Holborn State Penitentiary for his much tamer extra-vehicular incident.

I saw Snapper later that day; I was surprised he was still in the building. Perhaps someone senior was coming in to give him a proper bollocking. His sharp eyes sat in large grey bags after what must have been one hell of a hangover and one hell of a 'What-the-fuck-did-I-do-last-night?' moment.

'Still here, then?' I asked.

'I take it you've heard?'

'I think everyone has, at least twice; you're guaranteed to be the hot topic for months to come. What are they going to do to you?'

'Nothing.'

'Yeah, right. And I'm shagging Pamela Anderson tonight.'

'No, really, Cam – the whole thing's sorted.'

'How the hell did you manage that?'

'Let's just say I cashed in all of my IOUs. I've done more than my fair share of favours in my time.'

And that was it. I never found out what favours Snapper had done but, my God, they must have been something exceptional to make that colourful incident disappear. That was soon forgotten about, however, as I picked up a very interesting little call as soon as I returned to my desk.

UKM1: Yeah. It's me.

UKM2: Where are you?

UKM1: I'm wiv da missus, she wanted to go shopping up west.

UKM2: You got da money?

UKM1: Yeah. Free 'undred [thousand] in the car.

UKM2: You gonna drop it off?

UKM1: Nah, not yet. We're going to the cinema, blood; she wanna see that new Jim Carrey film, you know what I'm sayin'?

UKM2: Girl flic. Safe, blood. Laters.

One hour later:

UKM1: Yeah, blood, it's me. Any ting?

UKM2: No ting; all quiet, my frien'. Where you at?

UKM1: Mulitplex in Finchley, yeah.

UKM2: Where's da paper [money]?

UKM1: Wid me, under da passenger seat.

UKM2: Wotcha gonna do with it?

UKM1: Leave it there, ya get me? Dis car park has cams and guards and everythin'. I gotta go, I gotta get popcorn.

UKM2: 'Kay, blood, safe.

UKM1: Laters.

My fingers drummed on the desk.

I knew the registration of the car.

I knew which cinema they were at.

I knew I could get there in less than an hour.

I knew that no one else on the planet knew about that money.

Only me.

I could delete that call, stroll out of the office, quietly break into the car, pick up the money and return two hours later, £300,000 richer and no one the wiser. Of course, UKM2 would probably end up dead as he was the only one who knew where the cash was – unless they were smart enough to figure out they were being listened in to (considering they were happy to leave £300k in cash in a multiplex car park, I didn't think they had too much brain power) and I'd get onto them again when they went back to Jimmy's to clean the next lot.

I drummed my fingers a little longer.

'Well, well, well,' I said out loud, 'that's a first.'

'What's that then?' Mike asked.

'Two guys who've been laundering money through Jimmy's bureau have just told me that there is £300,000 in freshly washed, untraceable notes, sitting in a BMW. I know the registration number and I know its location. The owner is going to be occupied for the next two hours, watching *Eternal Sunshine of the Spotless Mind* with his missus in the Finchley multiplex.

'What's stopping me from popping up there and using my well-honed skills to break into the Beamer and walk off into the sunset?'

'That's a very good question, Cam. I don't know. What

is stopping you – and now me, for that matter? I see you've obviously decided to drag me in to debate the hows, whys and whats.'

'I don't know. Something's stopping me.'

'Me too.'

'And it's certainly not my overdraft or maintenance payments . . . I suppose it's just wrong, isn't it?'

'Don't be daft.'

We sat in silence for a bit. I'm not sure what would have happened if one of us had stood up and said: 'Right, well, I'm off, then.'

'Me too,' probably.

But we didn't. We just stayed put, got on with the day and went home.

I liked the walk home. Whitechapel was an interesting part of the world. The area has a long and dreadful history; it was where London's poor were traditionally housed, although the expansion of the City and the recent trendi-fication of Whitechapel and Bethnal Green meant that more and more City types, along with fashionable young folk, had started to push prices up. They'd also started to push the poor further down the Commercial Road towards Mile End.

Petticoat Square, where I lived, was a real mishmash of old and new and rich and poor. As well as the City folk, much of the estate was still council owned and given over to local people, many of them working in the famous Petti-coat Lane market and in the surrounding bars, boutiques and curry houses.

I passed by a bench in the square and nodded 'hello' to

the three old blokes who seemed to spend every day there drinking cans of Special Brew. They always seemed to be enjoying themselves and, as I stopped in at the offy to pick up my own night's supply, I wondered for a second if they had the best approach to life after all. Back at my block, I noted that the door-entry system was buggered yet again and ascended the stairs to my flat.

It was a strange place to live, hidden behind Aldgate tube, a stone's throw from the 'ring of plastic', the fenced-off section of the Square Mile that is the City of London. It's as about as urban as it's possible to get. The twenty-five-storey tower could have passed for an office block were it not for the telltale signs of domestic life in the windows – an abundance of England flag curtains, tie-dye sheets and colourful sparkling Indian drapes.

The estate had a dystopian feel about it, which I actually quite liked. I'd spent my entire working life hanging out in the 'in-between places' on the fringes of cities – the warehouses, factories, motorways, Holiday Inns – so I found this urbanism reassuringly familiar.

As I walked up the stairs Harry appeared. An old codger and World War II veteran, Harry had nothing better to do but look over his balcony and natter to anyone he heard coming up. If it weren't for the job I'd be as isolated as he was: nothing but the TV, a microwave dinner and a few cans.

Harry was always going on about the local 'trouble-makers'. Although I hadn't seen them at that time, I had heard them, shouting and screaming late at night, the occasional firework popping and shrieking. Every now and again I'd wake in the middle of the night to see the walls of my bedroom flashing blue with the lights of the City cops who were trying to quell the tearaways' over-exuberance.

Here on the estate, City types hoovered lines of coke at dinner parties while the arty types popped E's and acid in trendy bars and the poor inhaled their seven-quid hits of crack anywhere they could. I sometimes spotted the telltale signs: balls of scrunched-up foil in odd corners of the estate, little piles of matches, discarded lighters and so on – the detritus of broken lives.

It was amazing. What other business hooks both rich and poor, successful and derelict, without any advertising or branding? We've spent decades warning people about the awful consequences of drug abuse – the unimaginable pain and poverty it causes in the countries where it's produced, the misery it visits upon the poor across the planet, the associated crime, the prospect of prison, the effects on the human mind and body, etc., etc., etc. How could it be, then, that hard drugs remained so popular, with no drop in demand?

I was supposed to be a big part of the solution to the drug problem, but despite the armies of law enforcement officers, despite the tens of thousands of people we'd put in jail and the billions of pounds we'd spent, it just didn't seem to be getting any better – if anything the situation seemed to be steadily worsening. The bad guys still had full control of the price, purity and quantity of every illegal drug going. Nothing we had done had stopped them. Although I was getting tremendous satisfaction from the seizures Alpha were making it really depressed me that all our efforts seemed to be having no effect whatsoever at street level.

My flat was on the sixth floor. A feeling of isolation came over me as the door closed and left me in empty silence. I missed the boys, even though I'd hardly seen them while we lived under the same roof. At least before we'd shared an address; now there was no connection at all.

I flicked on the TV and quickly downed a beer. I stared from my window at the opposite block with the City skyline behind it and contemplated the odd juxtaposition of unimaginable wealth and grinding poverty before my eyes. I also thought about my own strange job that had led me to sacrifice my family life to fight an unwinnable fight.

And then I thought about Slim.

He seemed happy. He ran a successful business, was hugely wealthy, had a palatial house in a leafy part of Finchley and a beautiful wife and son to whom he was able to devote nearly all of his time.

Discussions about the morality of drug dealing hardly ever took place in Customs. The American agencies were always very keen to hammer home the 'drug dealers are evil' message and they still seemed to genuinely believe that the Nancy Reagan/Grange Hill message of 'Just Say No!' would get through if it was repeated often enough.

Sure, many drug traders could hardly be described as 'nice people', but the same applies to the City folk who trade in weapons, pharma companies who withhold vital medicines from poorer nations, or others who asset strip their acquisitions with no thought for the thousands who lose their livelihoods as a result. All's fair in business, legal or not. All the dealers were doing was giving the people what they wanted.

But something about Slim bugged me. Did he have no

fear of justice? Did he have no fear of what might happen to his family if he ever got caught?

Slim called Billy Scrote and then his cousin Neal (whose phone we had, so I got Slim's new number). Neal then sent one of his more intellectually challenged boys called Steve to Australia to explain why the E that the Aussies were expecting had been seized, and to reassure them that a replacement consignment would be sorted asap.

Steve took a phone with him that worked in Oz, and so every time he phoned his missus I got every word.

Steve had got himself into a major side deal that he outlined in enough detail for us to pass to the authorities in Western Australia. At 3 o'clock one morning Steve and his two new Ozzie chums, tucked up in their cots in some flyblown motel in the middle of nowhere, had their sleep rudely disturbed by a dozen or so heavily armed Mad Max lookalikes crashing through their doors and windows.

They found three machine pistols, twenty kilos of amphetamine and about three million Australian dollars in cash. Bonzer! To celebrate, Ranjiv and I headed out for a shandy in the Litten Tree, another popular Custom House boozer.

'Aw, shit, look who's here,' Ranjiv said.

The pub was busy with after-work drinkers but we could both hear and see know-it-all Perry, who was talking animatedly with two senior Martians. He was pissed and so didn't see us. 'Bad-mouthing us, no doubt,' Ranjiv said. Still, our bust in the bush had got the office all abuzz, so I thought they'd get to hear about that soon enough.

'Never mind,' I said. 'Onwards and upwards, to the bar, my friend.'

As we supped our pints I overheard Perry say something that made me prick up my ears. 'Yeah, that's right, I just put together a major seizure.'

*Hello*, I thought, *what's this?* I hadn't heard anything back at the office.

'Yeah, it was in Australia,' Perry drunkenly continued. 'Guns, ammo, twenty kilos of amphet and three mil in cash.'

I listened, open mouthed, as Perry told the two senior police officers that all the Intel had come from him and on the back of this he was off to the Australian High Commission for tea and medals.

Ranjiv, sensible chap, was forced to restrain me.

Perry eventually left and young Thomas appeared and came over to join us. 'Watch out, Cam,' Ranjiv whispered quickly as Thomas came over. 'Word is, him and Ali have had a big row. Might not be in the best of moods.'

'Me and him both,' I replied, still fuming over what Perry had said.

Thomas was indeed in a foul mood but it wasn't anything to do with Ali; he'd just come from a major meeting about the future of UK law enforcement and the so-called 'war on drugs'.

For some time we'd been hearing the odd whisper from the government that they were planning to set up a new FBI-style agency to deal with serious crime. We didn't have much time to think about it but senior management had, since 2004, been told to prepare for the inevitable. The Serious Organized Crime Agency was coming, like it or not.

'We're going the way of the Americans, lads,' Thomas said. 'Unbelievable. You might think that the management of the British end of the war on drugs is bad but that's nothing when compared to the US. I mean, how can you work with the country whose government sold crack to its own people?'

It's hard to believe, but it's true. Back in 1979 President Ronald Reagan saw the right-wing Nicaraguan Contras as allies in the global fight against communism. He wanted to support them in their guerrilla war against the country's left-wing Sandinista government.

Congress refused to back Reagan. The Contras were strapped for cash to buy weapons so Colonel Oliver North sold American weapons to Iran, supposedly a US enemy, to raise money for the Contras. That story was reported everywhere, but it is less well known that the CIA also approved and supported the Contras in the trafficking of cocaine into the United States.

The Contras would take delivery of planeloads of goods that had been sent by supportive Nicaraguan expatriates from the United States. But on their return flight, the planes were packed with cocaine, paid for by Californian drug dealers. While Californian hippies were joking about putting LSD into the water supply, the CIA got the whole of California, rich and poor, black, white and Hispanic, high on coke and crack. Tens of millions of hard-earned US dollars were handed over to weapons manufacturers or were simply pumped straight back to support the Contras.

The CIA put cocaine within the reach of many more Americans, and paved the way for the crack epidemic that swept through the inner cities of the United States in the 1980s. Between 1982 and 1985 the wholesale price of cocaine in Miami, Los Angeles and Baltimore dropped by half.

Working hand in hand with major criminals was nothing new for the US authorities. As far back as the 1940s they had helped to turn the Italian-American Mafioso Lucky Luciano into the world's pre-eminent heroin dealer. They reportedly allowed Lucky to run his empire from his prison cell in upstate New York in return for his cooperation in helping the US war effort in Italy (his connections there passed on intelligence to the US government) before going on to help them combat communism. Meanwhile, Lucky's heroin flooded into New York and Washington, and once those cities got a taste for the drug, they were permanently hooked.

The CIA also allowed the importation of opium and heroin into the United States by their allies in south-east Asia during the Vietnam War. The movie *Air America* is based on these true events. The same organization also turned a blind eye to heroin trafficking by Mujahideen rebels in Afghanistan because the profits paid for Afghan resistance to the Soviet Union's occupation of the country in the 1980s.

'The C-I-bloody-A,' Thomas said over his fifth pint, 'are worse than any drug dealer we've ever encountered in this country. They murdered half a generation of young people with hard drugs, sent the other half to die in Vietnam and Afghanistan. Meanwhile, it seems as though half of the present generation are working for the drugs trade which the CIA helped create.'

By 1991 (the most recent figures available), the number of Americans selling drugs, either full- or part-time, was estimated at 1.8 million.

'And now the UK government, in its infinite wisdom,

wants to turn us into the C-I-flaming-Arseholes. I need anozzer drink. Shame 'gain?'

Ranjiv and I nodded. As Thomas wove his way to the bar, we looked at one another and shrugged. 'Well, can't get any worse than how it is now, can it?' Ranjiv said.

'Let's bloody well hope not,' I replied.

# 19. Call That a Tip?

'Come on, Cam, you know you want to. I know you've been checking out Jimmy's bureau; I know you live right next door to the damn place.'

'I don't know about this, Snapper,' I said cautiously. 'Jimmy's is one thing – I mean, I can't help but pass by it every day. This is taking things a bit too far.'

'Look, I'm going to have do it when the time comes to nick him anyway –'

'You don't know that.'

'We're close, Cam. I'm sure of it; and you know my gut's never wrong. Come on, let's take a look.'

I wasn't sure. A career in which you spent weeks at a time following criminals every waking hour attracted some unusual types right enough, but I wondered whether Snapper was a bit too wild for this line of work. His recent and miraculous escape after crashing the Tommy car had made me a tad wary of him. I'd be taking a huge risk going on the plot – it was against all the rules; if it ever got out, I'd be up for the chop.

On the other hand, it wasn't as if I was a surveillance rookie, and I really, really wanted to check Slim out.

Snapper was looking at me intently, guessing which way I was leaning. 'Come on, Cam, what's to think about? You've waited this long, you might as well say yes, mightn't you?'

*

Slim's house was one of a kind. Just on the north-eastern edge of Hampstead Heath, a few short streets across from the famous millionaire's row of Bishop's Avenue (home to a £50 million super-mansion with its own tropical island in the middle of an indoor pool). Slim's house was large but understated.

Snapper whistled. 'Not bad at all.'

'Very tasteful. Crime may not always pay, but drugs certainly seem to,' I said. 'I mean, how much powder would you have to turn over to make enough to buy a house here?'

'It wouldn't have taken long at sixty grand a deal.'

'True enough.'

It was incredible. Slim had carved out a life here, amongst all the millionaire accounts, hedge funders, oil magnates and property developers. He'd done it; he was a made man.

Being in such a posh part of town made surveillance quite tricky. The local cops are always quick to react to blokes in stationary cars, so we'd brought two vehicles and covered the area in a looping fashion, taking turns to drive and wearing different jackets and tops.

'Wanna do a walk-by?' Snapper asked.

I was dead keen but played it cautiously. I missed the heart-pounding excitement of being out on the ground. Yeah, all right, but then we go.'

'Fine by me. See you in a bit.'

I left the car and strolled casually down the road. It was very broad, the lamp posts were of an aesthetically pleasing Victorian design. It was perfect; blossom was on the trees and the day was fresh and clear.

Then I saw them.

The door to Slim's house had opened. A man stepped

out. He was smiling and talking to someone. A young woman and a child – obviously his wife and son – appeared next to him. His son, whom I knew to be coming up to his fifth birthday, was clutching a football.

They were dressed for a walk on Hampstead Heath, and looked like the perfect little family unit. Slim was as thin as his name suggested. He had short dark hair, was just over six feet tall and wore a scarf loosely round his neck. His wife, gorgeous of course, was a few inches shorter and had a figure it was hard not to stare at, even when wrapped in a Burberry. They looked like they didn't have a care in the world.

I was almost upon them when their kid, whose name I knew was Archie, in his wisdom, decided to boot the ball down the drive. It rolled out and hit me on the foot.

Oh, crap. What's the most natural reaction? Give the kid his ball back. Bugger, bugger, bugger.

I bent over and rolled it back towards Archie. Slim's wife, who'd been wrapping her husband up in his scarf, saw what had happened. 'What do you say?'

Archie turned and said: 'Thank you.'

'Good lad!' Slim enthused, scooping his son up. I nodded, smiled and kept walking.

Snapper was waiting a hundred metres down the road. 'And?'

'Just drive,' I said.

I couldn't help but make the comparison. Slim and I were the same age and on opposite sides of the fence. And who was happier?

Jimmy: There's been a problem.
Elton: What?

Jimmy: Our mate hasn't come back, he might 'ave fallen over [been arrested].

Elton: What the fuck are you talking about, Jimmy?

Jimmy: The paper's gone. My guy, the guy who's worked for me for three years, has vanished. My hawaladar says my guy came and picked up the cash, got into a black cab and vanished. I knew as soon as he said he got into a black cab. He's never took a black cab, man, said it was too rich. I was always telling him get a black cab, it's safer.

Elton: What the fuck, geez. That ain't my problem, that's your problem. I'm coming over.

Jimmy: Didn't you hear me? It's been pinched.

Elton: I don't fucking care if it's gone or not, I'm coming to pick it up and it had better be there.

Jimmy: We should look for him. He's the one with the problem.

Elton: You're not hearing me, mate. I'm not sure I fucking believe you but if your guy has done a runner then you're fucked. This is London, mate. Ten million people, six fucking airports, hundreds of train stations. I don't fancy your chances. No, I'm coming to pick up a large one and it had better fucking be there otherwise you're fucked!

Blimey! I set the system to record and went outside for a breath of fresh air and a fag. I exhaled and looked across the Thames, admiring the view. Somewhere out there was a man with a hundred grand in untraceable euros in a sports holdall.

One minute a desk jockey for a skinflint money launderer, the next one cash-rich lucky bastard. Did he have a plan? Was it spur of the moment? I thought not. One of the things that kept many minor players in the drugs trade on the straight and narrow, so to speak, is the fact that their families would suffer if they did a runner. He must have nothing to lose. Fair play. I imagined what that must feel like.

Liberating, probably.

Finally, and most importantly, I wondered how Jimmy was going to play this most unexpected development.

I shook my head at the craziness of it. 'Fuck me,' I said out loud.

'I didn't know you cared, Cam.' It was Ali. Suddenly, despite the cold winter's air, it felt very warm. I turned bright red.

'Sorry, Ali,' I replied, 'but you're not going to believe what I've just heard.' I explained the phone call. 'This could fuck everything up, everything.'

'Don't worry about it. There are more than enough bad guys to go round.'

'Sure, but Jimmy's bureau is . . . Well, I've never seen anything like it.'

Ali paused for a bit and took a sip of her coffee. 'Do you believe in what we do, Cam? I mean really believe.'

'Well, I'm not stupid enough to think we're winning the poxy war on drugs. Prisons are awash with coke, dope and smack. If they can get in there, then the rest of the country isn't going to fare any better. As long as there's demand, we'll be up to our necks in it. The way I see it is I'm paid to put away bad guys, and so that's what I do.'

'But then why not sell fruit instead? It's a lot easier and the same principle applies.'

I laughed. 'You know why. Cos I'm addicted to the adrenaline rush of working these jobs, of getting big high-value seizures. I'm addicted to working my way up the ladder, taking out the useless twats as I go before getting to the smart guys, the ones who, had they been able to take another path, would be CEOs just down the road from here.'

'So it's a game?'

'A high stakes, rock 'n' roll one. Prison or paradise. Death or glory. Putting away Mr Drug Dealer is a lot more fun than selling him fruit. As an aside, the people he's hurt get some kind of justice.

'And it's not as if we're going to run out of work,' I added. 'I mean, it can't get much worse than it already is because it's pretty damn bad right now. Nick a burglar and there's a reduction in burglary, but nick a drug dealer at any level and the tide of drugs flows on unchanged.'

'What do we do, then?'

'Us? Nothing. It means we've got jobs for life. And no one's going to take our jobs from us, especially since young police officers today are only trained to make meaningless drug arrests on the street to provide vote-winning stats. All we can do is fight the good fight, enjoy the rock 'n' roll lifestyle but don't take it too seriously.'

Ali nodded. 'Indeed, you take this lark too seriously, then the fact that most of our budget and effort is spent on the war on drugs for no effect will drive you nuts.'

I finished my second fag and went back inside. Unsurprisingly, there were some recorded calls waiting for me. 'Well, well, let's see what the hell the Scrote twins' next move is,' I muttered.

Elton: We got a little problem.

Billy: What?

Elton: 'E says he's lost the money.

Billy: [pause] Come again?

Elton: 'Is mate didn't come back wiv it. He ain't got it. The bloke done a runner, mate.

Billy: Fuck, he'd better have it or he'll be fucked over big time.


Oliver: Slim, we gotta problem.

Slim: What?

Oliver: The Paki's mate done a runner with the cash. Jimmy won't pay. Say's it's not his fault.

Slim: Talk to him.

Oliver: I have done.

Slim: No, you ain't listenin' to me. I said *talk* to him.

Oliver: But . . . oh.

Slim: Talk to him or someone's going to come and talk to you.

Oliver: I'll put the Jockney on it. Don't worry, mate, this'll all be sorted by tomorrow.

Slim: It had better be sorted. That's gotta be done. This kinda shit has repercussions, understand?


I grinned. The trials and tribulations of drug dealing and money laundering. Sure, the profits are astronomical, but when the shit hits the fan, then it really hits the fan. Rather perversely, all I hoped was that this didn't affect Jimmy's bureau. Jimmy had to do the only sensible thing and cough the cash before the Jockney (whoever or whatever the hell that was) put the screws on, so things could keep ticking over.

Meanwhile, Slim had other fish to batter.

*

Slim's dad, Terry, was less of a villain than Barry and Conner in that he had a proper job that took up most of his time. He'd also, as per Slim's suggestion, started to change his phone regularly, so the amount of Intel coverage I was getting from the pair of them was pretty patchy.

On this occasion I was very lucky that we had his dirty phone.

Slim: Awight, Dad?
Terry: Not bad thanks, son. What can I do you for?
Slim: Got some paperwork that needs collecting.
Terry: Luverly. When?
Slim: Friday. I'll call back from another line with the number.

Which he did, but he called the same phone, so I still got the info.

Slim was sending his dad on a money collection. One of the great ironies of the drugs trade is that, considering it's full of rip-off-merchants, a huge part of it works on trust; a dealer will get a kilo of coke that is 80 per cent pure which he will cut down to produce 1.5 to 1.75 kilos. He owes £28,000 on the kilo he bought and selling at £40 per gram for the cut amount will gross him £70,000, a profit of £42,000. Once he has made what he owes he will be expected to pay it back before getting another kilo. If he is a 'new' customer, he will only be able to have small amounts of credit until he can show he is able to pay it back on time.

This money was part of a deal that Slim did on a shipment of coke to some Scousers a few weeks previously. Terry had been told by his son to go to the London

Gateway services on the M1 where the Scousers would arrive with £280,000 in cash. It would be delivered in two batches over two days.

Ali ran things from the ground and contacted the local traffic cops to warn them what we were up to. She also managed to persuade one of the SIOs in Manchester to put a team out to ID the Scousers. Once the handover had been completed, a surveillance team would follow them back up the warpath to their hidey-hole.

On the day, Terry did a bit of dicking around before getting a call from Slim.

'Head up there now. I've given them your number so they'll be in touch.'

Terry was pretty relaxed. As usual if it all went pear shaped, he'd just say he was a cabbie doing a courier job. No jury will convict an old cabbie with that little evidence.

At the services, Terry did the usual thing of sitting in the caff, twiddling his thumbs, looking at his watch, waiting for the call. Snapper and the representatives from Old Bill were parked in their usual base, outside a small office round the back of the main building.

The surveillance team were plotted up all around. They had two roles, one was to take Terry back onto the warpath until the Old Bill were in a position to pull him over for a 'routine check', and they also had to lock the Manchester surveillance team onto the Scousers. We knew that the Scousers weren't part of an Alpha op and so we hoped these would prove to be new faces.

The time for the meet came and went. Everybody got pretty tense, especially Slim, who kept calling. It was evident that he needed this to go smoothly.

Finally, over an hour late, Terry got the call.

UKM: Alri' la; we're on our way but runnin' late. Our idiot driver took the wrong turning and we're somewhere on the M14.

I could here some high-pitched animated discussion in the background, something about who'd misread the map and whose fault their lateness was.

UKM: Yeah, we'll be with you in thirty.
Terry: No problem, I'll be here.

I alerted Ali.
    Terry alerted Slim.
    Everyone was heads up. We needed to evidence the physical handover, then get the Scousers back to their mode of transport. The services were busy and the team, spread out over twelve vehicles and twelve footmen, were out to cover every eventuality. The Manchester team were all plotted up as well. They were on a different radio frequency so that there was no confusion when the targets left. Terry was not a problem, we had all his details and we'd catch up with him pretty quickly, but the Scousers were another matter.

UKM: Hiya, pal; yeah we're here, finally. Whereabouts are ya?

I rang Ali.
    'Hi, it's Ali.'
    'It's Cam, the Scousers are in the car park on foot looking for the cab.'
    'Thanks, let the games begin.'

When time is of the essence and I ring the operational commander there is nothing worse than them answering the phone with 'Hello'. I then have to confirm who it is on the other end of the phone, without saying who I am (a standard precaution in case I'd rung the wrong number). All this takes precious seconds which can make the difference between getting the gear or not. Anyone who has worked in Alpha or with Alpha always answers the phone with their name, so there's no time-wasting.

Before Ali had finished putting out the Intel she was interrupted by one of the team.

'From Lightning: That is two unknowns chilli with Zulu 18 [Terry] at the passenger side of X-ray 18.'

'Ranger: Yes, yes.'

'Lightning: Each of the unknowns has a holdall, wait . . . Yeah, the bags are going into the front passenger door of X-ray 18.'

'From Ranger: We will concentrate on the unknowns.'

Ali let the Old Bill know it was all systems go.

As soon as the Scousers were compromised our foot team handed over control to the Manchester team and made their way back to their own vehicles.

Terry left pretty much straight away, doing a circle of the car park to make sure he wasn't being followed.

Terry was shadowed by Ali's team straight back down the M1.

Terry had phoned Slim to let him know he was on his way.

I called Ali.

'OK, time to pass the football over to the Martians,' Ali replied.

The Scousers, meanwhile, having got rid of the £140,000 they had been lugging around all morning, went off for a celebratory KFC, relieved that no one was now going to find them holding all that cash.

As Terry convinced himself everything was cool, he rang his son to ask him where he wanted to meet. About five minutes later he found himself on the hard shoulder being asked searching questions about his £140,000 fare. He kept shtum and pleaded ignorance as he watched the bags disappear into the boot of a police car before being sent on his way with a receipt.

Funnily enough, we didn't hear much else for the rest of the day from Slim or Terry. I handed over to Ranjiv and went home as usual, taking a peep into Jimmy's grotty little world as I strolled past the bureau, nodding to the three wise drunkards and popping into Oddbins for a few cans. I joined the queue to pay and saw what was quite possibly the largest man in London. He was about six and a half feet, had long sloping, rounded shoulders, his arms were too long for his body and his hands were the size of watermelons. He was wearing a Scottish national team rugby shirt but spoke in a cockney accent. I followed him out and watched as he walked in the direction of Liverpool Street. I then looked back towards the bureau. Was that the Jockney? Shaking my head in disbelief, I picked up a pizza, had a quick chat with Harry and gratefully closed my front door behind me.

Then something very odd happened.

At 8 p.m., just as I was about to ring the kids, my phone went. It was Ranjiv.

'You won't believe this, but I think they're going ahead with the second lot tomorrow.'

'You're kidding!'

'Slim is desperate for the money, especially after the gear we took out last time. They've convinced themselves that today was just really bad luck and his old man is happy that he didn't get nicked. He was gonna get a grand for each run, so he wants the cash as well.'

'Jesus, and they're still using the same phones?'

'Terry is. He's rung Slim on an old one. Slim would have chucked the one today as soon as he knew it had all gone wonky. You'd have expected him to give his dad a bollocking for using the same one, but he didn't even mention it. He must be losing his touch. He can't have told the Scousers about the pull because he said that they were coming back down tomorrow, same time but different place.'

'OK, call Ali and Snapper and see if they want another job and I'll be in first thing. Leave anything else on the overnight note and I'll speak to you tomorrow. Happy days, mate.'

The following day Terry did lots and lots of counter-surveillance and proved he couldn't spot a tail if it was stapled to his arse. This time Snapper got the seizure. Once again, Terry kept shtum and pleaded ignorance. The police officer beamed. 'So, you won't mind if we take this, will you?'

God knows what Terry felt, waving goodbye to £140,000 for the second day running. But however bad he was feeling, Slim must've felt worse. He'd just given away a small fortune of coke to a load of Scouse bastards. And these were very mean Scouse bastards indeed. I'd caught one brief snatch of conversation on one of their phones that went: 'I heard he was making tea for the screws [informing on fellow criminals] inside.' 'We'll do 'im, all right.'

They were seriously unpleasant and liked to take grasses apart with bats, knives and axes – just to make sure everyone got the message. They were known for ramming any car they thought might be following them and exerting brutal force on whoever was inside, be they Old Bill in hot pursuit or OAPs on a jolly to Southport.

The Manchester team successfully locked on to their operation. 'These are quite probably the most disgusting, dangerous, sadistic maniacs I've ever had the misfortune to encounter,' the team leader said when he called me. 'I'm sure they won't hesitate to kill anyone who crosses them.'

Slim had helped put us on their tail. If they ever got wind of that, then Slim was a dead man walking.

# 20. Mr Football

I was out the back, enjoying a ciggie and admiring the view with Mike, when Snapper appeared beside us with an enormous cat-that-got-the-cream grin. 'Haven't you heard?' he said.

'No, what?'

'Major shit storm this morning. You're not going to believe this.'

'I'm all agog,' I said.

'You will be. You know Perry?'

'That lying prat? He's made my life a misery, or at least added to my miseries. Why? What's he done now?'

Snapper grinned. 'You're going to like this one. He was working a major drugs deal, or so he told everybody. Turned out to be no great shakes, but one of the guys he was listening in to was into fixing horse races.'

'Don't tell me Perry . . .'

'Damn right. Perry only went and bet on the races that this guy had fixed.'

'What a dipstick! Who would have thought?'

I turned to look at Mike. He simply raised his eyebrows and grinned. 'Some people would, some people wouldn't.'

The news stunned the office. No one could believe that someone working for Alpha could be so very stupid, let alone break the law. Alpha management was completely freaked. So freaked that Perry got away with it. Oh, sure, he was booted out of Alpha faster than you could say 'Shergar', but it was all hushed up and no charges brought. If something like that ever got out, the reputation of our elite department would be forever tarnished.

Oops!

As it happened, I was about to get my own insight to another sporting scam.

Slim: Awight, geez!

Mr Football: Fella, what you up to, son?

Slim: Up west, mate, Debbie's in Harvey Nicks with the little 'un, I'm stood outside feelin' me wallet gettin' mugged.

Mr Football: Nice one.

Slim: Yeah, anyway, we still on f'later?

Mr Football: Course. You spoke to Longshanks?

Slim: Yeah, he's bein' a prize prick but it's all sorted f'next week. We need to have a little chat tho'.

Mr Football: No worries, my friend, where do you wanna do it?

Slim: I'll be in the Archers wiv Unc later. See us in there, we can go for a bite after.

Mr Football: Cool as. Later.

Slim: Yeah, see ya. Be good.

'You'll never guess who I've just been listening to!' I called out to Mike.

'Who's that, then?'

I said the name.

'Bloody hell, who's he in with, then?'

'Slim, Conner and Barry.'

The name I'd given was a very, very famous former England football star.

We had more pies than fingers to put in them by this stage. Thanks to Jimmy, we'd been listening to coke dealers, launderers, racketeers, enforcers and, with no little interest and wonder, celebrities. Still at the centre of our sphere of interest were Jimmy, Barry and Conner, the Scrote twins and Slim. Amazingly a number of famous names started to crop up within surprising range of some of the heaviest criminals in town.

Gangsters and stars have always liked to mix it up, ever since the Krays. As well as Mr Football, I'd also recently heard the name of a very famous model. One of her relatives was the girlfriend of a serious dealer who got his thrills from orchestrating major drugs deals in London's top nightspots surrounded by models, pop stars and footballers; he loved to name-drop.

Although most celebs were innocent bystanders, a surprising number were right up to their necks in it. Mr Football had most certainly crossed the line and played a very active role in Slim's operations. He clearly loved hanging out with Barry and Conner. I couldn't understand why; it was hard to imagine that there were two more racist, sexist, humourless and boring bastards in existence. Nevertheless, Mr Football liked nothing more than spending the night driving round the West End with them in their limo, drinking champagne and snorting coke.

The phone conversations they had were hideous. Conner was on the phone to a mate and told him a story about a mutual acquaintance: 'Yeah, so Johnny fucked this prossie in the French farce a bit rough and she bled all over the missus's sofa. When the missus came in through the door,

Johnny grabbed the cat, nearly cut its leg off, and plonked it on the sofa, saying it must have got in scrap.' Hilarious.

Mr Football loved the fact that he was right in the thick of the north London criminal fraternity; he felt it gave him some kind of kudos, and vice versa. Barry and Conner loved him because he was an English icon.

After hearing Mr Football's name I checked our database. I wasn't disappointed. 'Bloody hell!'

'What now?'

'Did you know we'd intercepted Mr Football's phone before?'

'Really?'

'Says here he was hooked up a few years ago because he was, and I quote: "knowingly concerned".'

While Alpha had got nowhere near him, the gang had eventually been put away for donkey's years for bringing in cannabis resin by the boatload. Now it seemed he was at it again.

I put in the application (which raised a lot of eyebrows, including the Home Secretary's) and was soon listening in.

Mr Football: Awight, mate, just ordered a new batch.

UKM: Not the club ones?

Mr Football: Nah, course not; why waste decent money on the punters, eh? Get some England ones too, we'll get a ton for those.

UKM: Better warm up me signin' hand, then. Who we gonna say these are signed by?

Mr Football: A few by Becks, yeah?

UKM: Naturally. Got that one down pat, mate.

\*

Bastards. Mr Football and a famous friend were buying hundreds of fake replica shirts (the greedy bastard wouldn't even buy proper ones sold from the club shop), then forging the team's signatures on the back, adding their own real ones, and selling them to anyone who could afford them for between £75 and £200 a pop. Getting a shirt from this pair should have been a guarantee that everything was genuine. Not a bit of it. What made it all the more galling was that this guy was someone who came across publicly as a proper gent; he was someone that I'd long admired.

Not any more.

The greedy bastard was turning over a tidy fortune.

But it didn't end there, oh no.

Slim: Hiya, mate.

Mr Football: Slim! What can I do yer for?

Slim: You're seeing Conner on Saturday, aren't you?

Mr Football: S'right, yeah, we're goin' to Stringfellas.

Slim: Need somethin' collecting from Terry for Conner.

Mr Football: Sure, where and when?

Slim: Terry'll be in touch.

This time, blinded by the celebrity, Slim was being really stupid. He had the mobile number of this famous person and he'd started using him to move 'packages' around for him. I don't think Mr Football actually knew what was in the packages (money), but it was clear he was in deep.

Mr Football was the one person who couldn't and wouldn't change his mobile. He relied on people from all over the UK being able to get hold of him for work – public appearances, after-dinner speeches, etc. – so, once

Mr Football was hooked up, I had a wonderfully easy way of getting everybody else's numbers.

He was a cracking source of Intel. Soon he was giving me the number of every major villain in north London. Snapper even put out an ops team to trail him, to see if he'd lead us to the lair of any other Mr Big.

I was a little concerned at the sheer scale of Operation Undo; it was getting a bit too big for us to cover. The objectives at the beginning of the operation had been more than met. A number of previously unknown drug gangs in London and the north-west had been identified and were currently being worked on, all the parties in Jimmy's team of launderers had been identified, and a number of seizures had been made and could be put to them. Ali's team had also identified a few addresses that were thought to be stashes.

I was as keen as Snapper to see just how far it would take us, but I also realized that events were rapidly spiralling towards a chaotic climax and we knew we needed to take control soon and take everyone down before we lost the plot. The amount of money being laundered was ridiculous, and the speed at which it was being done was unlike anything anyone had seen before. There had been no more mention of the Jockney; Jimmy had repaid the lost money and was really going for it, trying to make it back up as quickly as possible. It was almost as if he were caught in a whirlpool and was being sucked towards its centre with ever increasing speed. I now had thirty targets on my Alpha board: top of the list was Slim but there were operators from all over London, as well as their runners (such as the Scrote twins), lovers, wives, friends and business partners.

Jimmy had stopped taking his daughter's calls and I reck-oned her hubby was becoming more abusive towards her, relying on the fact that Jimmy was too busy and too wrapped up in his own world of crime to care.

God, it's so tempting to reveal the bastard's name.

Jimmy was really cracking up and I didn't think that he would survive for much longer before another fuck-up meant he would disappear permanently. He was really under pressure from the sheer amount of work he'd taken on; you could cut the atmosphere at his bureau with a knife, mainly because the runners exchanging money with Jimmy were all working for guys who'd lost lots of gear thanks to Alpha, and they were extremely stressed.

I did wonder whether these guys might start talking to Jimmy about it all coming on top for them and he would put two and two together, realizing that he was at the centre of it all.

Listening to them all became quite depressing really, like a very bad radio soap opera. One thing was becoming clear: while crime could make you rich, it didn't bring much happi-ness – only paranoia, stress and misery by the gallon.

Slim, Barry and Conner were the only ones who were even vaguely happy, as far as I could tell, and they were right at the top of an enormous pyramid of pain. Every-body else who saw or touched the drugs and cash, the ones who took the risks, were doomed. They were the ones who we'd end up prosecuting and it was they who would go to jail, not the guys at the top. Slim was just too far removed and as for Barry and Conner – well, forget it. To us, they were untouchable as far as the law was concerned.

But, I knew we were at least becoming a real pain in their

collective arse. Slim was already out of pocket by at least £1.5 million in cash, and that's a lot by any dealer's standards. Plus, we were starting to hurt his reputation – he relied on other criminals, and rumours were flying that Slim wasn't the safe a pair of hands he'd once been. Now, with those nasty Scousers in the background, I suspected Slim would be very worried about anything going amiss – he couldn't afford to piss them off: there were worse things than going to jail.

It was the end of the road for Jimmy. New guidelines meant that we could now charge him with money laundering without having to demonstrate that he knew where the money had come from. This was thanks to a famous case involving one Ussama 'Sammy' El-Kurd.

El-Kurd, an Egyptian, laundered £70 million of criminals' cash through his tiny shop in Notting Hill. The cash came from those crazy Scouse drug dealers who bought their gear from Amsterdam (from our old friend the Dutchman, quite possibly), which was then resold on Merseyside.

When he was arrested, El-Kurd was found to have £1.2 million deposited in fifty-one bank accounts across Europe, a £50,000 collection of jewellery, £750,000 in two safety deposit boxes and a 'float' of £250,000 in his bureau's safe.

He was cleared of knowingly laundering drug-trafficking proceeds, but convicted of money laundering nonetheless. Judge John Samuels told the father of five: 'It must be plainly understood that laundering the proceeds of criminal conduct is, in its consequences, just as grave an offence as being involved in the primary criminal activity which generates the illicit proceeds.' El-Kurd was handed a £1-million fine and a fourteen-year prison sentence.

Hitherto, the only people imprisoned for money laundering had been provably involved with drugs, terrorism or some other nefarious offence. El-Kurd was not a drug dealer; he just washed the money and said he had no idea where it had come from, but ignorance was no longer bliss.

Problem solved, you might think, but dodgy bureaux de change still thrive today despite this new approach and the new regulations. In its 2008/9 threat assessment of serious organized crime, the Serious Organised Crime Agency (SOCA) still identified bureaux de change and the hawala system as high-risk areas open to abuse by money launderers.

Of course, the bureaux' clientele isn't limited to drug dealers. Terrorist organizations also avail themselves of the launderers' services. Although the amounts spent by terrorists on their ops are small (the 7/7 attacks in London only cost about £8,000 to set up), financing the day-to-day running of a terrorist network is extremely expensive: SOCA estimated that al-Qaeda spent about £30 million on running costs in between 2000 and 2001. They raised a great deal of those funds through illegal drug and diamond dealing, the proceeds of which were washed by money-changers across the world.

I noted earlier that one outfit in Bradford took £3.3 million in notes in a single day and paid over £80 million into the banks for just one client. The ring involved the laundering of some half a billion pounds over four years, using the hawala system. The clean money was deposited into business and personal accounts at various banking outlets, converted into foreign currencies, then transferred to accounts in the United States, the United Arab Emirates and across Europe.

In 2007 a successful, decade-long Customs operation ended with more than seventy-five years' jail for the main players. The most amazing thing to me about this operation was that it took Customs ten years to nick one money-laundering outfit, which shows how ridiculously difficult it was – and that criminals could quite happily carry on making hundreds of millions for ten years (investing it in whatever they wanted, perhaps even funding al-Qaeda) while Customs watched powerless, trying to build a case against them.

Did this operation change anything? Hardly. One major bust in ten years is not exactly a deterrent. There were and are plenty of others ticking along under the radar. It certainly didn't affect the criminals whose money was being laundered. In this case the drug dealers weren't even prosecuted.

Regulations are one thing; enforcing them is another. The law says that anyone who is operating a hawala business is required to register. Their directors have to be subject to a fit and proper persons test. Hmmm. Many hawaladars operate from the back rooms of greengrocers, butchers, and newsagents within tight-knit ethnic communities. Getting these guys to register is unlikely; regulating them is simply out of the question. On top of this, the majority of overseas agents are both unregulated and unknown to any authorities, making the tracking of transfers nigh-on impossible.

That's why Alpha was amazing. Within a few weeks I was deep into Jimmy's bureau and, thanks to a bit of decent legwork from the ops team, we were ready to do him for money laundering and drugs offences. We were certain he was bigger than all of the cases that had gone before. I was fairly certain he was laundering money with a hawaladar who had links to terrorism (there I go again, sexing up the dossier).

Jimmy's contact was too smart for us; he changed his phone as fast I could type out an intercept application but kept his business going without any trouble. He cast no shadow and left no trace.

We didn't have time to find him. We had to strike soon before this got too big and Customs prosecutors wound up snowed under for years trying to get all the cases through the courts. If we were going to bring the house down, it had to be soon.

I grinned when I thought about the day of the knock. It was going to be a beast.

Like Jimmy, Slim was getting desperate and taking unnecessary chances to make some fast money. He'd even started to buy gear on credit. Never a good idea, especially when working with a bunch of Scousers who wouldn't think twice about decapitating late payers with a rusty fireman's axe.

Good old Mr Football was still proving invaluable; Snapper and Ali were on his tail all the time, collecting addresses, picking out likely stash houses and dealers and plotting out all the routes of runners, dealers and launderers that Mr Football met. It all added up to a lovely spiderweb of red lines around Jimmy's bureau. But then came the fuck-up moment.

Mr Football: Wotcher, mate. Just wanted to letcha know I dropped off those fings last night.
Slim: Nice one. Unc sends his regards. You still coming to the match Saturday?
Mr Football: Of course, wouldn't miss it.

I called Snapper. 'Look's like Mr Football's clean today, whatever he was doing last night was for Slim.'

'Great, that was another new address for us. We'll keep on him for a bit longer today, see what he's up to next.'

Snapper's team stuck with him and all was going smoothly, until –

'From Belgium: Target is nine-one, ah shit, it's a dead one, we misread the map . . . wait . . .'

'Jesus Christ!' Belgium yelled. Suddenly, I could hear the sound of some very hectic driving; gear revs going through the roof followed by an almighty crash.

I called Snapper. 'Blimey,' he told me, 'the idiot spotted Belgium all right but he's only shat his pants and driven over two bollards at the end of the cul-de-sac and into the next street. That's some pretty desperate measures.'

'Did they give way?'

'Yeah he made it through; left glass, metal and a bumper behind him, though. Not sure how he's going to explain that one to the insurers. I'm standing the team down. Sorry, Cam, major fuck-up on our part.'

'Not to worry, mate. Let's see if he calls Slim.'

He didn't. I never heard Mr Football's voice again, and neither did Slim. Mr Football knew he was up to his neck in it and quickly realized when Snapper's team showed out that what he was mixed up in must have been pretty damn serious to have some sort of surveillance team behind him.

If he'd ever been nicked, the club and his fan base would have dropped him like a sack of hot King Edwards. As it turned out, he got clean of drugs and booze and has behaved himself ever since.

Good to think we helped to make a difference.

# 21. Knock, Knock, Knock

Presumably, Mr Football didn't say a word to Slim, Barry and Conner. He just upped and went, which was of great relief to me. The only catch, of course, was that when the knock did come, somebody might remember Mr Football's strange and sudden disappearance and might wonder if he talked, *then* his past would have most definitely have come back to haunt him.

This close call was another clear sign we needed to take down Jimmy, Billy, Elton and all the other money changers. Ali Mooney's team had found a couple of addresses linked to Conner, Barry and Slim that were holding a serious amount of stash, so if for nothing else we had a damn good chance of relieving them of their cash.

Discussions had been ongoing in the ops team as to when to call the knock. As the Alpha officer, I wouldn't be going out on the ground, so I didn't attend the lengthy briefings during which the logistics were hammered out. Every now and again I'd get a call from Ali, updating me and asking me to keep an eye out for a possible handover of cash at Jimmy's bureau, which would trigger the knock.

Billy: Yeah got one-fifty for you.
Jimmy: Right. Tomorrow?
Billy: Safe.

*That'll do nicely*, I thought, and called Ali. This would be a handover of cash between Billy, Elton and one of Jimmy's runners. Billy had already taken around £150,000 sterling into Jimmy and they were waiting for the return of high-value euros (high-value notes are much easier to conceal when sending them abroad to pay for the next/last load).

Billy and Elton had become really complacent. They'd stopped employing basic security measures and had even started making the handovers on the street instead of inside the bureau. This was perfect; it made things so much easier for the ops team as they would be able to see the exchange happen – if it had been done out of sight in the basement of the bureau then there was still room for Jimmy and Billy to plead not guilty as we couldn't be sure what had gone on between them out of sight. But if they were caught red-handed in the street then there would be no room for denial.

Ali agreed. 'Sounds good, Cammo. Tomorrow it is.'

As ever in these situations, I was in the suite with the head-phones on, feeling pretty useless. I wanted to be on the ground, see the takedown, be a part of it, feel some collar. But I still had plenty to worry about – Ali and Snapper were after twenty-nine targets connected to Jimmy's bureau. About fifty lines would light up as the knock began and gear and cash was dumped. I needed to be at my best to catch any vital new Intel. Invariably, most of the villains' wives and mistresses were going to make the mistake of calling all of their husbands' mates to ask if anything needed to be to 'done', e.g., go to a particular address and burn paperwork/move gear or money, etc. It was always nice to get an address that we didn't know about.

Snapper called. 'We're on our way, Cam. Jesus, that briefing was a monster, just about every operational team member going. It was like that bit in *Star Wars* before they go and blow up the Death Star.'

Despite some pretty intricate organization, Snapper's raid didn't exactly go to plan. I was on the phone to him as he was driving towards Oliver Scrote's gaff to put the door in. As they came up the road, Oliver had just climbed into his car, saw all the vehicles speeding towards his house, put two and two together and his foot to the floor.

All I heard from Snapper was a lot of Anglo-Saxon, followed by a huge KER-RUNCH and the sound of breaking glass as Snapper rammed Ollie into an unfortunate neighbour's garden, then silence.

When Snapper asked to be let into the house, he was told to boldly go where no man had gone before. Snapper shrugged with a 'have it your way, then' expression and Big Mac, a Scots officer the size of the Hulk, opened Oliver's door with our very own set of 'keys': a big lump of iron with a handle.

Snapper reached through the huge hole and opened the latch. Inside, it was chaos. Oliver had about six kids and he'd trained them well.

'Stop the little bastards!' Snapper yelled. The little horrors dived between legs and dodged past coppers in their bulky gear, causing complete and utter mayhem. The worrying sound of excessive and over-enthusiastic toilet flushing came from upstairs. Snapper charged up and grabbed one little sprog as he dropped another one of Daddy's mobile phones down the toilet.

Oliver was sitting in the front room, hands cuffed behind

his back, grinning with obvious pride as his kids continued to cause mayhem. Snapper was actually in the process of 'bagging and tagging' the main mobile when it was nicked off the kitchen table right under his nose by a 'small, dirty urchin', never to been seen again. Yep, Daddy was real proud, he'd raised a proper little clutch of mini-crims.

Meanwhile, as doors went in across London, my screen was lighting up like a Christmas tree on steroids. 'Here we fucking go!' Everyone in Alpha stopped what they were doing and watched, fascinated, as the calls kicked off.

As we'd predicted, many wives who'd seen the cops coming down the road had called their loved ones for instructions. Once word reached one criminal connection, the calls grew and grew in number from just about all of the phones we had, those whose owners weren't already eating carpet or staring at the business end of a copper's truncheon.

I worked through the flashing lights in a master-class of Alpha ops. As if I were conducting the 1812 Overture, my hands flew from screen to keyboard to phone, updating Snapper and numerous other teams as any new Intel came in.

It was beautiful . . .

Every now and then I'd update Snapper: 'Someone's called in to clear an address just round the corner from where you are now.'

Snapper dived round there to find a bloke hurriedly loading two hundred mobile phones into his car boot. Yes, that's two hundred. These weren't pay-as-you-go – you could make as many calls as you liked without topping up and they were all registered in the same fake name. This guy supplied anyone in the underworld who needed an anonymous phone. No doubt he charged well above the odds for this service; an extremely lucrative business.

Once all the teams were in their target addresses and the phones were under control, things started to settle down. To their credit, villains' wives usually take such unexpected drama in their stride and get a brew on sharpish, realizing from previous experience that if you give the search team tea and biscuits then they are far more likely to put everything back the way they found it, or at least in one piece.

One arrest did go awry, however. Elton had been nicked at home, on the ninth floor of a block of flats. While his drum was turned upside down, he sat meekly on the sofa. After nothing of interest was found, he was given a few quid so he could buy fags and sweets while he was in custody. We're nice like that. He was left alone for thirty seconds while the lead officer had one more look round the kitchen. When he returned Elton had done a runner.

The stairs were outside his door, the lifts were out of order but he was long gone before anyone could do anything about it. I can only imagine the palpations the three officers who'd mislaid him must have had. Not only had they let one of our suspects go, they'd be laughed out of court for incompetence and have the Mickey taken for evermore. No need for any disciplinary action; they would never again leave a suspect alone.

We threw every resource we had at trying to pick him up; I had his phone and managed to triangulate it all over north London (this was still quite a slow process back then so we were always one step behind) before the trail went cold early the next morning.

Despite this, all the main targets, all twenty-nine of them, were nicked and were carted off for interview. In my experience, villains had three different responses during questioning. The career crims say nothing at all. Nada. The stupid ones spin a story and quickly tie themselves into knots, ensuring that they look both gormless and guilty in court. The third type tended to be greedy men who were not career crims but had believed the others when told their role would provide them with big profit for little risk. They tell us everything about their role but keep shtum about the others.

A few hours after the knock, Ali called. 'How much cash did you think was in Jimmy's bureau?'

'On a good day, I reckon about half a mil.'

'Try £2.5 million in sterling, dollars and euros.'

'Holy crap.'

'He must have been doing a lot business off the phones,' Ali said.

Not a bad day's work. We even lifted a few unexpected kilos of coke, speed and ecstasy from the various addresses we'd crashed into.

At least some of that £2.5 million belonged to Slim. He was definitely not having a good year. And things were going to get worse. His house hadn't been raided because, apart from the Alpha Intel, we still had nothing on him evidentially that we could use in court.

'We stay on Slim,' Thomas said, 'to the death.'

# 22. Catch 22

Slim: I'm thinking of ending it.

Terry: What're you on about?

Slim: This fucking game. It's finished. All of it, down the pan. Just a load of big bollocks and never mind the flash crap. I could have done so much more with my fucking life. I had dreams.

Terry: Take it from me. In gangster-land, dreams don't come true. Look, take some time off, find somewhere to cool down. You're just in a rut.

Slim: Rut? I'm in a fucking trench, that's where I am.

'Keep going, Cam,' Thomas ordered. 'Keep stamping on Slim.'

Slim was a wounded rat in a trap; his days were numbered. Ranjiv, Snapper and I had been chasing him for months. We had heard him arrange massive class-A deals, taken hundreds of thousands of pounds off his team, and used his Intel to make numerous seizures all over the UK and abroad.

Barry and Conner had vanished off the phones; they'd realized the heat was a little too close to home and had decided to take an extended holiday in the Costa del Crime (Marbella) or the Costa Nostra (Malaga).

If ever there was an argument for using intercept material in evidence, Slim was it. Our phone intercepts would have proved that he'd been involved in the importation of massive amounts of heroin, cocaine, ecstasy and cannabis, that he'd moved large amounts of it around the country, and that he'd been laundering proceeds running into tens of millions. But so far as the courts were concerned, none of it was admissible. Still, we had him reeling; now he was on the ropes, awaiting the knock-out.

I went and sat outside Slim's house. This was against all the rules but I didn't care. I needed to see Slim. I still didn't get him. He had the beautiful girlfriend, a healthy son with a bright future and an amazing home paid for. He had once had millions and could have retired. Now, thanks to me, we'd hit him so hard his business had been turned on its head. He was in for a few hundred grand to various evil people and, on top of this, he'd lost his reputation for reliability. Word had spread that anyone close to him seemed to get nicked. After all, we'd just taken out his entire network. The fact that he was in debt to the Scousers meant that his wife and son were now kidnapping targets.

I watched as they came out, a happy family unit. How could Slim stay so cool, as if nothing was wrong? How could he risk the lives of his wife and son? She didn't yet know about all that had been happening and Slim made sure it stayed that way. Still, while I may have known Slim's working life better than his own wife, I still didn't understand him.

The problem was, we couldn't nick him. Apart from the wiretaps, we didn't have the evidence, so all we could do was carry on seizing his gear, forcing him into more and more debt. In a way, it was torture by proxy and I almost felt sorry for him.

Almost.

Meanwhile, I was close to burn-out. The endless booz-
ing, the long hours, the huge operation — although
successful — had taken its toll and I was sinking fast.

Before, when I'd been on the ground, I hadn't thought
that much about the bigger picture; I simply had to arrest
the couriers and thereby disrupt the flow of drugs. Now,
having seen it from Alpha's viewpoint, it all seemed such
a mess, a lot of time, money and effort expended for no
real change. What was I doing all this for? Throwing my
life away taking down these idiots while hundreds more
stood ready to replace them. I'd been getting plenty of grief
for not being there for my own sons and I deserved it.

I tried to push the thoughts and feelings of powerless-
ness away. I reminded myself that I was simply a player in
a game, tried to pull myself together, but I seemed to be
stuck in as deep a rut as Slim.

Then, just when I was ready to chuck it all in as pointless,
something happened to wake me up and remind me why
I was doing this job.

A few weeks later, after we got back with the right
phones, Slim arranged for two gophers to collect an
amount of coke from a third party somewhere in south
London.

And that was when I heard him.

I never forgot a voice, and this one was easy, with its
strong accent.

The Dutchman.

'Fuck! I don't believe it!'

I was delighted to be on the Dutchman's case again, and
this time I wasn't going to let him get away.

Snapper did the job with the Old Bill and was in the command car on the night. They were parked just south of the river, waiting for the off. Eventually my phones started lighting up.

Slim called the meeters in Camden and told them to head south and wait to get the mobile number of the supplier.

They had obviously used other phones to make most of the arrangements because after an hour or so of nothing, with the Old Bill and Snapper getting impatient, the meeters called the buyer. I rang Snapper.

'The meet is at the Black Prince in Bexleyheath, very soon. The meeters are on the A3 now.'

I could imagine the scene, the Old Bill screaming down the A3, hoping for the right result but also looking at Snapper and thinking, *Is this long-haired weirdo really gonna get us a result?* The same person who only a few weeks before had got rat-arsed in the Custom House bar, taken a tracker car home, crashed it into a black cab and run off?

After some more calls between the baddies, I phoned Snapper again. 'The meeters are already there, the supplier is on his way; he'll be five minutes.'

I could hear the car's engine accelerating in the background. Frantic radio calls putting the info out to the team.

Two minutes later. 'The buyer is in a silver Audi, the meeters are in a blue Astra, the handover is in the pub car park.'

'OK, we have one call sign here already,' Snapper answered, 'the rest are a minute behind.'

I called back thirty seconds later. 'The supplier is in a blue and white striped T-shirt.' Snapper stayed on the line while that was put out to the team. A pause, then I heard in the background, 'Yeah, we're eyeball on that.' The line went dead.

Silence again.

Snapper phoned me an hour later. They had got all three handing over 15kg of coke and a suitcase full of cash. They'd then gone back to the Dutchman's flat and found another 18kg of coke.

Yes!

Slim was massively out of pocket and up to his eyeballs in debt. As usual, he'd set up the deal from home using the mobiles, so we couldn't nick him.

Then he made an extraordinary move, considering what had happened.

He made a small deal with a close mate rather than associate, to get a kilo of amphetamines for him. This time, Slim made the mistake of going to collect it in person. This was it.

Snapper put the Intel through the local drugs squad. They rocked up and nicked Slim just after the handover. He was bailed but incredibly he continued where he left off.

'Bastard must have a death wish,' Snapper said.

# 23. The Axe Falls

But then Slim's calls stopped. He was setting up deals one day and the next – nothing. Operation Undo was over and my time in Alpha was coming to an end. The Serious Organised Crime Agency was about to come into being and the plan was to split up, rename and move Alpha, changing the way it was run, how operations were organized – it would be transformed into something else entirely.

I was given a couple of weeks' leave and was told I had two options: join either the Financial Team or the Dedicated Surveillance Team (DST). Hmmm . . . sitting at a desk examining bank statements or screaming round the UK in fast cars chasing after badass drug dealers and murderers?

The DST would be based in my old stomping ground of Bristol and my old pals Pat and Jed had already signed up. Happy days.

The DST was a new concept for Customs (and law enforcement in general). Previously, all Customs and National Crime Squad surveillance was carried out ad hoc by investigators from the team running the investigation. Now investigators from all over the country 'tasked' the DST to work on targets for a set time. The DST could be chosen to do the surveillance for any job, from drug dealers to hit men, from Newcastle to Brighton. It was about as rock and roll as it could get. I returned from my break refreshed and excited, relishing the chance to get back out on the street again.

First came the farewell drinks with some of the team and it wasn't long before things started to get messy. After five pints of Guinness, we ended up in an uber-trendy wine bar.

Thomas was also leaving, not only Alpha but Customs as well. He was ready to move into the private sector as some sort of security consultant. He was in high spirits (and they in him) and it seemed as though it was all back on with Ali. Thomas ranted about the UK's drugs policy to anyone who'd listen.

'The government's out of ideas,' he said, 'to stop coke getting into the UK. Besides, too many people on the criminal AND legal side of things are happy with the way things are. Take us, for example. We're paid tens of millions of tax pounds every year. At the moment it's a booming industry and recruitment is the way forward.'

'Who else benefits?' I asked, curious to hear his answer.

'The politicians,' Thomas said. 'Talk tough on drugs and you're onto a vote winner. Then there's people like me, the private sector. Now that's where you can really make a legal killing from the drugs trade, from advisory groups, think tanks, consultants, the security industry, from people who sell burglar alarms to people who sell growing lamps for skunk farming.'

'Not to mention the terrorists,' Snapper added. 'An easy way to make money to keep things ticking over.'

'Yeah, well, it's going to get worse,' Thomas added with sudden bitterness. 'We're making the mistake of copying the American model. We're not America and their policy hasn't exactly worked for them anyway. We're handing over the war on drugs to a bunch of bureaucrats who are going to dazzle the media with a deadly combination of statistics and secrecy.

'But I'm sure surveillance will continue to play a big part, Cammo,' Thomas added jovially, 'So don't worry, there will be plenty of demand for guys like you. After all, how on earth are we going to gather intelligence otherwise?

'If drug use goes down, that tells us that government policies are working. Drug use goes up and that means not enough is being done. Either way, it means we can demand more money for the war chest. Meanwhile, the people of this great land still want to get blitzed every night of the week and nobody seems too bothered about finding out why that is.'

At that moment, some bright spark spotted that that this bar sold absinthe. I knew all about the history of the drink, that it was supposed to have sent Van Gogh mad and had been banned in most of Europe. I had never tried it and, now that we were nicely 'warmed-up', we decided that this would be the perfect time to have a tipple.

The barman pointed first to the small print that said that they would sell no more than two shots to each customer. He handed us some paraphernalia and explained the procedure. We had a shot glass with the beautiful green liquid, a small tumbler half full of soda water, a spoon, a lighter and a sachet of brown sugar.

'You pour the sugar onto the spoon and caramelize it with the flame from the lighter, holding it over the shot glass.'

'Isn't this what crack addicts do?' I asked.

The barman ignored me.

'When the sugar has turned to liquid, whizz it very quickly round in the absinth before pouring it into the soda water and knock it right back. Got it?'

We nodded as one and followed his instructions to the letter. After five seconds a potent warm feeling passed through my body and I waited for the sledgehammer.

Nothing.

It was rather pleasant, not at all like the knockdown feeling I'd been expecting. We looked at each other and wondered what all the fuss was about. So we had another one. Same feeling. Nothing that would suggest a deep dark depression or complete brain failure was imminent. Boring, we thought.

Then we tried to get off our stools.

We appeared to have lost the use of our lower limbs. And our speech was strangely incoherent.

Then everything went blank.

I woke up the next day with a half-eaten vindaloo all over the bedroom floor, a traffic cone by the door and no recollection of how either had got there. It really felt like there wasn't much difference between the crackheads and me at that point. I spent the rest of the day packing my things and trying to get the spicy smell of curry out of the flat.

*DST, here I come*, I thought, slamming the door behind me.

## *Extract from Alpha Intercept*

Elton: Slim didn't have a clue it was bang on him.

UKM: Fucking shit ain't right, mate.

Elton: They put a shell in the back of his leg, blew off his kneecap.

UKM: That would have been enough.

Elton: But it weren't though, fuck. Dozen times with a fireman's axe. Deadest cunt there ever was.

UKM: Any word on the fucker wot done it?

Elton: Nah, and I don' wanna know neither.

UKM: Make you right.

# 24. Thundercats, Ho!

'Have you seen *The Bourne Ultimatum*?'

I looked back. This man, the man in his fifties with the huge grey beard, was SOCA's senior manager in charge of all surveillance matters.

He was also nearing his retirement.

He had an annoying habit of repeatedly telling us all about his past exploits. As we were mostly former Customs officers with countless ground ops under our belts and as he was a former cop who'd spent most of his years in senior management, these stories, from two decades ago, did not impress.

We christened him 'Uncle Albert' (from *Only Fools and Horses*), or 'Jewrin'-the-Wohwa'.

I told him that, yes, I had indeed seen *The Bourne Ultimatum*.

'Amazing, wasn't it?' he asked with wide-eyed enthusiasm.

'All right, I suppose,' I replied.

'That control room they had, the Americans, why don't we have one like that?'

'Control room?' I answered, a puzzled expression on my face, an expression that was becoming all too regular these days.

'Yes, that's what I said. Like the one the Yanks had when they were orchestrating the chase for Bourne, they were running things from a control room, directing officers on the ground and so on.'

Was he serious? I looked at Jed for assistance but he was, with a slight trembling smile, staring straight ahead at his monitor with laser-beam eyes as if his life depended on it.

I could just see the sort of fantasies that played through Uncle Albert's mind on a loop; he was standing in front of a huge LED screen with Matt Damon's face on it, shouting things like 'Get me the schematics!' or 'Activate the asset!' or 'Analyze that audio. Bring up the satellite imagery – I need this done yesterday, people!'

He wanted the gizmos and the glamour, something to play with, something nice to look at in the run-up to his retirement. Problem was, in SOCA, he actually had a good chance of getting it.

After the cell door slammed behind Jimmy (he got off lightly, seven years) and the axe came down all too literally on Slim, I really looked forward to leaving Alpha. I'd practically had a mental breakdown from being cooped up for so long (even now, I was still on the verge) and I was keen as mustard to get back out on the ground and have some fun hunting the bad guys under the auspices of the bright and shiny Serious Organized Crime Agency.

The government had spent the previous year selling us the concept of SOCA at several events. The entire DST had been press-ganged along with the Old Bill into going along to the government's million-pound SOCA road show that visited London, Birmingham, Manchester, Leeds and Bristol.

Despite having duitfully RSVP'd to our invites, and despite phoning in our confirmation of attendance, when we arrived the receptionist couldn't find any record of us. It was busy and there was quite a queue building up behind us. 'Don't worry,' he said, 'I'll just print you up some passes now.'

Nice security. If we'd been journalists or villains we

would have had a field day learning all of SOCA's planned strategies. Inside, however, I must admit it all looked very exciting.

All we heard from the moment we walked in was that, as SOCA officers, we would be working on better targets for better pay with better equipment. They didn't really need all the road-show glitz to sell this concept to us; we got it straight away.

Nonetheless, some bright sparks had made a video about surveillance to help our more intellectually challenged colleagues get the idea. It featured on ongoing story about a SOCA-led operation to catch some heavy-duty drug importers. There were some surveillance shots taken on the street and of a hotel room, filmed meetings on a boat, and then the legend 'To be continued' flashed up on the screen. It reminded me of those old Nescafé coffee adverts.

The reason for all the hoo-hah was that they wanted as many people as possible to apply. The selection procedure would take about six months and so they needed to get cracking as they only had a year before SOCA was due to go live. The road shows had New Labour's stamp of expensive PR slickness all over them. Lots of top managers gave PowerPoint presentations selling SOCA and we all bought it, lock, stock and smoking barrels. After all, none of us wanted to be left behind in Customs working on VAT fraud.

In a nutshell, SOCA was an agglomeration of 4,200 officers from the investigative and intelligence sections of HM Customs Investigations on serious drug trafficking, the National Crime Squad (NCS) and the National Criminal Intelligence Service (NCIS). Its aims were to gather more and better intelligence and to tackle major crime. SOCA

spends 40 per cent of its operational effort on drug trafficking, 25 per cent on organized immigration crime, 10 per
cent on fraud and 15 per cent on other organized crime.
The remaining 10 per cent is devoted to supporting other
law enforcement agencies.

To understand what went wrong with SOCA, I'd better
quickly explain what the NCS and NCIS were. The National
Crime Squad was formed in 1998, itself an amalgamation
of the seven Regional Crime Squads (RCS). It was made
up of detectives seconded from the police, and selection
was seen as the pinnacle to any detective's career. They dealt
with drug dealing, armed robberies and high-tech crime.

The NCS was formed partly thanks to a corruption scan-
dal at the South East Regional Crime Squad. Officers
moving over from RCS to NCS had to sign a contract
promising not to be corrupt. (It apparently didn't occur to
anyone that a corrupt officer would be as happy to sign this
as an honest one.) NCS senior management hated Customs.
They thought that only the police force should be allowed
to work on top villains. And they hated two things about
Customs in particular: (1) the fact that we had officers all
over the world doing really sexy stuff and (2) we had what
was called 'The Writ of Assistance' on our side.

The Writ was a search warrant peculiar to Customs. It
allowed any Customs officer to enter any premises in the
country to search for wanted persons, 'dutiable goods' or
other contraband. It was the only warrant that didn't require
a magistrate's approval: a number of copies all signed by the
Queen were kept in little purple pouches in SIOs' safes
around the UK. The Writ gave rise to the legend that Customs

had more power than the police; the Old Bill would have loved to have had it, but would have abused the hell out of it. I used it only twice in fifteen years. It was never over-exploited because we knew it would be revoked the moment we overstepped the mark. NCS lobbied and pushed the government until it caved in and said the Writ violated Joe Public's human rights. Really, they were just jealous.

The National Criminal Intelligence Service was formed in 1992 out of the old National Drugs Intelligence Unit (NDIU), which was part of the Home Office. The staff were all seconded from the police/NCS/Customs/Immigration. NCIS was quite possibly the biggest waste of money in law enforcement (until SOCA), with five hundred staff who probably wouldn't know a villain if he punched them in the face. I don't know anyone in Customs or the NCS with a good word for them. Funnily enough, SOCA's current objectives bear an uncanny resemblance to those of NCIS back in 1992.

NCIS didn't have an operational arm so they couldn't do any surveillance. They only gathered strategic intelligence regarding trends, so they could write a nice report for the Cabinet that outlined whatever the latest big crime phenomenon was. But anyone who reads trend reports from the DEA (the US Drug Enforcement Agency), the FBI or even the United Nations can do that.

They did have specialist informant-handling cells, but no worthwhile informants to handle. The best informants are recruited in the kitchen while the main man with the gear is being nicked in the lounge. Because NCIS never went out on the ground they were always on a loser to begin with so far as acquiring CIs (criminal informants) was concerned. It might surprise you to learn that most villains sign up as informants at some point or other. Honour among thieves? I don't think so. And not just the toe-rags, either. Almost every major criminal I've known has suddenly become much more talkative after being sent down for a decent stretch, looking at the four grey walls and the sad old padre, in the hope of just a little time off.

The other major function of NCIS was to provide intelligence analysts for police and Customs operations, if we let them. They basically took our intelligence and produced nice reports that showed little pictures of people and cars to confirm associations that we already knew about. I've seen dozens upon dozens of these reports and not one of them was ever of the slightest use to us.

HM Customs Investigations was made up of 1,200 investigators who were responsible for targeting the highest echelon of drug smugglers and money-launderers worldwide. Customs managed the Drugs Liaison Officer network, with staff in forty-odd countries. And then, of course, there was Alpha, the only 'live' Intel feed in UK law enforcement.

Customs staff were permanent, having undergone a rigorous interview and vetting process. Customs were extremely successful at what they did but were sometimes criticized for allowing operations to run longer than necessary in an attempt to build a stronger case. This was especially so regarding cigarette and alcohol smuggling, where I have to admit there were some pretty major screw-ups. We had a love–hate relationship with the NCS.

I'm the first person to accept that any large new agency will inevitably encounter teething trouble, but when my SOCA ID card arrived with someone else's picture on it

I should have taken it as an omen. Especially as the ugly mug staring back at me looked suspiciously like someone I'd arrested a few years back. And it wasn't just me. Altogether, two thousand SOCA officers ended up with the wrong face on their cards.

Besides that, we had the strangest badge I'd ever seen. It depicted an unidentified species of big cat (sabre-toothed tiger?) leaping over a stylized globe, in metallic grey and racing green. Its fangs were bared and its front claws were outstretched as if it was just about take down a mastodon. One of our younger officers said it bore a strong resemblance to the logo of the 1980s children's cartoon series *Thundercats*, which featured humanoid cats battling evil mutants in Earth's distant future.

I had no idea how much was spent on branding, but someone should have asked for a refund – the badge design was appalling. Criminals and Joe Public were never in doubt if we flashed a Customs badge at them. It's large, made of thick shiny metal and pretty elaborate. It looks 100 per cent genuine and screams 'The Law'. The SOCA badge looked like it belonged on a scout leader's woggle. Anecdotal reports started to some in from officers who said that criminals were resisting arrest because they didn't believe the badge was genuine. Imagine someone saying 'SOCA' and flashing a green tiger badge at you. I think that most people's first response would be 'Where's the candid camera?'

I was more troubled by the use of the word 'organized' in the title. I and every other officer of my rank knew that British crime had little or no organization. There were some loose groupings who shared a few connections, but that was as about as far as it went. I was also rather worried to learn that SOCA would be focusing almost exclusively on 'intelligence gathering'. This was fine so far as it went, but would we actually get to arrest any criminals?

The government said we would. SOCA's leadership repeated that we would work on better criminals for better pay with better equipment. We were told that £400 million would be spent on setting up a state-of-the-art agency with a staff of 4,200 selected from the best of the best that British law enforcement had to offer. All that was missing from the sales pitch was 'no expense spared'. But perhaps that was unnecessary: since inception, its annual spend has rocketed to £521 million (for the financial year 2008/9).

Things had gone downhill from Day One. For a start, although we were still in the old DST office, we had no idea whether we still had the right to use the equipment contained within it, or the cars in our garages as they belonged to Customs.

Essentially, the whole of SOCA had rolled in to work on 1 April 2006 with nothing to do. Until then, there had just been a small group of senior managers trying to get things set up – an impossible task. There was no infrastructure and to us it seemed as if there was no plan. Former coppers and Customs officers argued over who got which vehicles and chaos ensued as our cars were shuttled from Bristol to Ipswich to Glasgow to Manchester and all points between. It took months to sort out. We lost our black cab because one of the fleet managers, an ex-copper, couldn't get it into his head that it was one of the most useful vehicles we had.

My colleagues and I were then somewhat puzzled to discover that we'd been given a pay cut.

I was on £34,000 a year in Customs (£22,000 basic plus £12,000 allowance), plus overtime (of which there was quite a bit). In SOCA I was to be paid £30,000.

'Oh well,' I said to Jed, 'once we're on a mission and doing the overtime, it'll start racking up.'

'Too right.'

By the time we were called to our first briefing with Uncle Albert we were straining at the leash, not least because our bank balances were looking bulimically undernourished.

'This, gentlemen is a list of one hundred and thirty core nominals. The top criminals in the country, the targets that we need to focus on. Take a long look and get familiar with those names because you're going to be hearing them a lot from now on.'

We looked.

'This can't be right,' I said, 'I know nearly all these names and they're all has-beens.'

'Didn't you work on this case?' Jed asked another officer, pointing to a name.

'Yeah, the old git died of a heart attack a couple of years ago.'

'Good grief.'

The SOCA board comprises mostly ex-spooks who have never met a criminal (let alone know how to catch one) and ex-NCIS senior managers. Someone amongst this band of worthies had come up with a mission statement to target the country's top crims. The list had obviously been drafted by pulling names from the outdated NCIS database of core nominals, adding targets that the NCS were already working on and presenting it as current intelligence.

'Your target,' Uncle Albert continued, 'is the Ahmet family, based in north London. Big-time heroin importers.'

'I know them,' Jed said. 'They're a spent force now since that bit of argy-bargy with the Greeks a couple of years ago.'

'Oh yeah, isn't the father dead now?'

'It was all over the papers.'

The Ahmets were Turkish-Cypriots who'd been targets for about a decade. They'd all-but retired. I later discovered that they were on the list only on the say-so of a former cop who'd failed to nick them back in the nineties and was out for revenge. Hundreds of thousands spent on an old copper's grudge. Brilliant.

SOCA's oft-stated aim is to 'reduce harm'. 'Reduce harm to whom?' Jed said. 'The criminals?'

'Oh, just one other thing,' Uncle Albert said as we were on our way out, 'overtime is limited to four hours per week.'

The entire room stopped dead.

No overtime? You have to be able to work the hours the villains work in order to catch them. Very few work a forty-hour five-day week.

'OK,' Jed said as we headed back to our desks, 'let's break this down. We've got to hold a briefing before we go out so we all know what we're doing and who we're after, so that's forty-five minutes.'

'Yep,' I replied.

'Then we have to travel to the plot and back.'

'Average journey time, there and back, will be about two hours.'

'That leaves us with a total of three hours and forty-five minutes to follow the targets.'

'If the job's more than two hours from the office then there's no point in doing any surveillance at all.'

We took our calculations to Uncle Albert.

'Well, to save on overtime,' he said, 'instead of coming back to base, you can stay in a hotel.'

'But surely that's more expensive,' I said.

'That's the way we're going to do it.'

Management was happy to spend about £1,300 a night putting up a full team in a hotel rather than a few hundred on overtime and getting the officers home to see their families. Apparently they liked the fact that hotels gave receipts, while officers could only say how long they'd been working. SOCA didn't trust us.

In Customs we had a simple system for claiming expenses. It was all computerized and connected to the pay section. You merely filled in a form, sent it by email for approval and three days later the money was in your account. When you had to shell out hundreds of pounds a month on hotel bills, you wanted reimbursement before the credit card bill arrived. SOCA decided to use the police system. We had to photocopy every receipt, transfer the details onto a handwritten form and pass it to our line manager at the end of the month. He would then have to spend hours going through each one before posting them to the pay section. If you were lucky, you'd get your money in three to four weeks.

SOCA also demoted me by default. In Customs, I was a Band 6 officer. Band 6s ran operations, prepared cases for court, instructed barristers, ran surveillance teams and, allowing for experience, needed very little 'management' from above. My designated SOCA grade was G5. So what do you think a suitable equivalent in the police force might be? Detective inspector? Detective sergeant? No. Detective bloody constable, that's what. All DCs and all Band 6s were graded G5 at SOCA.

Band 6 had far more responsibility in Customs than any DC. We virtually ran our own ops; DCs didn't go to the toilet without permission. So many of us – Jed and I included, were now in a situation where we were mere cannon-fodder in a police organization.

Also, we soon learned that many of the policemen joining SOCA had been promoted in the run-up to their termination so that they could join the new organization at a higher pay grade. Such self-serving cynicism was pretty much unheard-of in Customs, who tended to play by the rules.

NCS also brought with them their corruption problem, which was transferred straight into SOCA, along with a healthy dose of institutional racism and sexism to boot. Ironically, soon more than half our unit's time was spent dealing not with organized villains but with corruption emanating from our own side of the fence. We were asked to take on so many surveillance jobs on bent ex-coppers-now-SOCAs that we weren't able to take on any more work.

Occasionally we found the time to do our proper job: keeping tabs on the semi-retired Ahmets. One day we were waiting and watching in a obs van just off the Seven Sisters Road near the Arsenal football stadium, waiting for a Colombian target to appear when a black Range Rover turned up and scored some gear from a scrote on the street. It was nothing to do with our job.

'Nice wheels to be scoring from the street,' I observed. 'Let's run it,' Jed said.

It was owned by the wife of a very well-known footballer.

'Is there no one in this country who's not dealing or scoring drugs?' I wondered aloud.

As it happened, this job didn't prove to be all bad, as some of the people the Ahmets associated with were at least moving some drugs; not massive amounts mind you, but they were class-A and so we switched our attention and had some fun in and around the Docklands area of east London and found a few new collars we could feel in the process. Problem was, the powers that be didn't like us using our initiative – they only wanted the bad guys locked up if they were on the list. The Turks we'd targeted were of no interest as SOCA had no intelligence on them.

'But how are we supposed to get intelligence in the first place?' Jed asked. It seemed like a sensible question. 'Stick to the list, and you won't have to,' said SOCA. Genius.

So we ignored them, just for long enough for us to discover where the handover would be.

It was due to be made in an underground car park attached to an exclusive block of flats in Docklands. There was a security guard on the door between the foyer and the car park. We reckoned that the security guards must be onside with the villains, so the problem for the ops team was to get an eyeball in the car park to witness and record the exchange so that the Ground Commander could call the knock at the right time. That way, there was no chance any of the villains could claim they were an innocent bystander.

In the end we decided to approach one of the tenants – a doctor. He agreed to drive an obs van into the underground car park with the Ground Commander in the passenger seat and one of our team hidden in the back.

They parked up and the doc and the pair sauntered over to the internal lift, allowing the Ground Commander to survey the area. The surveillance officer would be staying there for three days straight . . . I did not want to be the first person to open the van doors.

The Turks, by sheer coincidence, parked up slap bang behind the obs van on the night of the handover. Fortunately there were no innocents on the scene. Our man had a ringside seat and whispered a running commentary as the bags went into to the boot of the recipient vehicle.

The knock was called on the slipway of the car park, just as the dealers' car ascended the slope, heading towards the barrier. We'd called in armed police for this part as there was some evidence to suggest our targets might be tooled up. Subtle as ever, the boys in blue brought the car to a halt by throwing a sledgehammer through the windscreen; when the occupants declined to exit the vehicle in conventional fashion, they were dragged out through the hole the hammer had made. Our work was through. We melted away and went back to sitting on our numbed arses watching hairy old Turks play backgammon for hours at a time.

'Please God, tell me we aren't going to spend the rest of our careers doing this,' I moaned. As it happened, though, a bit of excitement was just round the corner. But it wasn't the kind I'd been hoping for.

# 25. What a Truck-Up

For many years Customs have run 'controlled deliveries'. Most of the substances smuggled into the UK such as drugs, cigarettes and alcohol are sent through in anything from a small postal packet containing heroin to a forty-foot shipping container packed to the roof with seven million cigarettes. Whether they were seized on the back of an intelligence report or on the hunch of a uniformed Customs officer, one thing was usually clear: we had the gear and the baddies didn't yet know we had it.

Let the fun begin.

We usually had a couple of days to get ourselves organized and take over the delivery run. If the suspicious parcel was fairly small and was being delivered to the buyer's door we'd hand it over to them or wait for them to come and pick it up from the post office. I'd done this before with a large woodcarving packed full of Bolivian's finest marching powder. Now who on earth orders a totem pole from Bolivia? You're just asking for someone to check it over.

Along with Mickey, I removed the head, placed light and movement alarms inside along with a little explosive surprise: gentian violet. This harmless chemical is very difficult to remove from the skin. When placed in a fairly airtight container such as a jar, once the lid pops it goes everywhere. We screwed and glued the head back on and carefully repacked it.

A few hours later, after an officer dressed as a postie had dropped it off, we had a bright purple drug dealer in custody. Every time he screamed denial we fell apart in hysterics, until he was forced to give up and join in. He stayed that colour for weeks. I could hardly give evidence for laughing when he appeared in court the next day.

If, on the other hand, we had a lorry load of gear to contend with, then we'd replace the driver with an under-cover Customs officer. I'd acquired an HGV1 licence precisely for this reason. I loved driving artics and playing undercover.

The drugs were almost always replaced with dummy packages. The only time we couldn't do this was when we intercepted a lorry load of six million fake cigarettes from China. The paperwork said the container was supposed to be full of beds from Italy, but when the local Avonmouth officers noticed two non-existent addresses on the manifest, it was obvious something funny was up.

Now fake fags are *really* lethal. The packaging is perfect; you wouldn't know a proper one from a snide one until you lit up. Then, when you're doubled over puking your guts up, you'd think it was time to quit. There's no tobacco in them, just sawdust and tiny shaved pieces of orange plastic, all bound together with a lovely carcinogenic paste. Smok-ing does kill, especially when bought for £20 a sleeve in your local boozer.

I replaced the driver and took over the delivery of the fags. The team pounced in a lorry-park, nicking the buyer – a sixteen-stone skinhead fascist with a penchant for extreme violence.

Stopping cheap fags getting to the street is arguably not

as important as stopping heroin or coke entering the country but, as we always said, it's not the commodity that matters, it's the quality of the villain. Some of the most dangerous and nastiest villains I have ever put away have been convicted of relatively minor offences. Nevertheless, these 'second-prize' convictions were worthwhile if it meant getting them off the streets, even if only for forty-two months.

Thousands of containers enter the UK every day. The majority are transferred between known and respectable companies who make hundreds of such shipments every year. The rest are sent by companies or individuals who have rarely or never transported goods this way before.

How is it possible to pick out containers filled with contraband with no prior intelligence? Ask the boys and girls of the EPU. Entry Processing Units are located at all of the UK's major ports, both air and sea. The EPUs' main job is to ensure that billions of pounds' worth of legitimate goods enter the UK quickly and on time – and, of course, to weed out the rest.

The uniformed staff at Plymouth were the best I worked with. They knew every scam, excuse and concealment point in every vehicle and vessel. If they were onto you, you might as well put your hands up and ask to be taken straight to chokey. They had given us plenty of jobs over the years and had helped lock up more boat smugglers than any other port.

EPUs keep an eye out for consignments that don't quite fit the profile. Maybe the delivery address looks dodgy. Maybe the description of the goods doesn't sound quite right. If the officer is at all suspicious, then he or she will carry out a few background checks and if they are still not satisfied, they will get the container examined.

When an officer in Avonmouth examined the paperwork for a container from Pakistan, she was immediately alerted to the fact that the names and addresses, apart from the delivery address, were extremely vague, and just referred to a surname or town. On further delving the officer found that there had been two previous deliveries with similar consignee/consignor addresses, so she had the container pulled.

It was packed with boxes of shoes. Thousands of them, all identical. They couldn't open every box, it would take days and there simply wasn't time.

If you want to send some gear to the UK you want it to be as anonymous as possible. The solution is to hide it amongst thousands of other identically packaged genuine articles. At Portbury Docks across the river from Avonmouth, the officers knew from Intel they'd received that heroin was (and still is) being smuggled into the UK amongst the hundreds of thousands of new cars that are imported every year. But how on earth are you supposed to pick the dirty car when there are two thousand cars on every ship? The villains put a tiny sticker in the windscreen of the car that has the gear in, so that the guy unloading them, who knows what to look for, can grab the stash from wherever it's been hidden in the car and walk out of the docks with it once his shift finishes.

So this is what the Customs lads were looking for, something on the 'dirty' boxes that marked them as different. In this case – and I'm not kidding here – they found thirteen boxes with a red 'H' marked on one end.

In total, there was about 25 kg. And there had been two previous trips, so these guys could already have grossed upwards of £650,000 (the price of heroin is £13 to 16,000 per kilo). Time for a 'controlled delivery'.

I stepped forward into the breach and volunteered to deliver the goods. The briefing in Felixstowe was a bit of a monster. With the operational team, my surveillance team, the uniformed staff and dog handlers, there were about forty of us. The briefing was conducted by the operational case officer Carl, an old drinking buddy of mine from Alpha.

The objectives were pretty clear. The DST would follow me in my Volvo F12 tractor unit pulling a green container to the delivery address. At that point SOCA's operational team would take control of the job, until they either called the knock or locked our surveillance team on to an additional target, i.e., the vehicle that the baddies handed the gear over to after splitting it from the main load. This depended on whether they decided to test the gear or not – we'd dummied it up with our very own special heroin imitation, and movement sensors had also been placed in three of the boxes.

At the end of the briefing I gave a mini-brief about what should happen as far as I was concerned. I stood up in the gear I would be wearing the next day. Blue trucker's trousers, black steel toe-capped boots and a bright fluorescent jacket. I pointed out my own features and description and told them a couple of things they HAD TO DO.

One was that if the knock was called at the delivery address, with me anywhere near, I HAD to be arrested, cautioned, cuffed and put in the back of a car. This was imperative so that the villains would see me as a suspect.

If they saw me having a quiet chat with the boys then they would realize I was in on the arrest – there was always the danger that they'd think I was some kind of informer and they'd memorize my face and have me killed. Heroin smugglers facing a life sentence won't think twice about bumping off grasses. If they clicked to the fact I was an undercover officer, they'd circulate my description, making any future undercover work that much more risky for me.

I also pointed out that I would be in constant contact with my handler, passing whatever Intel I could about what was happening because it was likely I would have a better view than any observation point that the operational team could put in.

The last thing was that under no circumstances was the knock to be called without letting me know first. Not that I had any control over when and where but I needed time to react properly.

My artic was fitted with a tracker and the planned route – to a unit in Ferry Lane just off the A13 – was made known to one and all.

On the day, as I came down the A13 slip road I turned on the digital Dictaphone inside my jacket, its microphone covertly secured in the lapel of my jacket. It would record everything within a few feet for about six hours.

As I turned into the industrial area where the unit was located I understood why the operational team hadn't done a recce. It looked like a proper little den of iniquity. A large container depot was surrounded by scrap yards, small haulage firms, an exceedingly unhygienic-looking greasy spoon, a scruffy second-hand van dealership. From where I was sitting, everyone and everything appeared dodgy.

It was really busy and I didn't stand out at all. There were artics delivering and picking up containers constantly. I had no contact number for the baddies so I drove round the grubby little circular road that ringed the estate, looking for heroin smugglers. I kid you not.

I guessed I'd be looking for two guys of Asian appearance sitting in a car, hoping they could get the driver to go and deliver somewhere else. I completed the circle and saw nothing whatsoever.

I thought I might be in for a long wait. If I had 25 kg of smack to pick up I wouldn't make a move until I was damn sure there was no surveillance about. All call signs had been warned off the plot until I had spoken to my handler to confirm that contact had been made.

I knew that at some point the baddies would approach me. They wanted their gear and they would know that at some point a legit driver would return the box to the port of entry, incurring more haulage and storage fees. I pulled up outside the greasy spoon, pulled out my trucker's hot-for-ever mug, filled it with tea and ordered a bacon banjo with extra salmonella before sitting in the cab reading the *Sun*. I sent a text to the handler every twenty minutes or so to let him know everything was cool.

After forty minutes I drove the truck round and went through the main gates of the container depot. A huge yard was surrounded on three sides by stacks of empty containers fanning out into massive avenues of the things, which were piled three high.

I waited for another half an hour but nobody approached me, not even the depot staff. I drove out and back round to another spot and finished my tea.

I spoke to Jed, who detailed his navigator's shortcomings. Using the crappy new clumsy maps method beloved of SOCA, she'd somehow managed to send Jed the wrong way up the A12. From his colourful description of her talents, I guessed she wasn't sitting in the car next to him.

Another hour came and went. I decided to drive back into the depot. Just a hunch. As I did so I clocked a VW Golf parked just outside the entrance: two-up, both IC4.

I called my handler. He asked the small obs van, a battered old VW Caddy, to drive past and get the twist. I was certain they were there for the pick-up. They were probably waiting until the gear was unloaded by their contact in the yard before collecting it.

As I drove through the yard a fiftyish Asian man waved at me from a block of containers. I wound down the window.

'This load of shoes yours, mate?' I asked.

'Yes, yes, we will unload them into this one here,' he replied gesturing towards one of the containers.

I manoeuvred the wagon as close as I could to the containers. This done, I jumped down from the cab and broke the seal on the doors, making sure the guy saw me do it, giving him a bit more confidence that it hadn't been tampered with.

The guy then called over three or four blokes who looked to me like they worked for the container depot. *This could get really interesting*, I thought. They definitely didn't look in the know.

While the guy was talking to the three labourers I jumped back in the cab and called my handler.

'Right, you've got an IC4 male, traditional grey Muslim

galabaya, black shoes. He's offering the unloading work to three IC3s from the depot. I don't know if you can get an OP, but with the two in the Golf still hanging about I would rely on my word to give you the necessary info, OK?

'OK.'

It all seemed to be going to plan. But why wasn't I completely convinced? Something felt wrong, but I didn't know what.

The unloading began. I got out of the cab every now and again to have a mooch round, then got back in and relayed how far they had got towards the dirty boxes and what they were doing with the load.

I rang Carl to suggest they were getting near the gear. 'Yeah, I know,' he replied. 'We can just about see how much they've got out.' I looked around but I couldn't see where they had an OP; it must have been some way away. Still, they seemed to be in control.

I got back in the cab and rang Jed. I wasn't supposed to call anyone else but something felt wrong and I didn't trust Carl's judgement or his authority, especially in relation to my safety. Jed confirmed my fears.

'It's turning into a clusterfuck of the highest order,' he growled. 'They've got this brand new SOCA woman from NCS who's promoted out of her depth running things. For all I know, this could be her first op. Fuck knows where Carl's gone to. She's been flapping ever since they started unloading the box, I get the feeling she really wants to knock it early.'

'Thanks, mate,' I said and hung up. *Oh, what joy*, I thought. At that moment a guy I had not seen before appeared at the driver's door. I jumped down.

'Hi, I'm the depot manager,' he said. 'Would you mind moving the wagon slightly? Only it's blocking the way into one of the rows of containers.'

'No problem.'

I told the baddie that I had to move and jumped back in the cab. I drove the truck forward and swung it round in a big circle, intending to put it back closer to the containers. As I pulled round I was met with the screeching arrival of about eight cars.

'What the FUCK!' I yelled.

I stopped the truck and watched as SOCA officers piled out and nicked the four blokes who were stood waiting to recommence unloading. They were laid out flat and cuffed.

No one was paying any attention to me.

I called Carl. 'Carl, what the fuck's going on, why am I not being nicked?'

'I don't know, Cam, I don't know what happened.'

'Get someone to come and nick me asap before the targets start wondering why the driver of a truck with half a million quid's worth of heroin in the back has been allowed to sit in his cab and ring his mates.'

I looked out of the cab window. One of the baddies was looking at me, dead in the eye. He nodded and smiled. It wasn't a friendly smile.

Fuck. This was not good.

No one came to nick me and I sat there like a lemon.

Eventually, a bright voice said, 'Hello.' It was Sarah, the assistant case officer whom Jed was ranting about. I'm certain she wasn't expecting what came next. I exploded with all the force of an H-bomb.

'What the FUCK is going on? Did you attend the fucking briefing yesterday? Did you hear me say that I had to be nicked like everyone else? Did you fucking understand the bit about letting me know when the knock was going down?'

As I drew breath, Sara meekly said, 'We thought the truck was being driven off by the suspects.'

'Are you fucking kidding me? How could you think that? And if you did, what the fuck did you think had happened to *me*? Do you know what they would have to do to me in order for them to get my keys, jump in the FUCKING cab and drive off?'

'We had a call from the OP saying that an IC4 male had got in the cab and was driving the cab away from the container.'

By now everyone was looking my way.

'Did any of you CUNTS recognize me or my attire at the fucking briefing?'

No answer.

'Do I look like an IC4?'

No answer.

'Who called the knock?'

'Um, I did,' Sarah said.

'Well you better fucking stand by because I am not a happy bunny. They hadn't even finished unloading the dirty boxes. Why the FUCK weren't you monitoring the fucking movement alarms?'

With hindsight I probably overreacted just a tad. I should probably have calmed down a bit and put it nicely in an email. Tough shit. She wouldn't make the same mistake again and I would have hated making it official.

I stomped off and found Jed. 'I tried to phone when she

called it,' he said. 'Sorry, mate. Their OP was miles away; your yellow coat probably made your skin look dark.'

A thought suddenly crossed my mind. 'Oh, crap.'

'What now?' Jed asked.

'The Dict—' I stopped speaking and pulled out the Dictaphone and switched it off. It had recorded everything and it would be admitted in evidence. Whoops.

I found Carl and explained that the recording of the day's events contained a Tarantino-worthy burst of swearing. 'It's all admissible, isn't it?' I asked, hoping it wasn't. I tried to repress the horrible visions I had of me standing in a courtroom, red-faced, as the judge listened to the tape.

'Don't worry,' he said, 'I'll make sure it's PII'd.' Public Interest Immunity is where evidence is withheld because it's damaging to the public interest – in this case we could argue that it would help further reveal the identity of the undercover officer (me), and we couldn't therefore use it as supportive evidence.

I'd expected the guys in the Golf to play a part in the proceedings and they did. As soon as the knock went down they took off like scalded cats towards the A13 only to be stopped by the case team. Telephone billing had them in contact all day with the IC4 who'd arranged the unloading. They'd been waiting for the container to be unloaded before going in to collect their gear.

At the trial all three claimed not to know what was in the boxes marked 'H'. Luckily for us, the few dirty boxes we'd given them time to unload had been set aside in a separate pile. If this hadn't been the case, then there was no way we would have been able to show that they knew there was anything 'special' about them.

I gave evidence from behind a screen and was smuggled in and out of the court under a blanket like a criminal. The jury returned a unanimous guilty verdict in just a couple of hours. The judge gave them eighteen, fourteen and twelve. Nice one, Your Honour.

And my recording didn't get played. But these were troubled times. In my fifteen years in Customs this was the first major fuck-up I'd been a party to. Sadly, it wouldn't be the last.

# 26. Smoke and Mirrors

My eyes snapped open. I sat up. My heart was pounding, I was covered in sweat. Was I having a heart attack? I got up, got a drink of water and paced the flat for a bit before things started to settle. What the hell was that?

I arrived at work shattered beyond belief. The following night the same thing happened. And the next. And the next. On it went, I woke up several times a night in a state of panic and was a zombie at work. What the hell was going on?

A visit to the doctors proved to be a real eye-opener.

'How are you feeling?'

'All right, apart from the panic attacks.'

'How many hours do you sleep each night?'

'About four or five since the panic attacks.'

'What do you do for a living?'

'I work in law enforcement.'

'When was your last holiday?'

I thought for a moment. Not counting Christmas and the odd weekend with the kids in the school holidays, I couldn't remember. I shrugged.

'How satisfying is your job?'

I almost giggled. 'On a scale of one to ten? About minus four.'

'Married?'

'Just divorced.'

'Children?'

'Two boys, one's just been expelled, they're living with their mum near Bristol.'

'Drink much?'

'Yep.'

After a few more questions and a few physical tests the doctor concluded that I was suffering from reactive depression and I was so stressed I was on the verge of imminent collapse.

'You need a holiday. Go and lie on a beach, lay off the booze for a few weeks, then you'll be fine. Ask work for some time off.'

I'd been in law enforcement for twenty-five years and had never had so much as a day off due to illness and had always ripped into anyone else that had taken time off but suddenly here I was, clinically depressed. *And it's not even a 'proper' illness*, I thought mistakenly.

I would have loved a holiday. But we had a job on.


'You've got to be kidding me, we're briefing here?' We were standing in a freezing car park. The team leader, bigoted idiot that he was, proceeded to breach SOCA's own regulations and endanger all our lives by debriefing us in public because he didn't want to spend £100 on a Holiday Inn conference room. More money saved. Added to that was the fact he peppered his speech with racist jokes and used the word 'cunt' so many times that I wanted to give him five Glasgow kisses for every time he'd said it.

Where the hell was this half-a-billion-pound budget being spent?

We were supposed to be working on capturing some of the most dangerous villains in the country red-handed. If you're looking at being arrested for coke or heroin smuggling, something that is punishable by a life sentence, then killing someone in an attempt to escape won't get you any more jail time.

It is therefore imperative that officers going out to work on these types of case be properly protected. Cost restrictions meant that we often met crammed into a hotel bedroom, twelve or more in a double. And that was on a good day: other times we were in corridors, car parks, lay-bys or various corners of pubs, bars and motorway service areas.

Partly thanks to these godawful locations, briefings and debriefings in SOCA were generally conducted as quickly as possible. If management doesn't give a full briefing detailing current intelligence, where the nearest hospital is located, whether the targets are surveillance conscious, etc., it is obvious that the safety of the officers in the firing line is going to be compromised. As for debriefings, well, in SOCA they consisted of the log being read out and passed round to sign. The day's successes and failures were not addressed; fresh intelligence was not discussed and evaluated by the team. This had a detrimental effect on the next day's surveillance.

Both briefings and debriefings were conducted in wholesale contravention of SOCA's own regulations. Management was advised time and again that someone would end up being killed or seriously injured due to the way surveillance was being conducted. The only answer ever given was that it wasted valuable time and money in a situation where there was no scope to pay overtime.

To make matters worse, our target for this operation was a real old duffer, someone who'd been of major interest in the 1980s but had been out of the game for a long, long time. Another old copper's grudge. He was sixty-two and had retired to Devon. He still did the occasional small deal and was connected to people abroad who were moving some gear, but we wouldn't have got out of bed for him in Customs.

We'd been following him all over the south-west of England but it hadn't been easy. In Customs our surveillance system had evolved over a period of about ten years: a computer laptop in each car, with ordnance survey quality mapping down to street level, showing the position of each car in the surveillance team. It was brilliant. You didn't need to be a good map-reader, it told you where you were in relation to every other car out that day. It allowed you to predict where the target was going by using the map and listening to the calls over the air and to follow the target without putting yourself in a line behind the five-five car.

In addition we had our military-style of brevity codes and the junction-spot system. Instead of spending precious seconds on the radio telling the team the target's red Datsun Sunny was heading down Douglas Bader Avenue towards the junction with the B4097 you could just say 'X-ray 15 is nine-one red 63'.

So what did SOCA do? They got rid of the laptops and made us use the police system of having a huge Philips Road Atlas that covered the whole of the UK. Perfect if you're a double-glazing salesman on the road from dawn till dusk, but for our purposes completely useless: it didn't even have six-figure grid references. We chucked them away and used red book county street maps instead.

We were also instructed to use the clunky police 'glossary' system of radio language, which was uncoded. Our black cabs were ditched and we were ordered to follow the crooks in a long line rather than using our more complex looping system. Once again it was a question of expense, they said, in terms of training former police officers.

Again I ask, what were they spending that £500 million on?

I was with Jed and Fin when we decided to lump Mr Pensioner-Big's Bentley. At least then we wouldn't have to take the long-line-of-vehicles approach when we followed him.

He lived in a mansion that was overlooked by his neighbours. He also had guard dogs and what looked like a decent alarm system, so we knew to be careful. In preparation, we'd gone to a Bentley dealership and got them to raise a similar model on a hydraulic lift so we could have a good look underneath and decide exactly whereabouts we could site the tracker.

On the night, at 3 a.m., Fin dropped me off just down the road from the target. He would wait a couple of streets away while Jed would hover in a getaway car in case I needed to make a sharp exit.

I strolled down the street, drinking a can of Red Bull and smoking a fag, as if I were just returning from a night out. As I neared Mr Big's driveway I heard a car coming from behind. We were in a cul-de-sac. It could only be a cop car. I acted as if I lived there and kept walking past Mr Big's place, pretending I lived in one of the other houses. The car stopped. Window went down. 'Everything OK?' a woman's voice said. I turned and walked over to the car. 'Do you need a lift home?'

What the hell was she doing offering me a lift after I'd walked up a bloody cul-de-sac? I quickly reached into my jacket, pulled out my badge and held it discreetly in front of me. 'No thanks, I'm a little bit busy right now, OK?' To my relief, she mouthed 'Sorry' and quietly drove away. The street was dark. No house lights on. I turned back and walked slowly down the gravel drive.

There was the Bentley. I crouched down. No sign of any movement, great. I extracted the tracking device from my jacket and slowly eased my way under the car.

The hallway light came on.

Oh bugger.

The door opened, I turned my head towards it and saw a pair of suede slippers marching towards me. This was followed by a sharp whistle.

Fuck!

I wiggled out from under the car and there was Mr Big, bleary eyed, hair ruffled, in his dressing gown. 'OI!' he yelled. I looked past him and saw two Dobermanns run out of the house.

I legged it out of the drive so fast I would have passed Usain Bolt. 'Jed!' I yelled in my mic. 'Time to go!' He pulled up with a skid outside the gate, rear door open, I dived in and we screeched away. The Dobermanns chased us for about half a mile.

'Bastard must have a movement alarm!' I yelled.

Luckily for us, Mr Big thought we were trying to steal his precious Bentley and so we decided to have another crack at him, except this time we called in the experts: the covert means of entry team. They found a way in without too much trouble (even the Dobermanns in the back garden didn't spot them) while he was away golfing and stuck the listening device in the back of his sofa.

It worked beautifully. Practically the first conversation we got was a call between him and a golfing buddy:

Mr B: Some li'l fucker tried ta steal me Bentley las' week.
UKM: Sure it wasn't the pigs? They could be trying to bug your car.
Mr B: Nah, they ain't interested in me no more.

Mr Big continued to reject his wise friend's suggestions and we started to get some decent Intel. Things were looking up at last until the day a van came round to Mr Big's house and removed the sofa. It was brand new and he'd returned it to DFS. 'There's somefink wrong wiv the upholstery,' he said.

The DFS staff repaired the sofa and found a great big brick with a bloody great antennae stashed inside. So what did they do?

They told the target.

Killed the operation stone dead.

Not long after this, Fin applied for a posting in Africa as a SOCA liaison officer, hoping for more interesting and challenging work. This involved a very long, very involved selection process that dragged on for months.

Obviously, representing British law enforcement in Africa was a tricky job and involved working with military regimes, so a lot of role-playing was done to see how good applicants' diplomatic skills were. In one such exercise Fin was asked to placate an African general who'd stormed into his office demanding to know what had gone wrong with an operation to arrest a gang of drug dealers. Fin was supposed to calm him down without revealing the details of the operation. There was a fine balance to be struck between information sharing and cooperation, and this required an awful lot of political nous.

One of SOCA's central tenets is that it 'fully embraces the principles of diversity'. Why, then, did they feel the need to hire a white actor to play the African general in a role-playing session? That in itself might not have been not too bad had he not arrived 'blacked up'.

The team stood with open mouths as the 'African' ranted at them in a dodgy Jamaican accent before several of them complained. A slap on their blacked-up wrists was all the perpetrators received.

The reason for their light punishment became clear to me when I was called into a line manager's office to discuss a case. He kept racist and sexist memorabilia on his desk and openly made offensive 'jokes' during the meeting and made similar comments to members of his immediate team.

Besides this line manager, an acting team leader made no attempt to hide his contempt for people of Asian descent who were on our squad. Encouraged by him, one particularly revolting individual would hiss 'Get back to the jungle' whenever someone who wasn't white walked by.

One morning as I waited for a training session for under-cover officers I heard a conversation that totally stunned me.

'Can't fucking stand Pakis,' he said.

'Bet one of them's had your wife. What're you gonna do when a black baby pops out?'

'Fuck off, don't make me sick.'

'Bet your gynaecologist is Asian, they all are these days. Bet he's the dad, too.'

'Those heroin heads are all Paki cunts.'

'Now, now,' said the senior manager, 'watch your language, there's a lady present.'

Afterwards, I bolted from the room into the corridor with relief only to hear, hissed in a nasal voice: 'Get back to the jungle.' I turned, dumbfounded. The revolting individual, an officer of my rank and his boss were standing by a coffee machine. An officer of Asian descent had just strolled past them. They saw me looking and grinned as if to say, 'Gotta show 'em who's boss, eh, mate?'

It was just like . . . No, it was actually worse than listening to the criminals back in Alpha. Except none of the criminals ever seemed that bothered about skin colour – in fact they were happy to embrace diversity if it helped them with the task in hand.

About 99 per cent of our officers were white males. We had no one, absolutely no one, who could safely pass for an undercover officer in certain parts of the country. For example Birmingham has a huge Asian population, but a colleague of mine who was based there told me bitterly that their surveillance team contained not a single officer from an Asian background. As far as I was concerned, SOCA was full of racists trying to do nothing all day. My anxiety grew. So did my panic attacks. And still I didn't think about taking some time off. I had work to do.

As time went on, it became very clear to me that SOCA was failing in the battle to bring drug dealers to justice.

Alpha used to run nine major class-A ops in London at once, seizing an average of 40kg of class-A drugs each week. In 2006, SOCA ran one. Yet the headline from SOCA's first annual report read: 74 TONNES OF CLASS-A DRUGS SEIZED, A RECORD. Hoorah.

Bollocks, was it.

Everything about SOCA was a smokescreen, devised to fool the public that this new system was working. It wasn't.

In all areas of law enforcement, departments have always played the game of claiming seizures and arrests for other teams' achievements. A classic example came from the 'rummage team' at Avonmouth (uniformed Customs officers trained to 'rummage' or search vessels). They were once approached by the Manchester Target Drugs team and asked to keep obs for twenty-four hours on a Colombian freighter carrying wood while they sorted out a diver to check the hull.

Sure enough, the diver found a torpedo welded to the hull near the sea locker containing 200kg of coke. The seizure came after months of covert Alpha-led surveillance, probably thousands of man-hours. Avonmouth put those figures on their monthly returns, for only one day's worth of effort.

SOCA is playing the same game but on an international scale. SOCA liaison officers are based in many source and transit countries including half of South America, Asia, Africa and the Far East. They play a small part in many operations, mostly as a conduit for intelligence between the host country and the UK. For instance, a liaison officer might be involved – in a very small way – in a seizure of a tonne of coke by the Royal Navy in the Caribbean. Perhaps a few documents will pass across their desk and a couple of encrypted emails sent to apprise SOCA of the situation. SOCA will include the tonne as a seizure in its annual report.

The extent of involvement may be even more peripheral:

Dutch police: 'There's a boat coming into Southampton, can you please leave it alone as we'll be seizing it in Holland?'

SOCA: 'No problem.'

When the Dutch seize the boat and collect another tonne of coke, SOCA adds it to their total. Nice work, fellas!

Occasionally, there appears to be no involvement at all. In one of the seizures, a joint naval task force stopped a ship off the Cape Verde Islands in November 2006 and found 1.8 tonnes of cocaine. The Royal Navy was working with Spanish law enforcement authorities and both the drugs and those arrested were taken to Spain. The 1.8 tonnes was, of course, added to SOCA's total.

SOCA employs maybe 140 investigators worldwide, and even if they were *solely* responsible for the 72.45 tonnes quoted as being seized outside the UK (a fifth of Europe's cocaine supply), what the hell were the other 4,000 SOCA staff doing all year? Strolling up and down corridors, trying to look busy, that's what. SOCA recruited 2,500 investigators from NCS and Customs. Within six months they found that they had 400 more than they needed.

In the past there were strict rules about claiming non-UK seizures. A set of protocols was drawn up between the Concerted Inter-Agency Drugs Action Group and the National Audit Office. This meant that unless a UK agency was entirely responsible for a non-UK seizure then only a percentage could be claimed. There also had to be overwhelming evidence that the cocaine was destined for the UK. But SOCA won't follow these protocols. 'We are a new and different organization and our reporting is, in consequence, different, too,' a spokesperson said. Well, that's all right, then; why didn't you say so?

Part of the reason SOCA had too many staff doing nothing was because they weren't taking on the local drugs work. Our bread-and-butter jobs in Customs used to come from the eagle-eyed officers working at the UK's entry points. As soon as they nabbed a drugs courier they'd turn them into an informant.

Because couriers are paid a pittance for running massive risks they were usually pretty grateful for any opportunity to reduce their sentence. The port staff would then call a Customs investigation team and we'd zip down as fast as we could. Meanwhile the port team would swap the drugs for a carefully disguised replacement. The guys who did this were amazing, real artists, and made sure the fake looked like the real deal, right down to the type and colour of cellophane or the stamp of identification dealers sometimes used. We'd then help the courier complete their delivery and hopefully nab and gather intelligence on whoever was on the receiving end.

When the guys at the port called SOCA, the reply was, 'What do you want us to do? You're in Dover, we're in London,' or the old chestnut, 'They're not on our list.' In the first year of SOCA's existence, there were over 140 referrals of this sort. Out of all those referrals only three were taken on. All the remaining couriers were simply prosecuted and the men and women further up the chain didn't

have to worry about being caught at the handover by Thundercats. SOCA has left a huge gap in drugs law enforcement.

Read in isolation, the SOCA reports for 2007–2009 suggest
immense success. Take these reports apart and it seems to
me that the agency is spinning its success. Unfortunately, Joe
Public can't interrogate the figures because SOCA is exempt
from the Freedom of Information Act – and it doesn't have
anyone to audit them. The question remains that even if there
was, then how would they measure their success?

SOCA's stated aims are to 'gain knowledge' and 'reduce
harm', not 'seize drugs' and 'reduce crime'. These are objectives written by smart senior managers who have seen the
problems created by setting your sights too high, or in this
instance, at all.

In total, SOCA's aims are:

- to build knowledge and understanding of serious organized
  crime, the harm it causes, and of the effectiveness in tackling it;
- to increase the amount of criminal assets recovered and
  increase the proportion of cases in which the proceeds of
  crime are pursued;
- to increase the risk to serious organized criminals operating
  against the UK, through traditional means and by innovation
  within the law;
- to collaborate with partners, join up domestic and international efforts to reduce harm and provide high-quality support
  to partners; and as appropriate seek theirs in return; and
- to build capacity and capability to make a difference.

Senior management have already admitted that with
the exception of criminal assets recovered, these aims

(knowledge building, collaboration, innovation, making a difference) cannot be measured.

There is a smug attitude (quoted directly to me by colleagues of various ranks) along the lines of 'What we do is better than working for a living; who else would pay us £35k a year basic for doing fuck all?' One head of intelligence, who'd come to SOCA from NCS, had the gall during one of his introductory speeches, and only half-jokingly, to say: '. . . and they're paying me a hundred grand a year for this!'

Many board members are retired senior policemen who collect a police pension and retirement bonus on top of a SOCA salary. This example set by the men at the top was keenly followed.

For example, fifty-five-year-old Bob Lauder quit his £60,000-a-year post as deputy director of the Scottish Drugs Enforcement Agency on a Friday and started work as assistant director of the Serious Organised Crime Agency in Scotland on the following Monday. He didn't have far to move, either – his new office was just a few yards away from his old one.

He was entitled to his £30,000-a-year police pension, a lump sum of £120,000 (nothing wrong with that, of course, he'd served thirty-six years in the force). But then he was hired by SOCA for an additional £50,000 a year. (I'm not suggesting that Bob Lauder isn't worth every penny of his salary, I'm sure he is.) His new job will also entitle him to a second pension when he retires. In addition to a chairman, director-general and ten-member board of directors, there are thirty deputy directors. Yes, that's right, thirty.

SOCA has stated that it will actively continue to recruit

into managerial grades recently retired police detectives who are in receipt of their 75-per-cent-of-pay pension after thirty years' service. It says this is the cheapest option because these candidates require no expensive training. So at the top of the organization, we have a growing collection of Uncle Alberts reminiscing about the good old days while experienced operatives sit on their fattening backsides every day bored out of their minds. These Uncle Alberts should be pottering about in the garden enjoying their retirement while keen-as-mustard younger men and women battle their way into the boardroom. And people wonder why SOCA hasn't got the results the government hoped for.

SOCA has recently claimed that the prices of drugs have risen to record levels, citing this as evidence of outstanding success: a higher price means that less drugs must be getting through. Two years ago, the highest-quality cocaine cost £35,000 per kilo. But in the first few months of 2009 the price, according to SOCA, hit a record level; more than £45,000 per kilo.

Impressive? Not at all. What SOCA conveniently overlooked was that the wholesale cocaine market is based on the value of the US dollar. In May 2007, the US dollar traded at 0.505 to the pound, so that £35,000 was worth $69,300. At the time of writing, the dollar is trading at 0.656, so £45,000 is now worth $68,600 – a slight *decrease* in price.

SOCA is doing so badly that what's left of Customs and the police are setting up their own regional units to replace the regional and national squads that were disbanded at the formation of SOCA. Customs are setting up drugs teams to do the work that SOCA isn't taking on, in an attempt to stem the flow.

Do I sound bitter? I hope so, because I bloody well am. SOCA ripped the heart out of my job and investigation teams in general.

A central tenet of my working life has been that public service, whether to country or community, is a noble and honourable aspiration. I have a strong work ethic: if you work hard, you will be rewarded. Over the past twenty years that has proven to be a very naive view. During my time at SOCA I've seen greedy, self-serving, ill-educated, racist and inept individuals promoted into positions of authority they had no business holding. Of course, this doesn't apply to every SOCA employee, and I realize that all organizations have their share of bad apples, but there are simply too many people in SOCA who are quite happy to turn up for work and take home a very good salary, without giving a second thought to whether they are part of the problem or the solution.

I should have spoken out earlier, but the people I would have been lambasting were my direct line management. If I'd complained, I would either have been moved off the team, which I definitely did not want to happen, or I would have been going out on the ground expecting these same people to watch my back. So I kept quiet.

I shouldn't have waited.

# 27. Shadowing a Serial Killer

On the unseasonably sunny morning of 2 December 2006, water bailiff Trevor Saunders made his way down Thorpe's Hill to Belstead Brook. After a week of very heavy rain the waterways in and around Ipswich's River Orwell had become swollen and were full of debris. There was a danger of flooding.

As he made his way along the brook, working clumps of branches free from its narrow twists and turns, he noticed a bend in the stream that appeared to be especially clogged. When he reached the turning he spotted the lower end of a mannequin's dummy caught up amongst other debris, its legs poking out of the water towards him.

He reached over and brushed away some of the dirt covering the legs and grabbed hold to try and pull it out. It was then that he realized he'd found a corpse. The woman, who was naked, was lying face down with her arms above her and bent at the elbows. Her head was turned to the side, her eyes half open. She was wearing earrings.

The body was identified as Gemma Adams, twenty-five years old, a local prostitute who'd been missing for about two weeks. The cold water had slowed decomposition.

Gemma had worked at a local massage parlour before plying for trade on the streets. She had an expensive crack and smack habit to support.

'Heroin was her undoing,' her father told reporters. 'It

is just the most awful waste of a young woman's life and it has destroyed our family. We are praying that the madman who did this is caught soon.'

She wasn't the only prostitute who'd been reported missing. On 30 October nineteen-year-old Tania Nicol left the home she shared with her mother and her fifteen-year-old brother and caught the bus to work in the red-light area of Ipswich. She was still very young but the physical signs of her heroin addiction were starting to show: Tania was losing weight and her face was covered in acne.

Known as 'Chantelle' on the street, she'd managed to keep both her addiction and her occupation secret from her mother. She was last seen on CCTV at 11 p.m. on foot, in cut-off jeans and pink stilettos, walking past the Sainsbury's petrol station on London Road.

On 8 December 2009, police divers who were working their way up Belstead Brook found Tania's body. By then a third girl was missing: Anneli Alderton, aka 'Crackhead Annie', twenty-four. She also lived with her mother and also had a drug addiction. She was also three months pregnant. Her naked body was found just ten metres from the side of a busy road and just thirty metres from a school. Anneli had been laid out in the shape of a crucifix, her long blonde hair pulled straight behind her.

Her grandmother told the press, which by now had descended upon Ipswich: 'She was not the little girl I knew. She was a perfectly nice little girl and had a happy upbringing. I was gobsmacked to hear my granddaughter was dead, but she had died years before.' She was, of course, referring to Anneli's addiction to crack cocaine.

\*

I was preparing for Christmas when I got the call. Thanks to the severe limit on overtime I was cash-poor but time-rich. I had started a new relationship with a woman called Vicky, and as long as things stayed this quiet then it looked as if I might manage to hold on to this one.

I'd even made big strides forward with my sons. Ben had come to live with me as he was proving to be quite a handful for his mother, but he'd started to settle down and was making a real effort at school. My panic attacks had eased and for once I was actually looking forward to Christmas.

Vicky and I had decided we'd have a stress-free lunch, M&S turkey and vegetables, posh nibbles, treats and pudding, etc. I'd just booked and paid for the above when Uncle Albert called. 'Get yourself down to Ipswich; hotel details to follow.'

The story was all over the news so it could mean only one thing, the Dedicated Surveillance Team were about to shadow a serial killer.

I reasoned that the cops must have a suspect but not enough evidence, so no arrest could be made. We'd be expected to shadow the prime suspect without his knowing to make sure he didn't top anyone else before the murder squad had amassed enough evidence.

As soon as I hung up, Vicky's face fell. 'I should start making other plans, shouldn't I?' she said.

It was odd – for the first time in a long time I was hacked off about being called away on a secret mission. I'd been looking forward to Christmas. *Blimey, it must be love*, I thought.

But then the adrenaline kicked in, the old buzz I used to get from being called out on urgent missions was back. As far as I was concerned, this was the first job I'd had in two years that might actually mean something. I packed my bags and quickly got all my gear together: camera kit, covert stab vest, asp (extendable truncheon), cuffs, etc., all the while trying to look disappointed for Vicky's sake as my excitement threatened to bubble over.

'I'll be stood down before Christmas,' I told her confidently. 'They'll nick him and it'll all be over. The murder squad detectives are the best in the world at catching these bastards. You have about a one in a thousand chance of getting away with murder in the UK and this guy has done three. He's got no chance whatsoever. I'll be back on Wednesday at the latest, you'll see.'

The murder investigation was rated A+, which meant every available officer was put on the case. The pressure was on. Suffolk Constabulary had one of the smallest police forces in England and Wales. Suddenly, the world was watching as they began one of the largest murder investigations in policing history.

Our outfit had been called in to take over from a joint Norfolk/Suffolk police surveillance team. It was impressed upon us that we'd been summoned because we were the best and that meant we would not, under any circumstances, fuck it up.

At the briefing the branch commander told us sarcastically, 'Try not to lose the target.' Wanker. We didn't need him to tell us what the stakes were. Three young women had been strangled to death – so far. Another woman was missing.

'The prime suspect is thirty-seven-year-old Tom

Stephens, a supermarket shelf-stacker,' the commander said. 'Some of the girls who work in the red-light district get a lift into town with him – including some of the victims.'

Meaningful glances were exchanged.

'After he drops them off, he typically waits in the red-light area and sits in his car by himself and talks to the other girls. If any of them need a lift to score drugs or be picked up from where a punter had dropped them off, he obliges. Sometimes they pay him for a lift, other times he gets paid with sexual favours.

'Now for the bit nobody else knows about. And this is where it gets interesting. A counter-surveillance team has been hired by a national tabloid newspaper to actively hunt any surveillance teams down and ID you.'

'What the hell?' Jed asked.

'They have paid the suspect for his story; it's most likely they believe that he's innocent. The tabloid surveillance team are there to keep tabs on us, and at the same time to look for an opportunity to pick him up and deliver him to a location where his story can be taken down by a journalist.'

Yikes. 'The only people able to manage such a task would be ex-Special Forces,' I said to Jed as we left, ready for our Mission Impossible.

'Best be on our toes, then,' he replied.

Assistant Chief Constable Jacqui Cheer had warned prostitutes to stay off the streets. While this might have seemed logical, it was far easier said than done. The prostitutes were still out in force, not out of defiance, but because their need for crack and heroin outweighed their fear, yet another direct result of our unforgivable failure to stem the flood of drugs into the towns and cities of the United Kingdom. The killer had exploited this to his advantage.

As journalists dug into the victims' backgrounds they uncovered histories of likeable and ambitious young girls who'd fallen in with the wrong crowd at school. It was from there that their drug addictions seemed to stem.

Once such girl was Paula Clennell. When she was sixteen, Paula had appeared in the local paper after coming to the aid of a badly injured pensioner. The pensioner had made a public appeal for her 'mystery angel' to come forward so she could thank her.

Since then she had become addicted to heroin and now worked the streets of Ipswich to pay for it. The twenty-four-year-old was interviewed by a TV reporter after Gemma and Tania's bodies had been found. She told them that she had known Gemma and was afraid that what had happened to Gemma might happen to her. She also said that the murders would not stop her from working the streets because she needed the money to support her drug addiction.

Now Paula was missing.

We took over at midnight. As we headed into the city we spotted an old VW Golf, two-up, parked just off a round-about: exactly where I would put a car if I were looking for a surveillance team entering a city.

'Good job we split up,' Jed said as we drove in and put the car details over the air. The Golf stayed put. The team had entered Ipswich from four different locations around the city to flatten our profile. One–nil to us.

Surveillance like this is more of an art than a science. Some people have it, they are naturals and become extremely successful. Some people don't. Not all investigators and intelligence operators I know are naturals (and neither was I – I had to work really hard to master the art).

It's not just about fading into the background; the success of a surveillance team comes from being able to stay outside the target's field of vision and still keep him in yours. It also depends on some clever navigating to put you ahead of the target so you can just call through his position to your colleagues. This is much more difficult on the pavements of a medium-sized town late at night than staying with a car for half an hour round the M25. The fact that we probably had an ex-Special Forces c/s team looking out for us made us extra twitchy. We were all well used to handling third-party awareness, which is usually not malicious and not very hard to spot. It typically comes from the Neighbourhood Watch, independent curtain-twitchers, concerned passers-by or guilt-laden ne'er-do-wells.

Criminals are everywhere and I guarantee that in every street there will be people who believe they are being targeted, in addition to the one you are working on. You have to be aware of how your movements and plot positions can be picked up. Imagine what you would be looking for in your street if you were dodgy, things like the empty house with curtains open and closed over the course of a day, two men sitting in a car for a couple of hours, the same van parked in the same position for three nights running, someone waiting at a bus stop for thirty minutes but never taking a bus.

When we took over the plot, the target was in bed. After

a few careful circuits on foot and in vehicles we were certain that no journalists or burly ex-SF types were waiting to snatch our target.

Usually, on jobs like this, the crews would spend the night nodding off, in the knowledge that whoever held the OP would yell if the target moved and all hell would break loose over the air with excited breathless voices commentating at nineteen-to-the-dozen. Tonight was different. Everyone wanted to stay alert; flasks of hot coffee and Red Bull on hand just in case. We all knew that however heavy our eyelids got and however painful it was to force them to stay open, a moment's lack of concentration could spell disaster.

We were well concealed, in areas where we could move up to our plot positions in seconds, but remain hidden until we were needed. The only people who spotted us were the working girls, who would normally have given any car with two men in it serious attention if they thought they could score, or treated it with disdain if they thought we were 'vice'. Tonight, though, they instinctively knew we were on their side, giving us knowing nods or glances as they patrolled by, but nothing else.

It was the first time for many of us under SOCA that we felt we were achieving something tangible, even though we were really doing nothing more than getting deep-vein thrombosis. Most of us hoped that the suspect would decide that tonight was the night when whatever perverted compulsion possessed him would take hold and he would take a trip to the red-light district so we would have the honour of taking him down.

It wasn't to be. As dawn rose, our day relief kicked in and we stood down to one of East Anglia's finest hotels.

'Jesus, this job must be important,' Jed whispered as we checked in. 'Uncle Albert must have blown a month's budget letting us stay here.'

'I bet he nearly had an aneurysm when senior management told him to put two teams down here until the New Year,' I replied.

A top-brass meeting of police commanders was stunned into silence the following day when it was interrupted by the news that not one but two more bodies had been found.

Paula's body had been found by a passer-by in an area that police had already searched. Forty minutes after this discovery, the body of twenty-nine-year-old prostitute Annette Nicholls was uncovered nearby. Both Annette and Paula had children. Both were addicted to heroin.

That made a total of five bodies found in just ten days. All of the victims had been strangled. The killer, now christened the 'Suffolk Strangler' by the media, was picking up speed and growing more confident by the day.

We were either following the wrong guy or there was an accomplice. Either way it looked as if we were here for Christmas, so I called Vicky to let her know. Then news came in that we were to stand down and head home. I was just calling her back when that order was revoked and we were called into the briefing room at 7 a.m. on Thursday 14 December.

'Forget Tom Stephens; let the press have him. New target. Steve Wright, a fork-lift truck driver. The objectives are the same, except that he has no idea there's any interest in him.'

'If he has done it, he should fucking well expect some interest,' I whispered to Jed.

Sure enough, the *Sunday Mirror* got their scoop and despite his best efforts, Stephens managed to make a pretty good job of convincing everyone he was the killer. 'I am a friend of all the girls,' he said between sobs, 'but I don't have any alibis.' He also said he became the girls' 'protector' and would have had 'complete opportunity' to carry out the crime as 'the girls trusted me so much'. Still, both the murder squad and the prostitutes who knew him were certain he wasn't in the frame, so it was time to move on to suspect number two.

We stuck to Wright like invisible glue as he went to work, did his shopping, watched news reports of the murders while eating his wife's lasagne. It continued for three more days until forensics officers, who'd spent days recovering DNA from the bodies of Anneli, Annette and Paula found an identical profile on all three victims. The results were rinsed through a police DNA database and a match popped up: Steve Wright. He had been convicted of the theft of £84 in 2003. If there ever was an argument in favour of a DNA database, this was it.

Two days later, at 4.45 a.m. on 19 December, Wright peered out from between his curtains as he heard the plod pull up and march down his garden path in their size elevens.

When he opened the door, Wright looked just like any stocky middle-aged man; he was dressed in blue tracksuit bottoms and a white polo shirt. When the charges were read, he became unsteady on his feet and was escorted back into his front room.

Wright will die in prison. As to what actually motivated him to commit those murders, we'll never really know. He 'no commented' for six hours straight, except to deny the charges.

While forensic psychology has its place, its significance has been hugely overblown by various TV shows, movies, authors of both fiction and non-fiction and soundbite-hungry psychologists. Sometimes there is just no satisfactory explanation that satisfies. He did it, that's all. I think we just have to accept that there are, and always will be, evil people in this world.

I went home for Christmas, counting myself one lucky bastard to have my friends and family all alive and all (relatively) content.

Although Wright might have been a killer by nature, the Ipswich murders were a damning indictment of how our failure to slow the illegal drugs trade made finding victims so easy for him. It has been estimated that as many as 95 per cent of those involved in street prostitution are using crack or heroin. No such detailed investigation into the lives of streetwalkers in the twenty-first century had ever been made before these murders.

It was eye-opening to see how young the girls were, how similar their stories, and how hard drugs had gripped them at a very young age, either at school or shortly after, how the dealers had foisted their trade upon them, telling them they'd like it, knowing that almost inevitably they'd be prostituting themselves in the future to keep the same dealers in business, knowing deep down that they'd been duped by these smooth-talking bastards but now unable to live without their help.

And I knew that it was getting worse. Although the role

we playcd in Ipswich had been vital, I knew I was essentially working not for a crime-fighting body but a bureaucratic institution. I could have made a fortune if I'd decided to play the game; I knew how the system worked and I knew how it could be manipulated to make SOCA look good. But to me, the people I was employed by were no better than the drug dealers we were supposed to be putting out of business. They were deceiving the public, taking a healthy pay packet from them for doing sod all.

I'd had enough.

# 28. The Nightmare

I'd been sprinting at top speed after this fully paid-up Colombian cartel member for at least three minutes now, which wouldn't be so bad except it was night time and we were running against the traffic down Park Lane towards Hyde Park Corner, one of the busiest, most chaotic intersections in London.

Something wasn't right. I had the strangest feeling of *déjà vu*.

It had all come on top after we'd been tailing a black cab containing a bag lady and five kilos of coke about to make her drop. She'd become twitchy so we'd pulled her over.

Afterwards, Fin, who was standing on a street corner watching the entrance to the Dorchester Hotel, had spotted a couple of Latino-looking blokes staring intently at us. He approached them and identified himself and the response from both was to fuck off in separate directions. Finbar quickly got hold of the first one and introduced his face to Mr Macadam. I'd seen all this from a side street and started out after the other one, Mickey and Jed in my wake.

The Colombian dashed across the first four lanes of traffic and ran for the huge roundabout just thirty metres ahead. I was gaining on him and shouted: 'Armed officer! Stop or I shoot!' I wasn't carrying but it made the Colombian think twice and he turned, slowing slightly. It was just enough. At the edge of the roundabout I launched myself through the air and brought him down with a rugby tackle. We crashed to the ground, rolling right in front of fast-moving London traffic. Horns beeped, cars took avoiding action. Arrest and restraint procedures went straight out of the window. I grabbed the Colombian's head and smacked it into the tarmac, hard.

He rolled over.

Slim's cold dead eyes stared straight back at me.

I sat up in bed in a cold sweat, panting. The sheets were knotted all around me. I rubbed my eyes and, trying to shake the horror from my mind, I got up, went to the kitchen, ran the tap and drank a glass of water.

The first part of that dream had actually happened, I had once chased a Colombian down Park Lane. The main difference was the ending, when we were nearly run over, conveniently enough, by an ambulance. That and the shape shifting.

My panic attacks hadn't subsided. Things at work hadn't improved. I'd decided to talk to my management and Human Resources about all of the bigotry I'd witnessed and the problems I thought SOCA were creating. They listened politely, pushed a few bits of paper about and did absolutely nothing about it.

In the meantime I'd carried on regardless. We were asked by Manchester's Financial Investigation Team to take on what was shaping up to be a pretty worthwhile job. I'd met Cassie, the FIT officer (in every sense of the word) running the case, during a foot surveillance course. She'd never forgotten me for scaring her half to death by appearing out of nowhere after she'd thought she'd given me the slip in Leeds city centre.

Once again we were following a dirty money trail from a bureau de change, this time in Birmingham. It soon took us to a second bureau in West Yorkshire and then to bureaux all over the north of England.

Two money men based in Birmingham were at the heart of the operation. Our mission was to follow and gather as much Intel as possible about them. One guy was an Asian businessman called Sidhu with a clean record. The other was Michael Jones, an ex-armed blagger and enforcer, well known to the police although he hadn't been nicked for years. They were both in their mid fifties and were thought to be laundering millions of pounds in cash that was tied to drugs, terrorism and tax fraud. Cassie hoped we'd be able to put meat on the bones.

We didn't have much to start with, just the home addresses of the two men. We began with 'lifestyle surveillance' and followed the targets to get a clear picture of their daily routine. We needed to know how much time they spent at home, where they laid their heads at night, what they did during the day, where they drank and socialized, who they met (girlfriends, legit partners, business contacts) and what their hobbies were. We weren't reacting to any outside Intel at this stage although we were able to respond if Cassie rang up and said, 'We're expecting Sidhu to meet an unknown tomorrow,' in which case we would wait for them to show up at their arranged meeting place.

Cassie was very inexperienced operationally, but unlike a lot of case officers she appreciated the dark arts of surveillance. We'd had quite a few run-ins with other case officers who had tried to tell us how to do our job. Cassie accepted that she didn't know that much about our work and just trusted us get on with it. She made a name for herself as a brilliant officer to work with because she expected everyone else to be as dedicated as she was, without her breathing down their necks.

Sidhu drove a brand new Mercedes 600SL and lived in a huge house in Edgbaston. Ditto Jones, although he had two Mercs (another one for his missus). The hard man had obviously found out late in life that the easy way to get rich was through money laundering, not sticking up banks and security vans with a sawn-off. He also had a flash apartment in the Mailbox (a very exclusive development in central Brum), where he met his off-the-record shag and, more importantly for us, carried out all his money laundering.

It took us ages to find the exact place. We kept losing Jones when he got close to home; there were dozens of underground garages with multiple entrances, so we had no idea which one he was in. Eventually we swamped the area with footmen and we got him going into one of the underground car parks. After that, we plonked a lucky volunteer in an obs van for a few days to see which part of the block he went to, before putting footmen out to see which lights came on after Jones entered. Then it was simply a matter of carrying out background checks to find out who owned it.

To our delight, the job suddenly got really busy. I wondered whether we were on to something good at last. The Asian met dozens of different people every week, some of whom looked legit, others not. Everything was fed back to Cassie, who drove the job along.

The pair were clearly a good team. It looked to us as though Jones was introducing criminals to the Asian, and they would then agree the rate at which he would launder their money using the good old hawala network.

We spent about four months behind them, tagging both of their vehicles. We took out a couple of their couriers as they left Jones's off-the-record shag-pad, confiscating their cash. We made it look like a cold pull and they bought it both times, thinking it was just bad luck. We also followed Sidhu to a local mosque where he did some of the handovers and where we discovered he had a money stash.

At one of the meets, at the Birmingham Marriott, Sidhu met a previously unknown IC1 male. He looked tasty so we followed him to Nottingham. He in turn met another couple of guys and when their background checks came back they ran to several pages, all of it linked to class-A importation, so it was clear we were on to a good thing.

We spent a month or so following these three on an ad-hoc basis (we continued to work on the main targets which took up most of our time). We wanted to build a case for these new guys to be taken on. The fact that we thought they were serious coke dealers who were obviously connected was not enough; we needed something concrete.

Then we got a break.

We got word that the coke dealers were holding a planning meeting at their local boozer. They all arrived in brand new motors: Mercs, Beamers and Rangers. It was clear to us that these guys had just cleaned a shedload of money, which must have resulted from a pretty damn big shipment; their cars added up to over £150k in value, so they were obviously not without a hefty regular income. We put everything we had to senior management.

Not a chance they said. The targets weren't 'on the list'. That was it, no arguments.

So we simply stuck with the primary targets and the knock came at Jones's shag palace. He had £130,000 in grubby cash in his Merc and another £50,000 was in the flat. By the time the op was done, we had a half a million in cash and a handful of other misfits behind bars, but they were all small fry. The serious coke dealers – the outfit that we'd been following – were continuing to operate without let or hindrance and with SOCA's full knowledge. That really grated.

'This is bollocks, mate,' I told Jed after management's rejection. 'I can't do this any more. The bosses just aren't interested and I'm not going to spend the rest of my days watching criminals getting away with it.'

Jed nodded glumly.

I took a long hard look at my life and career and decided to resign. I typed up my letter and took it with me to work. Something made me hold back, though. I couldn't bear the thought of giving Uncle Albert the satisfaction. I knew he'd be pleased when I handed it over. One less troublesome officer to pay; more money saved.

Then, with spectacularly good timing, the FBI called.

# 29. The Mafia Comes to Town

I walked into the briefing, where the atmosphere was already electric. Rumours abounded about a massive international job. By the time the meeting was over Jed, Mickey and I were bouncing around the room with excitement, any notions of resignation forgotten.

Uncle Albert showed less than a modicum of enthusiasm, however. It was like listening to a speech by John Major on ketamine. But the content was dynamite.

'The FBI has asked us for their assistance in their war in the global drugs market,' Uncle Albert said glumly. 'Apparently, London has become the meeting place for a syndicate of Italian, Russian and South American criminals who are planning to buy a Colombian bank in Bogotá for £80 million.

'Once the purchase has gone through, these gangs will have the wherewithal to launder as much money as they wish, opening hundreds, if not thousands, of bank accounts which will allow them to operate legally in the international money market.'

'Holy crap,' I said. Other teams gave whistles and sighs of amazement and wonder as the news sank in. We would be following senior representatives from the three world's largest criminal organizations: the Italian and Russian Mafia and the Colombian Cali cartel. All at the same time.

'I knew London was supposed to be centre of world

business,' Mickey said, 'but this just takes the custard cream . . .'

'The FBI has asked you,' Uncle Albert continued, 'to follow the main players as they do their business here and report back to them. Essentially, you are to wait for their call before dropping everything and covering these guys for the whole time they're in the UK.'

Fin voiced the one-word question we all had on our minds: 'Overtime?'

Uncle Albert frowned. 'On this one, I've been told whatever it takes.'

We beamed back at him like Cheshire cats.

'Wow,' I said afterwards, that's like the ultimate dodgy bureaux de change,' I flicked through the Intel report. It was sketchy but we had a list of names and photos of everyone the FBI knew to be involved.

'Talk about a licence to print money,' Jed said. 'Does that mean this weekend's cancelled?'

We were planning to go to France on a bit of a rugby jolly. Fortunately, we had been told the meeting of the Mr Bigs was still a week off, so we Eurostarred ourselves over to Paris.

We'd arranged to meet up with Billy Peters, a friend of mine who was in the SAS. I'd known him since my days in the Marines. Jed and I were on our third Stella Artois when he walked in, a massive brute of a bloke.

'My papers are up soon,' Billy told us, 'then I'm going where the money is.'

'Private contracting?' Jed asked.

'Damn right. A mate of mine, ex-regiment, has a job

next week in London. He's been travelling all over the world with these guys on a twelve-grand-a-month retainer.'

Jed and I exchanged glances. It couldn't be, could it? We immediately went into extract-Intel mode.

'Was that Jimmy Browning?' Jed asked innocently, 'I heard he was doing well.'

'Nah, mate, geezer called Brian Dowler, was in the Reg for twelve years.'

I tried not to spit out my pint. As soon as Billy had left for the bar we held an urgent confab. 'I don't fucking believe this,' I said. 'Dowler's name is on the bloody FBI list.'

'What do we do?' Jed asked.

'Well, nothing, I suppose. We're going to be seeing him next week anyway, whatever the score. Just one of life's little coincidences.'

'Twelve grand a bloody month.'

It was easy to see why these SAS guys didn't ask too many questions about the people who hired them. Criminals were the only ones who paid that well, and who provided the most interesting work for men like Dowler.

It was a sobering thought. The SAS had incredible skills, honed over many years in the toughest of environments. They provided the best possible protection and wouldn't blink an eyelid at arranging security in any city in the world, from Belize to New York from Bogotá to London. No other outfit was better trained in counter surveillance; they knew every trick in the book.

Now they would be trying to spot us.

The following week, we got ourselves prepped. At that time, the DST was entirely made up of ex-Customs officers, so I broke out our old laptops and navigators.

'We'll go back to using the old brevity codes now as well,' I said. 'And the old vehicle surveillance techniques. SOCA has said they won't fund us any replacements for this old gear but it's all still working, just about.'

We'd literally stuck some of our old laptops together with masking tape and bastardized those with broken screens so they just worked, albeit with the occasional heart-stopping flicker.

We also went back to briefing in the pub. 'Right,' I said, clearly unable to contain my glee, 'we're going to be up against the finest counter-surveillance teams on the entire planet, so we're not going to bugger about. We blow this one, then we fuck up one of the largest counter-crime operations ever mounted. Failure is not an option.'

Everyone agreed. We would go back to the old team, using the old methods. Mickey even joined us on his Fire-blade. God, this felt good.

I went home and had my first decent night's sleep in months.

The FBI had very little Intel; the job had started with a fairly recent tip-off. They wanted to know everything we could find out about these guys. We were going to follow them, photograph them, search their rooms at the Park Lane Hilton. Find out exactly what they were up to. No holds barred.

This job was going to rock.

We placed one man in the hotel's basement security office to monitor and redirect the CCTV in the corridor outside their room and at front reception; that way he'd be able to give us a heads-up if the targets were leaving/

returning as the bugs we'd planted wouldn't always give us enough warning.

The hotel's security team were really jealous of the work we were doing, especially when we were rushing in and out of their office and taking it over without explanation. Fortunately, the security manager, Juris Pauls, was right behind us. Jay was Latvian and he really hated Russians, so made sure everyone bent over backwards to help.

Another officer would stay in the lobby to ID the targets to the rest of the team positioned outside in vehicles and on foot. He was also on hand to cover a possible meet in the reception area.

'From Control [hotel security]: That's two males from the area of room 2214 generally towards the lifts . . . that's both males unsighted to control.'

'Cammo: Yes, all call signs stand by, stand by.'

There was now an uncomfortable sixty-second wait. The officers in the lobby got twitchier with every passing moment, the collected breath of the team was held until:

'Yeah, Cammo has eyeball. Zulu 17 and Zulu 32 from the lift nine-one the broccoli; wait for description . . . Zulu 17 dark blue suit, light blue shirt, bright yellow tie carrying briefcase-sized black shoulder bag over right shoulder . . . Zulu 32 grey sports jacket on dark trousers, open-necked shirt carrying traditional brown briefcase.'

'Sweden.'

'Cam: Both Zulus complete the broccoli.'

We could relax as the ground commander repositioned his troops for a probable taxi lift off. After breakfast the targets had a smoke outside the main entrance while waiting for a cab.

After following our targets for forty-eight hours we were certain no one was watching the rooms. While we doubted they'd risk leaving anything of importance behind, the FBI had asked us to have a root around and damned if we weren't going to do just that as soon as they'd taken off. We also took the chance to install bugs in every room.

We hadn't been in the room five minutes when my phone rang.

'Cam here.'

'Control: Zulu 32's nine-one the lift, en route to you!'

Shit. Our first rummage of Mr Mafia's five-star hotel room had been rudely interrupted.

'Zulu 32 complete the lift.'

We performed a very, very quick tidy-up, making sure everything looked just the way it had when we came in. We heard the lift bell ping at the end of the corridor.

'Zulu 32 from the lift, nine-one the room.'

We bundled out and into the corridor. A second later Zulu 32 appeared in front of us, patting his pockets as we passed him, heads down. Then suddenly finding whatever it was he'd thought he'd forgotten, he turned back and followed us straight into the lift.

None of us could be described as being waif-like. It's not easy to look natural and relaxed when you're nose-to-nose with your target in such a confined space. Fin made the logical leap that we looked like a bunch of fat German tourists over here for the beer festival (he spoke the lingo fluently) and said something in German, to which I nodded seriously and replied: '*Ja, ja, das ist gut.*'

It seemed to do the trick. Mr Mafia was relaxed as he left and headed straight out the doors in a hurry while we went to the bar for a quick debrief – and to slow our beating hearts.

Our second attempt ran clockwork-smooth and we actually found some good paperwork, so I broke out the Nikon and started snapping away. We soon got to the heart of the concept of what they were planning to do and it was breathtaking – they had all the ambition of a James Bond villain.

Ever since Colombians started to export drugs, dealing with the vast amounts of cash the trade generates has been a major problem for them. As sales of cocaine took off, it soon became more of a hassle to count the mountains of money and stack them neatly than it was to sell the stuff in the first place. People would have to count and recount it over and over again to make sure they had an accurate total before anything could be done with it. It takes several days to hand-count half a million dollars of varying denominations – tedious as hell. Amazingly, money had become an obstacle; it removed all the fun from the game.

In the old days, the gangs used to fly planeloads of US dollars to the Bahamas (the same planes they used for the coke), where they were deposited in hundreds of offshore bank accounts, no questions asked.

Legend has it that one successful coke exporter couldn't get his money to the bank fast enough, so buried millions of dollars all over his land. He died unexpectedly and no one knew where all the cash was hidden, so the whole area was dug up. It must have been like the California gold rush. A decade later, villagers were still finding the odd sack of US dollars washed out of its burial place by heavy rains.

The problem for the dealers was that a fistful of offshore

dollars was of little use in Medellín or Cali: safe havens but also virtual open prisons they were wary of leaving. They needed their money turned into pesos so they could live day-to-day as well as spend it on villas, Dobermanns, security guards, guns, women, water features, priceless works of art – and bigger and better planes to ferry their product.

To turn the drug-tainted dollars into shiny new pesos, the Black Market Peso Exchange was created. This relied upon a network of illegal money traders. For a substantial commission, the dodgy broker handed over a load of clean pesos in return for access to the drug dollars held in American bank accounts (the dealers employed dozens of runners who took the cash and deposited it into hundreds of bank accounts in the United States in amounts of less than $10,000).

To restock, the broker tells dodgy Colombian importers that he has foreign funds to buy foreign products, duty free. The Colombian importers place their orders and the broker's contacts purchase on their behalf, using the broker's drug money. The broker is then paid in pesos by the Colombian importers, replenishing his supply of Colombian currency. The goods are then smuggled into Colombia where the importer takes possession of them without having to pay import tariffs.

The system works, but what a hassle.

Now, suppose you had ownership of your own Colombian bank. You could do whatever you liked. You could fill it full of dollars transferred from the little accounts in the US and move them between other countries/people/organizations using the international banking system. Transferring money between the US, Colombia, Italy and Russia or anywhere else in the world would be no problem whatsoever.

That's what our boys were planning. This multinational syndicate had their eyes on a medium-sized Colombian bank that had been operating for decades in Bogotá. The photos I saw of it reminded me a little of the banks you see in old cowboy films. But to the drug dealers it would make their lives extremely simple and massively profitable. At £80 million, it was a snip.

We also picked up some paperwork that the FBI didn't yet know about: agricultural subsidy fraud. The EU had paid out tens of millions of euros to Italian farmers during the period 2001–4 for buying and selling surpluses of citrus fruits under the EU's Common Agricultural Policy. However, neither the farmers, the fruit nor the buyers actually existed.

The Italians were finally getting a grip on the situation and so the Mafia were buying up land in the 'new' Europe – recently admitted members of the EU where inspectors did not yet exist or were easily bribed or intimidated.

They were making millions in a venture that was far less risky than dealing drugs, using fewer people and with much less effort. The Italians wanted somewhere safe to hide their money so kindly donated by the EU taxpayer, some-where no one would ever come looking. Where better than your very own Colombian bank?

Between them, the assorted mobsters had several hundred million pounds burning a hole in their collective pocket, so buying an £80 million bank was going to be a piece of cake. All the money was being routed through good old Dubai via Hong Kong.

Keeping tabs on them kept us busy between 6 a.m. and midnight. The overtime was racking up; Uncle Albert was ready to pop a blood vessel but the Foreign Office had the ultimate say on this one – we had to help our American cousins.

Our targets' routine was always the same: they stayed in five-star hotels before heading off to an office they'd leased in the City from a well-known UK villain whose name had cropped up on Alpha's radar a few years back. We managed to establish an OP in the building opposite the City office, in a disused block scheduled for demolition. It was weird being in a vast, empty building with no furniture, no phones, no people, just the odd banal postcard from some long-forgotten holiday sent to work colleagues.

'Would've been nice if they'd left some fucking chairs to sit on,' I moaned, stretching my aching back.

'It's your fault for being the camera nut,' Jed replied.

It was true. I love photography and broke out the gear at work whenever I had an excuse. The downside is that to take good surveillance photos you always end up in the weirdest positions. It's never like in the movies where you see the handsome operative stretched out on a sofa staring down a telephoto lens at the subject who conveniently hovers in view. The best, most revealing view of the action is never, ever from a comfy chair. I eventually perched on a windowsill, looking through a small hole in the blinds, with one foot on the floor and my left cheek pressed against the glass. From there I was able to get pretty good footage of the targets arriving and leaving.

'From OP: Zulu 17 and Zulu 32 from the premises, wait . . . Relax, that's both Zulus lighting up. With flourish.'

'France.'

Luckily they were chronic smokers and the building was

strictly no-smo, so I got lots of shots of them chatting away over ciggies on the pavement at least a dozen times a day. Unfortunately, I was trying to give up at the time and it was an uncomfortable reminder of my own addiction.

One day they were thus engaged when a load of black Mercs arrived and some old men who looked so Mafioso Martin Scorsese would have hired them on appearance alone stepped out. They hugged and kissed like long-lost brothers while I kept my finger on the shutter button.

Most of my colleagues couldn't see the point of my playing David Bailey, but I knew a good surveillance shot would look great in court, or might be used all over the world for ID purposes. I also knew that international police teams in Holland, Russia, Italy and the US would judge our work by the quality of our shots. I'd seen so many amateur-looking surveillance photos in my time that were simply binned because they were of no use to anyone. Good pics made us look good.

I also took my camera out and about and shot some great stills of the targets in front of Harrods using a 70–300mm lens from twenty feet away, pretending to be a tourist. I also got shots of them at night outside a restaurant in Covent Garden and again at night of them entering the Ritz with me one-up in Joseph – whom we'd managed to save from the breaker's yard – one hand on the wheel, one on the camera, slowing the cab in the middle of Piccadilly and firing off a few rounds.

Lots of people – some obviously legit, some equally obviously not – passed through their office. All of them departed in black cabs. No doubt this was Dowler's choice, since he knew we couldn't lump every black cab in town and they're notoriously difficult to follow. But we were well experienced. We were also so up for this job that the operational minutiae that might have seemed dull and tiring in the good old days was now utterly absorbing.

Along with our resurrected Joseph, we ran a standard surveillance set-up with a Volvo T5 (call sign Sweden), a Peugeot 406 SRi (Spain), a BMW 3-series (Denmark), a Honda Fireblade (Kilo) plus the Vito obs van (Lightning).

After a hard day at the office, the targets would head off to one of London's top eateries: the Ivy and Nobu were favourites. To avoid desperate scrambles for volunteers we worked out rotations and used our special 'gold passes' to get tables. Typically, dinner was followed by a long night out at a casino or a swanky West End nightclub.

One night we left them to it in a club at about 2 a.m. and drove back down Haymarket, through Trafalgar Square, down Northumberland Avenue and across the river to the office for a debrief. On the way we'd clocked a car that seemed to be in the first stages of a fire. An ambulance was already on the scene and a cop car with its blues and twos on screamed past us, so we assumed it had been reported. The next day we awoke to find that we'd driven by a terrorist car bomb filled with sixty litres of petrol, gas cylinders and nails.

While the Haymarket didn't go up in smoke, our fabulous operation did. We were called into the office on the following Monday, where we found Uncle Albert grinning from ear to ear.

'Seems that the Italian police, true to stereotype, have proven to be poor timekeepers,' Uncle Albert said, unable to contain his glee. 'The FBI had coordinated an international operation to arrest everyone at the same time. The Italians didn't realize they had to take into account the time difference when they synchronized their watches.'

They'd nicked the ringleaders at the Italian end of the operation too early and this had given everyone else plenty of warning, so while the baddies had at least called the bank purchase off, none of them would be going to jail anytime soon, thanks to a lack of evidence.

To say we were disappointed would be an understatement. But that's real life for you. Criminals are given every advantage. The larger the operation we have in place to catch them, then the more likely it is that someone, somewhere, will fuck it up.

To be honest, though – and this might give you an idea of just how much working for SOCA had warped my priorities – what I was most concerned about was the thought that there'd be no more overtime, no more fun and games, no more proper surveillance techniques and lots more of the shit Uncle Albert kept unloading on us.

It was then that I realized I'd just been delaying the inevitable. I took my resignation letter out of my pocket, walked up to Uncle Albert's desk, placed it neatly under his coffee mug and went home.

# 30. On the Outside

I was owed a lot of leave, so Uncle Albert told me not to come back until my last official day when I could hand over my kit. God forbid he should end up owing me for any unused holiday.

On the appointed day I arrived at the office to find it empty. Uncle Albert had clearly told the rest of the team to stay away. No chance of a farewell do, then, or even a goodbye chat. It felt strange to think that, when I left, I would be a civilian for the first time since leaving school, and no longer authorized even to enter the building.

I cleared out my desk, handed in all my official kit and my ID/warrant cards. It was all very perfunctory – no small talk whatsoever.

Afterwards, Uncle Albert escorted me to the basement car park; he barely said a word. When we reached my car, he said, 'Well, I don't like long goodbyes,' turned on his heel and walked off.

'You'll put the gold watch in the post, then, will you?' I called after him.

The door to the car park slammed resoundingly.

I felt strangely liberated.

The following weekend I met up with Jed, Fin and a few others at a Gloucester versus Ireland game at Kingsholm Rugby Club. It was better than any leaving do.

Our conversation inevitably turned to work, in particular the drugs trade and SOCA. We even started to talk about legalization.

There's a well-known quote from the 2004 movie *Layer Cake* in which Daniel Craig's unnamed coke-dealing character says: 'Always remember that one day all this drug monkey business will be legal. They won't leave it to people like me . . . not when they finally figure out how much money is to be made – not millions, fucking billions. Recreational Drugs plc – giving the people what they want . . . Good times today, stupor tomorrow. But this is now, so until prohibition ends, make hay whilst the sun shines.'

This is wrong. Drugs will *never* be legalized.

Politicians know only too well the profits to be made from legalizing and taxing the trade in cocaine. They also know that there are plenty of other reasons as to why this is a good idea. Hundreds of international criminal cartels would steadily disintegrate, money laundering would decline massively, associated crime which costs the UK economy alone billions of pounds each year would fall, billions more would be saved on law enforcement, the courts, the prisons, etc. Then there's the fact that kids under eighteen currently find it easier to find someone willing to sell them drugs than sell them booze. Licensing the drug trade would eventually make it much harder for them to get hold of hard drugs.

Despite these reasons, the powers that be still believe that legalization is more trouble than it's worth. Any UK politician daft enough to actually voice the idea will be shot down by the media and opposition MPs and will be out on their ear faster than you can say 'loony bin'.

Until the Yanks come on board (ever been hit by a snow-ball in the Sahara?), any attempt to legalize drugs will be futile. Their official policy of drug prohibition includes a policy of debate prohibition.

In the meantime, the government doesn't have any control over what's getting into the UK and no one has a clue how to stop the growing numbers of young people who are snorting, popping, smoking, puffing and injecting all these thousands of tonnes of pills and powders from coming back for more.

So what is going to happen, then? Things will just carry on they way they are. Politicians with goldfish-like attention spans will keep playing the stats game, winning votes by using SOCA to tell us we're winning the so-called 'war on drugs'.

Alpha was the best approach to drug prohibition we ever had (if only in terms of stamping on the dealers' efforts to get class-A drugs into the UK). If we had about fifty Alpha offices each supported by their own operational teams on the ground, *then* I could see us going some way to turning the UK into a no-go area for drug importers.

Whatever the case, my role in the so-called war on drugs was over – or so I thought.


After my 'leaving do' I spent a few weeks with the kids and then took off on a whistle-stop round-the-world tour with Vicky, something I'd wanted to do for years.

One place I wanted to revisit was Canada. I'd been there once before on a job, collecting evidence against an English-man who'd tried to set himself up as a professional money launderer. I'd made some good friends while I was there and so I looked forward to having a bit of a catch-up.

Sergeant Steve Smith, my opposite number on that op, met us at the airport. It wasn't long before we started talking about phone intercepts. 'Hey, why don't you come and have a look at how we do things here?'

'Are you serious?' Considering the way that Alpha operated, I was more than a little surprised at his offer to show me round their suite.

On the way, we talked about SOCA. Steve said that SOCA sounded more like the British equivalent of the DEA than the FBI. The DEA was created back in 1973 when several US drug enforcement agencies were merged into one. 'It took about seventeen years to get its act together,' Steve said. 'It only started to function properly once all the old-timers who still held grudges against former rival departments had retired. It was only when the new skins [young recruits with no baggage] took over that the DEA was able to get on with its job. Sounds to me like SOCA's in for a long and bumpy ride.'

I nodded. 'I can believe it,' I said glumly.

We arrived at their intercept suite. It was bright, naturally lit and looked friendly and comfortable. They had about sixty lines. Steve told me their biggest problem was the cannabis crops grown by biker gangs. The Hells Angels, the Outlaws and Bandidos have been a major thorn in the side of Canadian law enforcement since the 1970s. They'd controlled drug dealing and smuggling in British Columbia and Alberta for years, during which time they'd managed to kick off several wars costing the lives of dozens of innocent bystanders.

'The Royal Canadian Mounted Police are hunting out cannabis factories,' Steve told me. 'They're usually hidden in large detached houses in quiet anonymous suburbs. The only clue to their whereabouts are the unusually high electricity bills, caused by the continuous use of UV lights to produce up to three crops a year of mind-smashingly powerful skunk. Others use generators so the energy use doesn't show up on the bills.'

'So how do you hook up a line?' I asked. 'What's the application process?'

'We can hook up any phone immediately without too much trouble, as long as the operator has good reason to suspect that it's connected to the operation.'

'Wow,' I said, seriously impressed. 'If we were following a target in the UK and he popped in to a telephone kiosk to make a call, all we could do is "mark" the call by going in after him and using the same phone. We'd then be able to ID the number he'd called at a later date. If he used the same phone again and again, then we could apply for it to be intercepted, which would go before the Home Secretary and could take weeks.'

Steve laughed. 'I can't imagine working like that. It's a miracle you guys got *anywhere*. Here, if the surveillance team sees the target using a public phone, the officer in charge on the ground puts in a call to the intercept suite, the phone is hooked up immediately and we get the live Intel there and then. As soon as the target hangs up, the intercept is switched off.'

I drooled at the thought of running such a system in the UK. If only. We're so far behind in crime fighting it's ridiculous, yet the criminals are constantly seeking out and employing new techniques to make their job easier and ours that much harder.

There are more of them now than there's ever been, take it from someone who's seen it happen. Our cities are packed full of drug dealers and money launderers, the men and women who help keep the global underworld economy spinning – and they've never had it so good.

Seeing my slack-jawed, wide-eyed expression, Steve said, 'Come and work for us, Cammo, you'll have a blast!'

I grinned.

Who wouldn't want to chase drug-dealing sawn-off shotgun carrying biker gangs around Canada with that Intercept suite?

'Let me get back to you,' I said.

## *Eighteen months later*

Rhiannon focussed her binocs on one of the two roofless long brick huts inside the compound and tried not to think about the desert heat.

Inside were dozens of steaming forty-five-gallon drums filled to the brim with opium gum, lime and boiling water, part of a non-stop, 24/7, 365-days-a-year operation.

The lab technicians, Kalashnikovs slung over their shoulders, drew off the white layer of morphine from the top of the drums.

The morphine was re-heated with ammonia until it simmered. Eventually, the resultant clay-like brown paste, a seventy per cent pure morphine base, was poured into block moulds, many of which were now drying in the Afghan sun.

Once dried, they'd be ready to smoke – but that wasn't

the plan here. Rhi knew that a tonne of those dried blocks were leaving that day for another lab in Ankara, Turkey, for further refinement into heroin before being sent by various trucks on the remainder of their journey to the discerning European injector.

A former Alpha operative and informant handler, Rhi – who was tall, blonde and attractive to boot – had beaten off forty highly qualified male applicants for this top-secret 'advisory' role in the newly formed Counter Narcotics Police of Afghanistan (CNPA).

Her cover had been to train hapless Afghan recruits in how to combat drug smuggling. Her real job was to disrupt the supply of opium from the Kandahar and Helmand provinces, which produce eighty per cent of Afghanistan's opium – about ninety per cent of the world's supply – using those few precious recruits who were honest, willing, able-bodied, moderately literate and didn't use drugs.

Barely a year after she arrived, Rhi was leading them on desert operations like a female Lawrence of Arabia. I shouldn't have been surprised; Rhi had spent her whole working life on cultivating relationships and convincing people to trust her with their lives.

Still, not bad for a girl from the Welsh valleys.

Rhi checked in with her troops lying behind a series of rocks, looking down on the compound. They were all set.

A buzz in her earpiece.

'Cam,' I said.

'Rhi. Go ahead.' Even though she was half a world away, Rhi sounded like she was in the next room.

'The pick-up team's on their way.'

'Roger that, Cam, thanks. I can see them now.'

'No sweat.' Using her binocs, Rhi looked back to the north-east, across the rocky desert at the dust trail from two battered white Toyota Land Cruisers, packed full of armed neo-Taliban (that's the 'capitalist' Taliban, who are in it for the money). One of the men was carrying a past-its-best-before-date grenade launcher. It looked as though it belonged to the Soviet era.

Bouncing along between them was a large truck that was going to move the gear on to the next stage of its voyage, into Baluchistan, a mountainous border region, from where it would be smuggled across the border into Iran. This was the most dangerous stage of the journey; Iranian border forces could rarely be bribed, and enthusiastically operated a shoot-to-kill policy. But the risks were worth taking: the Afghan smugglers stood to make about $200,000 for organizing this little operation.

The Colonel, the man who controlled the Afghan border police, would take about a quarter of that for literally providing them with his seal of approval. The documentation he gave them would see the smugglers sail safely through dozens of checkpoints where robbery, murder, rape and corruption were rife.

If you'd have told me eighteen months ago that I'd be fighting the war on drugs in Afghanistan I'd have laughed you out of the room.

But life's like that; full of surprises. After a few months on Civvy Street, I missed the excitement of hunting bad guys. And then the opportunity I'd been waiting for came along: a chance to coordinate operations to take down drug lords from the comfort of an international communications hub. The aim was to track and stop drugs at the source country. Best of all, I could play the game on my own terms, free of the likes of men such as Uncle Albert.

I grinned.

Now *this* knock was going to be a beast.

# Glossary: Brevity Codes and Abbreviations

## *Numerical brevity codes*

**One/two of two** Inside/outside lane of two-lane carriageway

**One/two/three of three** Inside/middle/outside lane of motorway (called so that the six-eight car can identify the target from a long way back)

**Two-two** A call made by the Tommy car (tracker vehicle) when he has 'technical control' of the target. This is the Tommy car equivalent of five-five

**Two-four** I am in the convoy (called by other cars in no particular order)

**Three-one** Turned left

**Three-six** Convoy check, please identify (called by five-five car to confirm that all the cars are in the convoy and following the target; six-eight calls second; if no one calls six-eight, everyone tries to get into that position)

**Four-one** Turned right

**Five-five** I have control of the target and am going with him

**Six-eight** I am in a position to take over control of the target

**Seven-four** Handover of five-five to another call sign

**Seven-seven, seven-seven** Target is moving off

**Eight-two** I am at the back of the convoy

**Nine-one** Heading towards

**Nine-nine-nine** Target has stopped (not used if the target is stopped at traffic lights or simply waiting somewhere)

**Ten-nine** Telephone call

## *Other brevity codes*

**3P** Third party

**Alternative** I am travelling in the same direction as the target but on a parallel route in an attempt to get ahead of him

**Basket** Bridge

**Bedlight** Hotel

**Belt** Male suspect/unknown male (also 'UKM')

**Black** Business premises regularly used by target; combined with a number, e.g. Black 10

# Glossary

**Bouncer** Bus
**Bramble** Go past the target
**Broccoli** Restaurant
**Buckle** Female suspect/unknown female (also 'UKF')
**Bugle** Post office
**Canary** Telephone kiosk (also 'TK')
**Chilli** Meeting
**Complete** Gone into (a shop, car park, hotel, etc.)
**Crispy** Likely to be spotted (when tailing a vehicle)
**Dead one** Cul-de-sac
**Detached** I am not in the convoy but am trying to join it
**Dryer** Bureau de change
**Father** Airport
**Flood** Filling station (as noun); refuel a vehicle (as verb)
**Flourish** Photograph
**Flyer** Mobile phone
**Footie** Officer patrolling on foot
**Fridge** Bank
**From** Has come out of (a shop, car park, hotel, etc.)
**Handle** Door
**Hawk** Road junction
**Jug** Public toilet
**Knife** Pub
**Leek** Car park
**Lump** Tracker attached to a suspect vehicle
**Mahogany** Stand down, end of surveillance
**Martian(s)** Police
**Maze** One-way system
**Melon** Railway station
**Mini-warpath** Dual carriageway
**Mother** Ferryport
**Mud** Roadworks
**Multi-tankard** Shopping mall or precinct
**Multi-leek** Multi-storey car park
**Nest** Roundabout
**OP** Observation point
**Purple** Domestic premises used by target with corresponding number
**Rattler** Train
**Recip** Return journey
**Rose** Unknown suspect car
**Sand** Traffic jam

**Sauna** Debriefing
**Shaker** Taxi
**Slaughter** Cutting and repackaging drugs
**Slug** Lorry
**Sparklers** Traffic lights
**Spice** Anti-counter-surveillance manoeuvres carried out by target (called to warn the team)
**Starling** City/town centre
**Sticky** Child
**Sticky factory** School
**Swede** Motorway service area
**Tankard** Shop
**TK** Telephone kiosk (also 'canary')
**Tommy car** Technical surveillance vehicle kitted out to track a 'lump' or 'tag'
**Touch red** A request at night for the five-five car to touch its brake lights in order to let the six-eight car/team lock on to the five-five car (instead of going straight past)
**Trench** Underground railway
**Twist** Vehicle registration number
**UKM/F** Unknown male/female (also 'belt'/'buckle')
**Warpath** Motorway
**X-ray** Vehicle regularly used by target (*see* Zulu) with corresponding number identifier, e.g. X-ray 10
**Zulu** Confirmed target, given a number a random, e.g. Zulu 10

## Abbreviations

**ACIO** Assistant chief investigation officer
**CITES** Convention on the Illegal Trade in Endangered Species
**CME** Covert means of entry
**CROPS** Covert rural operations
**DEA** Drug Enforcement Administration (US)
**DST** Dedicated Surveillance Team (SOCA and Customs)
**LIO** Local Intelligence Officer
**NCIS** National Criminal Intelligence Service
**NCS** National Crime Squad

**OSC** Office of the Surveillance Commissioners
**PNC** Police National Computer
**RCS** Regional Crime Squad
**SIO** Senior investigating officer
**SIS** Secret Intelligence Service
**SOCA** Serious Organised Crime Agency
**Vmems** Vehicle-mounted electronic mapping equipment
**VODS** Vehicle on-line descriptive searching facility
**VTD** Vehicle tracking device (commonly known as 'tag' or 'lump')